THE ICONOGRAPHY OF HEAVEN

THE ICONOGRAPHY OF HEAVEN

edited by
Clifford Davidson

Early Drama, Art, and Music
Monograph Series, 21

Medieval Institute Publications

WESTERN MICHIGAN UNIVERSITY

Kalamazoo, Michigan
1994

Cover design by Jayne Cappelletti

ISBN 1-879288-48-6 (casebound)
ISBN 1-879288-49-4 (paperbound)

Contents

Illustrations

1. Angel roof. Church of St. Wendreda, March, Cambridgeshire.

2. Christ as Judge with angels and saints (nineteenth-century "restoration"). Church of St. Mary, Fairford, Gloucestershire.

3. God enthroned with angels above the cosmos. *Nuremberg Chronicle.*

4. St. Michael with sword (above), devils, and the damned at the mouth of hell. Wall painting, Östra Vemmerlöv, Skåne, Sweden.

5. St. Peter welcoming the souls to heaven; at the right is the Virgin Mary, crowned. Wall painting, Östra Vemmerlöv, Skåne, Sweden.

6. Communion. Historiated initial. Sarum Missal, Oxford, Trinity College, MS. D.8, fol. 158^v.

7. Extreme Unction (viaticum). Panel in Seven-Sacrament Window. Church of St. Michael, Doddiscombsleigh, Devon.

8. Extreme Unction (viaticum), showing an attendant kneeling and looking at Host. Panel in Seven-Sacrament Window. All Saints Church, Crudwell, Wiltshire.

9. Eucharist. Elevation of Host. Manuscript illumination. Book of Hours, Brussels, Bibliothèque Royale, MS. 1095, fol. 34^v.

10. Eucharist. Elevation of Host. Panel in Seven-Sacrament Window. Church of St. Michael, Doddiscombsleigh, Devon.

11. The Garden of Eden. *Bedford Hours*, British Library, Add. MS. 18,850, fol. 14^r.

12. Mary Garden. Woodcut. *Hore Beatissime Virginis Mariae.*

13. Enclosed Garden, with Fountain in center. Henry Hawkins, *Parthenia Sacra.*

14. Jesse Tree Window. Church at Llanrhaeadr-yng-Nghinmeirch, Denbigh.

15. Angel emptying censer. Apocalypse scene. Great East Window, York Minster.

16. Angel swinging censer. Angel Choir, Lincoln Cathedral.

17. Angel and Three Maries at Tomb. *Benedictional of St. Ethelwold*, British Library, Add. MS. 45,598, fol. 51^v.

18. Resurrection. Roof boss (oak) formerly in the nave, York Minster. Engraving from John Browne's drawing.

19. The work of four lacemakers lit by a candle and four condensers arranged on a candle stool.

20. Jerusalem. Mosaic, S. Maria Maggiore, Rome.

21. Apse mosaic, S. Pudenziana, Rome.

22. Heavenly Jerusalem. Valenciennes Apocalypse. Valenciennes, Bibliothèque Municipale, MS. 99, fol. 38.

23. Heavenly Jerusalem. Bamberg Apocalypse. Bamberg, Staatsbibliothek, Cod. 140, fol. 55.

24. Vault frescoes, entrance bays, San Pietro al Monte sopra Civate, Lombardy.

25. Botticelli, *Mystical Crucifixion.*

26. "Florentines succoring the Sienese." *Biadaiolo Fiorentino* (c.

1340). Florence, Biblioteca Laurenziana, MS. Tempi 3.

27. St. Francis and the Simple Man. Fresco, upper church, Assisi.

28. Ambroglio Lorenzetti, *The Effects of Good Government in the City*. Fresco, Palazzo Pubblico, Siena.

29. Ambroglio Lorenzetti, *The Effects of Good Government in the Countryside*. Fresco, Palazzo Pubblico, Siena.

30. Securitas. Detail from Ambroglio Lorenzetti, *The Effects of Good Government in the City*.

31. Broletto, Brescia. Early thirteenth-century courtyard and tower, looking toward the southwest.

Preface

The present book, designed as a companion to *The Iconography of Hell* (1992), focuses on the representation of heaven in art and drama, mainly during the later Middle Ages. Some of the papers were presented in preliminary form at the International Congress on Medieval Studies in Kalamazoo in 1993, and other studies have been added to provide additional perspectives on the topic. The book is intended as a collection of essays that will focus on the ultimate site of happiness as defined by medieval theologians and popular writers alike—a place in direct contrast to the stinking and dirty pit of hell with its frequently visualized punishments. In contrast to its modern stereotype as a place that would invite boredom because of its unchanging character, heaven as defined in the late Middle Ages has everything to recommend it and no negative qualities. Its beauty is described in the Middle English *Pearl* as a city "al of brende golde bryght/ As glemande glas burnist broun,/ Wyth gentyl gemmes anunder pyght . . ." (ll. 989–91). It is the residence of saints and angels, the heavenly Jerusalem where the blessed shall be happy forever. The first essay, my "Of Saints and Angels," is intended as an extended introduction to the present book and also as an independent study focusing on specific aspects of late medieval heaven.

As Ann Eljenholm Nichols demonstrates in "The Bread of Heaven: Foretaste or Foresight?" a preliminary view of heaven was available to worshippers through the Eucharist with its consecration of bread which becomes the body of Christ according to the doctrine of transubstantiation. Heaven could thus be brought into the life experience by means of ritual, an act regarded not merely as an abstract mnemonic device that would bring the events of sacred history to mind. In the liturgy, therefore, worshippers were able to become participants in a reality that transcended the distorted and transitory state represented by earthly life. Heaven became real to people in a more imaginative way because of its connection to the *Genesis* stories of the Creation, which took place in a paradisiacal garden that became closely linked to one aspect of the place of bliss. This matter is explored by J. T. Rhodes and myself in an essay ("The Garden of Paradise") that underlines the conception of heaven as a fertile and joyful place, though it will also be noted that there is a certain level of ambiguity because of the blurred line separating bliss-as-garden from the love garden of courtly love. Quite clearly heavenly love is not something absolutely discrete from human love, even of the erotic variety, as St. Bernard of Clairvaux seems to acknowledge in his sermons on the *Song of Songs*.

Heaven is also a place of fragrance and light. The essay on "Heaven's Fragrance" was to have been written by another scholar, who, through difficulties not of his own making, was unable to complete the project. Though this study perhaps takes me much further out of my field of expertise and skill than I should have allowed myself to wander, I nevertheless felt that the topic is one that could not be left out of the book. The principal fragrance of heaven, of course, is incense, which seems incidentally to be in conflict with the likely odor of some of the sources of heavenly light in stage presentations—e.g., "powdered sulphur mixed with aqua ardens," suggested as a way of creating flame coming from above in the Chester *Cain and Abel* play—described by Philip Butterworth. His "The Light of Heaven: Flame as Special Effect" illustrates how the medieval theater could have generated spectacular effects to represent the obligatory light of heaven in a time when electricity and electrical lighting were not yet dreamed of.

The desire for heaven, understood as the heavenly Jerusalem, might even have unusual consequences for city planning, as Robert D. Russell demonstrates in "A Similitude of Paradise: The city as Image of the City." The temporal city in this case is the Italian municipality of Brescia, which was remolded in the thirteenth century in a shape understood to be that of the heavenly City. The effort would seem to have been to define municipal space as distinct from Babylon, the earthly city defined by St. Augustine in his *City of God* and illustrated in a woodcut in an early printed book, the edition of Augustine's *De Trinitate* published at Basle by Johann Amerbach in 1489, as a place of temptation and danger on one side of a path representing the progress of one's life—in contrast to the City of God on the other. In the woodcut, angels on the battlements of the heavenly City beckon, and behind its gates is the place of safety from the devils on the other side who threaten and throw stones down at the path where travelers tread.

But one of the most exciting aspects of heaven was the close association of harmony and music with its depiction. The Middle English *Pearl* describes heaven as permeated by the "nwe songe" sung by angelic harpers "byfore Godes chayere" (ll. 881–85). Everyone familiar with the glorious music of the late Middle Ages—music which has never been surpassed in quality in any place or time—will need to agree that the heavenly repertory must have been a matter of very great interest. "Heaven: The Musical Repertory" by Richard Rastall provides a discussion of the sounds, more beautiful than any mortal being can imagine, that angels sing in the place of bliss.

Finally, I need to acknowledge those who have spoken words of encouragement and given assistance to the present project, especially to Thomas H. Seiler, Managing Editor of Medieval Institute Publications and my co-editor in the preparation of *The Iconography of Hell*, and also to Juleen Eichinger, Otto Gründler, Sarah Brown, Bengt Hernsell, Gunilla Iversen, and others. I am grateful to all who gave valuable suggestions and advice, and I also need to acknowledge the institutions which were indispensable to my work in both research and editing: the Library of Western Michigan University, the University of Michigan Libraries, the Library and Photographic Collection of the Warburg Institute, the Bodleian Library, the British Library, and the National Monuments Record. Kevin Glick produced camera-ready copy for Medieval Institute Publications, and Jayne Cappelletti provided assistance with the graphics and designed the cover.

Of Saints and Angels

Clifford Davidson

Heaven has become in the West a problematic concept. While Fundamentalist Christians insist on a literal understanding of heaven as a place and state, Catholics and Protestants alike have considerable difficulty visualizing it except as a place of great joy where the faithful will "be with Christ." Even the Roman Congregation for the Doctrine of the Faith, the successor to the Holy Office of the Inquisition, has officially stated that in

> dealing with man's situation after death, one must especially beware of arbitrary imaginative representations: excess of this kind is a major cause of the difficulties that Christian faith often encounters. Neither Scripture nor theology provides sufficient light for a proper picture of life after death. Christians must firmly hold the two following essential points: on the one hand they must believe in the fundamental continuity, thanks to the power of the Holy Spirit, between our present life and the future life . . . ; on the other hand they must be clearly aware of the radical break between the present life and the future one, due to the fact that the economy of faith fill be replaced by the fullness of life: we shall be with Christ and 'we shall see God' (cf. 1 Jn. 3:2), and it is in these promises and marvellous mysteries that our hope essentially consists. Our imagination may be incapable of reaching these heights, but our heart does so instinctively and completely.[1]

Karl Rahner, while admitting that heaven "can be evoked in imagery," notes that the place of bliss "cannot be described here and now in a report, and it is announced to man because he can only endure his present if he knows he is in movement toward his future, which is the incomprehensible God in his own very life."[2] But some have been content to follow the Protestant Paul Tillich in defining heaven—the condition of "blessedness"—simply as "the negation of the negative."[3] The difficulty encountered here is, however, a modern one. Heaven once had an elaborate though flexible iconography, which found expression in the visual arts, the

1

drama, and the literature of the Middle Ages.

First of all, the orientation of heaven was fixed: it was, of course, visualized in the celestial region, beyond the sky and filled with a luminescence brighter and more comforting than the sun. St. Paul had been reported to have been *lifted up* to the "third heaven," and manuscript illuminations show the saint being thus raised. A roundel in the Toledo Cathedral Library *Bible Moralisée* (Vol. III, fol. 132) illustrates the bare-footed Paul, standing in mid-air with other saints on his right and left, while God, who is above a cloud and flanked by angels, is blessing him; and a twelfth-century copy of St. Anselm's Prayers and Meditations (Admont, Stiftsbibliothek, MS. 289, fol. 44ᵛ) shows God grasping the right wrist of St. Paul, who, in mid-air with his legs and feet extended, has an angel with a scroll on each side of him.[4]

Imaginative depictions of the heavenly realm from very early times had placed it among symbols representing the sky. In the apse of S. Vitale in Ravenna, Christ, seated on the orb of the universe and positioned between angels and saints, appears against a background of clouds.[5] In the seventh-century mosaic at the Chapel of S. Venanzio, adjacent to St. John Lateran in Rome, Christ is flanked by an angel on each side as he appears above in the clouds, while below are Mary and other saints.[6] Entrance into this upper realm is always understood in terms of being raised up, and God's natural abode in both painting and theatrical event was normally depicted as "above."[7] Hence in John Thornton's Great East Window at York Minster, God, holding the book of Creation (with the words "Ego sum Alph[a] and [Omega]") which records all of history from the beginning to the end, appears at the very point at the top.[8] His position is in the highest opening in the tracery—above the panels of painted glass which show, in the upper portion of the window, the events of the earliest times, including the Creation, and, below, the apocalyptic happenings of the Last Days. In the York Corpus Christi cycle, the existence of God, the eternal Creator of both heaven and earth, is affirmed to transcend the beginning and end of human history as staged in the streets of the city,[9] and at the same time he is symbolically depicted as residing in a location above the earth. In the Doomsday play, it is Christ who comes back down to earth on a rainbow to judge the world, while those who are among the elect—his "chosen childir" (XLVII.365)—will be invited to enter into the place of perfect blessedness above. In such depictions as the wall paintings in the Guild Chapel in Stratford-upon-Avon and Holy Trinity Church in Coventry,[10] heaven had been located diagonally across from the pit of hell below Christ's left hand where the damned will suffer eternally.

The Old Testament confirms that God is at once above in the heavens (*Genesis* 28.12) and omnipresent (Psalm 139.8–10), the latter a requisite if he is to attend to the prayers of his people. The location of heaven, as the *Genesis* description of Jacob's ladder illustrates, is not so remote from earth that no connection is possible between this world and a higher realm which lies above— a stairway "standing upon the earth, and the top thereof touching heaven: the angels also of God ascending and descending by it." This image seems to be the source of the Ladder of Salvation of John Climacus—an image that appears as a way of escape from hell in the restored wall painting at Chaldon, Surrey, though in this example not all souls will be successful in climbing upward into safety.[11] Both the concept of heaven as located *above*—most magnificently and elaborately portrayed in Dante's *Divine Comedy*—and the idea of God as omniscient are simply affirmed by the New Testament, which describes the Incarnation in which God comes into time and the marvellous events of Jesus' Passion, Resurrection, and Ascension. At the Ascension, Christ "was carried up into heaven" (*Luke* 24.51) where he is seated "on the right hand of God" (*Mark* 16.19). In the *Acts of the Apostles* the description is as follows:

> while they looked on, he was raised up; and a cloud received him out of their sight. And while they were beholding him going up into heaven, behold two men stood by them in white garments. Who also said: Ye men of Galilee, why stand you looking up into heaven? This Jesus who is taken up from you into heaven shall so come, as you have seen him going into heaven. (*Acts* 1.9–11)

This passage is the principal source of the iconography which became most widely accepted after c.1000 A.D. and which shows Christ disappearing into the clouds; depictions in the visual arts show his feet and the bottom of his garment extending below the cloud as he rises.[12] There is, for example, a splendid illumination in the Hunterian Psalter (c.1170) which illustrates two angels with scrolls beside Christ's feet as he disappears into a colorful cloud (fol. 14ʳ).[13] But examples of this iconography abound in English art not only in manuscript illuminations such as the Hunterian Psalter or the Hereford Troper (British Library, MS. Cotton Caligula A.XIV, fol. 18ʳ) noted by Meyer Schapiro,[14] but also in other media; for example, several alabasters in the Victoria and Albert Museum show Christ thus rising into the clouds—the one exception showing him in full figure surrounded by a mandorla and ascending.[15] A particularly fine Continental wall painting appears at Kiaby in the Swedish province of Skåne in which two angels appear in the air immediately beneath the cloud into which Christ is disappearing; the angels in this fifteenth-century example are seen playing musical instruments, an organ and a lute.[16]

The Ascension scene is one that was depicted by the dramatists as a necessary episode in the Middle English Creation to Doom cycles. In the York Ascension play, Jesus prays to the Father that a "clowde" may be sent down (XLII.174) so that he might ascend to heaven. The usefulness of the cloud to conceal the device used to raise Christ up into the heavens will be obvious. In the Chester cycle, the ascent is accompanied by angels and enriched with appropriate liturgical music;[17] the angels thereafter descend and address the disciples who are standing below in order to instruct them concerning the significance of the event. In the version of the Chester plays preserved in Huntington MS. 2, Primus Angelus speaks as follows:

> Jesu Christe, leeve yee mee,
> that steede to heaven, as ye see,
> right so come agayne shall hee
> as yee seene him goo. (XX.157–60)

The past tense 'steede' here carries the same meaning as the present tense 'sty,' which appears in the remarkable indenture that inventories the York Doomsday pageant: "A brandreth of Iren þat god sall sitte vppon when he sall sty vppe to heuen."[18] In both cases the word is indicative not only of the technology involved but also of the assumption that to enter heaven one would necessarily rise up through the air.

It is important, however, to note that the practice of raising a figure representing Christ into the "heavens" also was found in a Church ceremony that was dramatic in character. In this ceremony a carving of the Savior was used that would be raised up into the roof of the church.[19] In connection with her survey of such stage properties in liturgical drama, Ulla Haastrup has called attention to a 1363 dramatic ceremony of this kind from Moosburg in Germany that is provided with a complete description.[20] The ceremony was performed following the Office of None. A tent, which had been set up to represent Sinai, was made to conceal a large image of Christ clothed in vestments (a humeral, alb, stole, and cope are recommended) and holding a vexillum. A hole in the vaulting of the roof was outfitted with a rope, which would be used to raise the image of Christ ("ymago Saluatoris") from among the apostles and the Virgin Mary upward until it eventually was drawn through the opening "as if into Heaven." At first Christ was impersonated by a live actor, who, following the singing of the *Silete* by accompanying angels, chanted the antiphon *Ascendo ad patrem*, whereupon the image, now substituted for the live actor, was raised above the tent. Then a dove representing the Holy Spirit was lowered from "Heaven" to a position immediately above the image's head, and an angel also descended. At the third singing of *Ascendo ad patrem* by the actor, the image of Christ disappeared into the hole in the vaulting. At the conclusion, "it is advised that roses, lilies, flowers of various kinds be dropped from above together with large wafers of the kind, if they can be had, often shared out like this in many churches." The flowers are symbolic of the Gifts of the Holy Spirit, and the wafers signify "the presence of the Host, the bread of the Eucharist which is with us until the end of the world."[21]

Haastrup happily is able to identify not only actual Ascension figures but also holes in vaulting that were apparently used for the Ascension ceremony. One such figure, from the Mariakirken at Visby (now Visby Cathedral) in Gotland, Sweden, is hollowed out to reduce its weight and has a back attached so that the figure might appear complete in the round as it was raised; the vaulting in the church also has a round hole at the crossing of the appropriate size for drawing the image through into "heaven."[22] In two other cases, Kalkar Church in Germany and St. Amandus Church in Urach, Switzerland, holes in the vaulting are provided with paintings showing angels, the former with the instruments of the Passion and the latter with angel musicians and prophets. At Urach, each figure holds a scroll containing a text associated with the Ascension.[23] In the case of an Ascension image from Viby Church in Närke, Sweden, even the bottom of the footrest is painted with clouds, which also encircle Christ like a mandorla.[24] An Ascension image from Kleinwangen, Switzerland, published by Young presents a figure of Christ holding a vexillum and surrounded by a mandorla of clouds to which were attached metal holders for candles, while below his feet is the face of an angel carved into the bottom of the mandorla.[25]

The most remarkable Ascension play of all, however, must have been the staging in the Church of Santa Maria del Carmine in Florence in 1439, when heaven was represented by an opening at the top of a scaffold, at first covered by a blue cloth painted with sun, moon, and stars; the lifting of this curtain represented the opening of heaven's gates to show God the Father, who

> looked down on the Mount of Olives, where his divine Son, the holy Virgin, and the Apostles are standing together. He blesses them, apparently suspended in mid-air. Around him are small children in great numbers with flutes, citterns, and chime bells. Among these children, who represent the angels, and around God the Father there is a vast number of burning lamps. At the top of the opening which represents Heaven is fixed a paper disc, the bottom rim of which points upwards; on this, life-size angels are painted. Seven thin and strong ropes with skillfully constructed iron gear wheels go from the opening of Heaven to the Mount of Olives. A young man representing Jesus Christ in the act of ascending to the Father is beneath these ropes.[26]

The heavens open when Jesus has climbed to the top of the "mountain"; and "God the Father can be seen miraculously suspended in the air, enveloped in a great light which pours forth from the innumerable lamps; the small children representing the angels move about him while harmonious music and sweet singing are heard. The taller angels which are painted on the disc also revolve around so that they seem to be alive." Then a cloud along with two angels will be sent down from the heaven. Jesus will be raised up to meet the cloud until he is enveloped "from head to foot and the two angels who stand one on each side of him kneel down before him." The cloud which covers Jesus and the angels is raised into heaven, and the lights are extinguished.[27]

While Ascension plays were demonstrably among the high points of the civic cycles at Chester and York, the only evidence of which I am aware in the English dramatic records of any

Ascension ceremony or play within an ecclesiastical building is a tenth-century Ascension trope, though there is a vitriolic attack on the practice of raising an image of Christ up to "heaven" on Ascension Day in Philippe de Marnix's *The Bee Hiue of the Romishe Church*, translated by George Gylpen the elder:

> upon Ascension day, they pul Christ vp on high with ropes aboue the clowdes, by a vice deuise in the roofe of the Church, and they haile him vp, asyf they would pul him vp to the gallowes: and there stande the poore Priestes, and looke so pitifully after theyr God, as a dog for his dinner.[28]

It will, however, be granted that in England the idea of the church vault or roof as symbolic of heaven was very widespread. Angels appear ubiquitously on church roofs. The churches of East Anglia are especially rich in this symbolism, with the church at March having over a hundred such figures (fig. 1).[29] At times, as in Holy Trinity Church, Coventry, the angels may hold symbols of the Passion,[30] while elsewhere, as at All Saints, North Street, York, they hold emblems and play musical instruments.[31] There are also records of a Pentecost ceremony at St. Paul's Cathedral in London that describe the use of a hole in the vaulting for releasing a dove as a symbol of the Holy Spirit, the third person of the Trinity who descended from heaven on the first Pentecost—an occasion, as the biblical narrative explains, when tongues of fire came from thence to each of the apostles.[32] The fullest account of the St. Paul's Cathedral ceremony, though written after the Reformation when it was no longer being performed, recalls its effect: "the comynge downe of the *Holy Gost* was set forthe by a white Pigion, that was let to fly out of a Hole . . . in the mydst of the Roofe of the great Ile, and by a long Censer, which descendinge out of the same Place almost to the verie Grounde, was swinged up and downe at suche a Lengthe, that it reached with thone Swepe almost to the West Gate of the Churche, and with the other to the Quyre Staires of the same, breathinge out over the whole Churche and Companie a most pleasant Perfume of suche swete Thinges as burned thearin."[33] In this instance, the odor of heaven was made to descend into the earthly church, for incense was associated with that place of bliss—the opposite of the disgusting and fetid odors of hell.[34] Another Pentecost ceremony involving not only a dove suspended from the vault of the nave but also an angel appears in the fourteenth-century records of Lincoln Cathedral. Very likely wafers and flowers were thrown down from the hole in the vaulting in this example of the Pentecost ceremony.[35]

Lincoln Cathedral also had a *visus* of the Assumption and Coronation of the Virgin which in the fifteenth century was performed in the nave on the Feast of St. Anne.[36] This ceremony or play, like other examples of the Assumption and Coronation drama, would have revealed the sight of a divine act in heaven, the reception of the Blessed Virgin Mary, who will be crowned Queen of Heaven. A play of this sort, with considerable modern accretions, is still presented for the Feast of the Assumption in August of each year at Elche in Spain.[37] In the Elche play, the depiction of Mary's death and her Assumption culminates in a substitution of a very special statue for a human actor, and then the statue, accompanied by angel musicians, will be taken up into "heaven," which is part of the architecture of the vault of the rebuilt cathedral.

In the visual arts, the Assumption and Coronation of the Virgin were among of the most popular subjects, often being repeated many times in the same building. The reason for the popularity of the Coronation in particular in both art and drama seems to have been its function in opening up a sight of heaven and of God, who might appear as the glorified Son or as the Father and Son along with the dove of the Holy Spirit. At the Church of the Holy Trinity, Goodramgate, in York, Mary is depicted being crowned by three figures joined under a single ermine mantle—a representation of the unity of the Trinity.[38] As Queen of Heaven, Mary will of course serve as intercessor for men and women below. She thus appears in many depictions of the Last Judgment, where her appeal to her Son for mercy for those devoted to her is expected to be effectual. In some cases she exposes her breast, the source of the milk which succored her Son and a sign that he must respond to her plea for mercifulness for the children of men.[39] In other examples in the visual arts, she places her hand on the scales which are being used to weigh a soul's good deeds against his bad with the result that one of her devotees might be saved and allowed entrance into heaven.[40] In a sense, she represents a prime source of hope for individuals since she is indicative of the possibility of their ascending to bliss where, clothed with white and radiant robes, they might walk among the angels.

The crucial moment in one's life is the moment of death since the condition of one's soul at that instant will determine whether one will in fact be admitted to bliss. For those who have been baptized and have devoted themselves to good works and to holiness of mind and body, crossing the river of death will mean that the veil will be lifted so that one might see God "face to face" instead of in a murky reflection. Such souls will be taken up into heaven to be with the angels and other saints. The death scene is established in the *Apocalypse of Paul* where the dying person is attended by good and evil angels, both hoping to take his soul away.[41] As the soul leaves the body—in later depictions in the arts, as in the wall painting at Vrå, Denmark, the soul is shown as a doll-like figure coming from the mouth of the person[42]—the guardian angels receive it and promise to carry it to "a place which thou never knewest."[43] Thereafter the soul will be taken to the presence of God where, among St. Michael and all the host of heaven, he is judged worthy and welcomed with music and rejoicing into the heavenly court.

The soul being taken off to heaven immediately after death is often depicted as a nude of diminutive stature within a napkin being carried up by an angel. In a carving of c.1470 in the central roof of the choir of All Saints, North Street, in York, an angel is lifting up a tonsured soul which may possibly be a donor, the clergyman John Gilliot,[44] while a similar scene in the north choir aisle depicts an unidentified soul being raised.[45] A funeral scene with a tonsured priest at an altar (he holds a scroll with the words "PRECOR TE MARIA"), a bier (in the foreground), mourners, and consolers appears in a wall painting at Starston, Norfolk; at the top of this painting is a pair of angels lifting the upright and nude soul, who is standing in a napkin, up to the clouds.[46] In a miniature in the Shaftesbury Psalter illuminated in the middle of the twelfth century, the archangel Michael with his feet on a cloud holds up a napkin containing several souls—nude except for a hood worn by some of them—before God, who appears in a roundel above (British Library, MS. Lansdowne 383, fol. 168^v).[47] The iconography is identified as a soul or souls being taken to Abraham's bosom, and in other examples Abraham, sometimes merged with God the Father, holds one or more souls in the napkin in his lap—e.g., on sculpture on the Percy tomb at Beverley Minster,[48] or on tympana at Bourges Cathedral and Reims Cathedral.[49] On an early sixteenth-century label stop at St. Helen's Church in York, God the Father and the Son (head missing) receive a soul in a napkin.[50]

Belief in the presence not only of Mary but also of other souls of saints in heaven led to the widespread veneration of those persons—at first the apostles and martyrs—recognized as having gone forth through death into bliss. Peter Brown has noted that initially people were anxious to be buried in close proximity to the bodies of saints in order to draw on their holiness,[51] and churches were erected where martyrs were buried.[52] Relics of the saints and martyrs came to possess power both in this earthly life and in the world to come, and churches and monasteries collected large relic inventories in order to achieve betterment for the souls in their care. Relics could be called on to bridge the natural chasm between the temporal world and the eternity of heaven. Some relics, such as those of St. James at Compostela and St. Thomas Becket at Canterbury, were especially believed to effect miraculous cures—cures that in the case of Becket were advertised in the painted glass at the cathedral.[53] Prayers to saints, often using the intermediary of an image before which candles might be lighted as an invocation, were a way of opening new channels of communication between earth and heaven. Feast days devoted to saints punctuated the calendar with commemorations not only of the Virgin Mary, the apostles, and early martyrs but also of widely venerated later saints and often local ones (e.g., the Yorkshire nun St. Everilda, whose head was preserved in a reliquary standing on four copper lions at York Minster,[54] whose feast day in the York calendar was 9 July,[55] and whose image formerly stood in painted glass at Nether Poppleton[56]). Pilgrimages were, of course, usually directed to such sites as Canterbury, Compostela in Spain, Trondheim in Norway (St. Olaf), Walsingham (Our Lady), and Rome, and their stated object, in spite of the modern popular conception which is colored by Chaucer's *Canterbury Tales*, was to achieve temporary alienation from worldly entanglements and therefore to be closer to the goal of heaven.[57]

Indeed, all of earthly life was rightly to be seen as a pilgrimage, reflecting the Patriarchs' view that we are but wanderers and pilgrims on this earth rather than permanent sojourners here. The proper direction that one was to take in this life was toward heaven along the biblically sanctioned narrow road, which was opposed to the broad and easily traveled way that leads to the everlasting bonfire. To be sure, there was a third way that led to

Purgatory, and this too was an unpleasant place in the suburbs of hell—a place, as the Imperator Salvatus reports in the Chester Last Judgment play, of "woe and teene" and "hard payne" like the suffering of souls in hell, though with the difference that such pain "shall have an end" (*Chester* XXIV.90, 97–100). Those in Purgatory thus are also in some sense pilgrims who, purging away their sins, are destined eventually for salvation, and they too can hence be assisted both by earthly prayers by people in this life and by the saints in bliss.

The attractiveness of the saints in bliss appealed even across the great divide of the Reformation, as George Herbert's poem "To All Angels and Saints"[58] demonstrates:

> Oh glorious spirits, who after all your bands
> See the smooth face of God without a frown
>   Or strict commands;
> Where ev'ry one is king, and hath his crown,
> If not upon his head, yet in his hands. (ll. 1–5)

The poet would "crave" the saints' "speciall aid" and "would addresse" his "vows" to the "Mother of my God," but he is prevented from venerating them because of his ideological Protestantism which demands that his devotion be directed only to the all-powerful God. In Catholic tradition there was no bar to such a practice, though the Church warned against directing the kind of worship appropriate only to God (*latria*)[59] wrongly to the saints and to angels such as St. Michael, who are worthy only of *dulia*, or to the Virgin Mary, who merits *hyperdulia*.

St. Ambrose had in fact recommended intercessions to saints, especially martyrs

> whose patronage we seem to claim for ourselves by the pledge as it were of their bodily remains. They can entreat for our sins, who, if they had any sins, washed them [away] in their own blood; for they are martyrs of God, our leaders, the beholders of our life and actions. Let us not be ashamed to take them as intercessors for our weaknesses, for they themselves knew the weaknesses of the body, even when they overcame.[60]

It was generally agreed that the saints and martyrs will make useful advocates at the Last Day before the divine Judge:

> The olde fadres a-fore tymes made fro bigynnyng the festyuites of holy
> apostles and martires whiche were before hem to be louyd and halowed
> as is i-seen, and specially in entent that we, the herers of here blessid
> commemoracions whiche ben in tymes of here festes redde and songen,
> myght be stired for to folowe hem in the same wey and also that we
> myghte þrough here prayers and medes be in here euerlastynge fellaschip
> and holpen here in erþe.[61]

In heaven, the prayers of the saints are like incense which ascends
to the deity (*Apocalypse* 8.4).

The saints in heaven join with the angels in singing praise to
God,[62] especially the *Sanctus* in which persons not yet released
from their earthly pilgrimage likewise participate in the song. As
Pamela Sheingorn indicates, the singing of the *Sanctus* from the
ordinary of the Mass—an item based on the canticle sung by the
seraphim in *Isaias* 6.3—in earthly churches "dissolved not only the
boundaries separating heaven and earth, but also those separating
time and eternity, for they participated in the 'Eternal Mass in the
Heavenly Jerusalem'."[63] Sheingorn also publishes a remarkable
Mass of St. Gregory illustration from a fifteenth-century *Biblia
Pauperum* (Munich, Bayerische Staatsbibliothek, MS. clm. 8201,
fol. 94ᵛ) that shows, below, the Eucharist being celebrated at an
altar at the moment of transubstantiation when the Host is elevated.
Over the altar is the figure of Christ as Man of Sorrows attended
by angels with candles, a censer, and an aspergillum; immediately
above and in the clouds are the nine orders of angels arranged in
choirs, while in the central position are Mary as Queen of Heaven
and the glorified Christ at the right with a cross nimbus.[64] A long
scroll reaches from the throne of the Most High down to the dove
of the Holy Spirit at the head of the Man of Sorrows figure, who
in turn holds a scroll reaching down to the Host being held by the
priest and containing words proclaiming "This is my body." The
earthly choir sings the *communio*, *Ave verum corpus*, in concert
with the heavenly choir, which is only in this illustration missing
the voices of the saints. Saints, however, appear in roundels
arranged around the margins of the page. So, as *The Lay Folks
Mass Book* insists, the object of the individual rightly should be to
yearn and strive with the assistance of the saints for bliss where
one might "with aungels . . . sing/ þis swete song of þi louyng,/
sanctus: sanctus: sanctus."[65] The *Sanctus* is, after all, given
additional authority as a principal item in the heavenly repertory by

the appearance of a variant text, the *Trisagion*, in the *Apocalypse*: "Holy, holy, holy, Lord God Almighty, who was, and who is, and who is to come" (4.8). C. Clifford Flanigan calls attention to two *Sanctus* tropes in the *Winchester Troper* that imply a direct connection between earthly worshippers and the throne of heaven; included in the second of these tropes are the following words added to the *Benedictus*: ". . . We, rising with You,/ We, now sitting with you in heaven as a sharer of the riches of the Kingdom,/ We, therefore, ask that when you come as judge to determine the merits of everyone,/ That you join us with the saints and angels,/ With whom we may praise to You."[66] As Flanigan notes, the point is made even more clearly in the ancient Liturgy of St. Mark in which the *Sanctus* is accompanied by the drawing back of a curtain to reveal "a depiction of choirs of thousands of angels standing in the divine presence and calling out to each other."[67]

The monastic poet John Lydgate commented: "Aungellys reioyse with lawde, honour, and glory,/ From the heuynly court by grace they ar sent,/ And at the masse abyte and be present. . . ."[68] Through a remarkable legacy of £10 in a will (dated 20 October 1502) by an alderman of Hull, Thomas Goisman, it is known that a mechanical device was to be made that would "rise and descend at the high altar, as angels go up and down, between the elevation of Christ's body [and of the Lord's blood, as in the church at Lynne], and the end of the chant, *Ne nos inducas in temptacionem*"—i.e., the end of the *Pater Noster*—in the Church of the Holy Trinity where he was to be buried.[69] Such a device would have provided visual affirmation of the presence of visitors from the "heuynly court" at the time of consecration during Mass.

The schematic organization of the heavenly choirs in the *Biblia Pauperum* illustration places the nine orders of angels[70] in the following arrangement in relation to God and Mary:

		Mary — God		
Chorus throni	Chorus cherubin		Chorus seraphin	Chorus dominiaciones
Chorus archangeli	Chorus principatus	Chorus virtutes	Chorus potestates	Chorus angeli

All the faces of the angels are turned toward the center in praise, and this requires the choir of Virtues, which is divided by the scroll descending between heaven and earth, to face to the center on each side. In the depiction of the heavenly host in the Last Judgment scene in the West Window of c.1500 at Fairford—a portion of the window (fig. 2) which is actually a nineteenth-century copy of the original glass—the various orders of angels circle around the descending Judge in layers, with Cherubim and Seraphim represented in the blue and ruby glass immediately surrounding Christ.[71] There is a sense of hierarchy, although the ranks are not distinguished by color, in Giotto's depiction of nine rows of angels in the Arena Chapel at Padua; and in Fra Angelico's *Christ Glorified in the Court of Heaven* in the National Gallery, London, the ranks of angels seem to be reduced to eight for the sake of symmetry, though this painting is of very great interest on account of the musical instruments being held and played.[72] But in the *Nuremberg Chronicle* (1493) all of the nine orders are carefully distinguished by their headgear, and their names are listed at the left of the circular heaven in which they reside (fig. 3).[73]

According to Pseudo-Dionysius, heaven was organized hierar-chically, with the nine orders of angels, arranged in three groupings or hierarchies of three each, in an exact sequence reflecting prece-dence. The arrangement described in William Caxton's edition of the *Golden Legend* follows Pseudo-Dionysius and St. Thomas Aquinas: (1) a "souerain" hierarchy of "Cherubyn, Seraphin, and the thrones"; (2) a "mydle" hierarchy of "the domynacions, the vertues, and the potestates" or powers; (3) the "last" hierarchy, which "conteynith the pryncipates, angels and archaungels." The text admits, however, that this order differs from the accounts presented by Gregory the Great and Bernard of Clairvaux.[74]

After listing the arrangement of the hierarchies and the orders within them in heaven, the *Golden Legend* comments on the function to which each rank is devoted. The angels in the first hierarchy minister to God and are wholly turned toward him: the seraphim express "souerayne loue," the cherubim represent "perfyght knowledge," and the thrones are the means by which God sits and rests since they rest in him. In the second hierarchy, which is devoted to the governance of "thunyuersite of the peple in comyn," the dominations "commaundeth to them all thyng" and have power over the lower angels, while the virtues, since nothing is impossible for them, are responsible for performing miracles; the powers, in turn, have the role of constraining—e.g., St. Raphael's

binding of the Devil in the Egyptian desert. Finally, the lowest
hierarchy has more limited authority; principalities have power in
a particular region, while archangels rule in a smaller area over a
group of people—e.g., the inhabitants of a specific city—and
angels are devoted "to the gouernance of one persone" and to the
performing of smaller tasks.[75]

The angelic orders are placed among the heavenly spheres in a
miniature in a fourteenth-century *Life and Miracles of St. Denis* in
Paris, Bibliothèque Nationale, MS. fr. 2090, fol. 107^v, which shows
the vision of Dionysius, who is seated below; it is a vision that
reaches even beyond the realm of the angels to the Trinity,
represented in the form of two men seated on each side of the Holy
Spirit depicted as a large dove with its wings extended and
touching their mouths.[76] The angelic orders are shown playing
musical instruments, which represent the harmony of heaven.
Dionysius' hierarchical arrangement was, of course, approved by
St. Thomas Aquinas[77] and transformed into great poetry by Dante
in the *Divine Comedy*. Hildegard of Bingen, whose *Scivias* lists the
angelic orders in a variant sequence which agrees with the arrangement set forth by St. Bernard rather than Aquinas, visualizes
them in a miniature as embodying a brilliant crown made up of
circles; each order is described, often drawing on traditional
iconography (e.g., the eyes with which the seraphim are adorned).[78]

The tradition of nine orders was retained by the dramatists of
the initial pageants of the Chester and York cycles. At Chester God
mentions the "greate beautye" of the "nine orders" of angels, and
describes them as walking "aboute the Trenitie" (I.65–67). In the
York play, Deus, creating the heavenly host, bids "Nyen ordres of
aungels full clere" to arise—angels which are to give him everlasting praise (I.20–24); the following stage direction announces that
they at once worship him in singing the canticle *Te Deum laudamus*. In the Cornish *Creacion of the World*, God first creates
heaven, then places in it the "Nine orders of glorious angels" who
"will worship me with joyful song."[79] Each order is placed on his
own throne, with the cherubim rather than the seraphim being in
closest proximity to God, and in the "second degree" the order is
changed to principalities, powers, and dominations. Finally, in the
"third degree" are archangels, virtues, and God's "messengers," the
angels. This arrangement, which differs from Pseudo-Dionysius,
Gregory, Bernard of Clairvaux, and Isidore of Seville,[80] is identical

to the ordering in Bartholomeus Anglicanus' *De Proprietatibus Rerum.*[81]

In Coventry, where a pageant of "9 orders of Angells" had been "set forth" in 1511 at Jordan Well for King Henry VIII and Queen Catherine,[82] some angels in painted glass currently remain from the Church (later Cathedral) of St. Michael, which was bombed in World War II; the fifteenth-century glass, now in St. Michael's Hall in the new Cathedral, illustrates six six-winged cherubim who stand on wheels (see *Ezeckiel* 10) with cross diadems and with amices at their necks.[83] There were also sixteen angels on the roof, which was destroyed. These apparently were intended to be connected with specific orders since a text listing the nine orders was painted on a cross beam attached across the nave:

1. Archangeli presunt civitatibus.
2. Potestates presunt demonibus.
3. Dominaciones presunt spiritus angelicus.
4. Cherubyn habent omnem scienciam.
5. Principalitates presunt bonis hominibus.
6. Virtutes faciunt mirabilia.
7. Seraphyn ardent in amore dei.
8. Troni eorum est judicare.
9. Angeli sunt nuncii domini.[84]

The carvings in this case seem not to have been arranged according to hierarchies, though the list usefully identifies the function attributed to each order in a way consistent with the scheme that we have seen described in the *Golden Legend*. Remains of nine orders of angels arrangements are extant, however, in various other locations; numerous instances of painted glass from such arrangements may still be seen in East Anglia, and there is an interesting, though very fragmentary example in a window at All Saints, North Street, York, that has been reconstructed in recent times from a drawing in the Bodleian Library.[85] The nine orders are illustrated in the *Queen Mary Psalter*,[86] and an extensive sculptural group, dating from the middle of the fifteenth century, is displayed around God the Father in the Beauchamp Chapel at Warwick.[87]

Even more remarkable than the sculptures at the Beauchamp Chapel is its painted glass, which presents the angelic company singing and playing in heaven. The notation identifies the antiphon *Gaudeamus* in the Sarum version, appropriate for the dedication of the chapel and its patron since this item was sung at the Feast of the Assumption of the Virgin Mary.[88] Indeed, Mary is depicted on the central boss in the roof as Queen of Heaven, crowned and holding an orb and scepter. The other music identifiable from the notation still visible in the painted glass includes the Marian antiphon *Ave Regina caelorum* as well as the *Gloria in excelsis*. But in viewing the windows in this splendid chapel from its interior we must be most impressed with the size and variety of the angelic instrumentarium, which has been presented with considerable attention to detail and thus has served to provide illustrations to Jeremy Montagu's very respectable popular guide to early instruments (*The World of Medieval and Renaissance Musical Instruments*).[89] Not only are stringed instruments like the harp—an instrument specifically associated with heaven because noted in *Apocalypse* 5.8 and hence illustrated in some Apocalypse manuscripts[90]—and the venerable organ present, but also wind instruments, including the shawm, and percussion.[91] The appearance of such a variety of instruments in one program should not, however, mean that they would all have been played at the same time in normal usage or that they would all have been imagined to sound together in concert in heavenly music. But in the late Middle Ages the music of chapel and cathedral was hardly always entirely unaccompanied, and hence artists like John Prudde, whose workshop produced the Beauchamp Chapel windows in c.1447–49, saw fit to imagine the music of heaven likewise as involving the joyous sound of instruments—including but not limited to instruments which approximated the ones listed in Psalms 149 and 150.

In the visual arts the angels are not costumed with consistency, though the basic garments seem to be the alb, amice, and perhaps the dalmatic or tunicle. Crowns are common, sometimes with a cross affixed. The feet are always bare, and sometimes instead of or along with liturgical garb they are given garments of feathers.[92] The sculptures at Beauchamp Chapel thus present, for example, the following: feathered seraphim, which stand on a sea of fire, radiate flames, and have their necks encircled with clouds and stars; crowned cherubim, shown with collars that radiate light, standing in water in front of clouds; feathered and crowned thrones; feathered dominions, in one case having a body nearly covered by a star with twelve points; powers, wearing armor and trampling on demons; virtues garbed in dalmatics; principalities wearing clouds and flower-stars as girdles; archangels appearing with emblems, spear and lily.[93]

While in the earliest Christian centuries angels, as in *Acts* 1.10, were simply described as young "men . . . in white garments," by the time of Tertullian they tended normally to be thought of as having wings,[94] and in the Middle Ages they invariably were winged. Records for the Coventry Drapers' play of Doomsday in the sixteenth century noted the making and painting of four pairs of angels' wings on two occasions.[95] The York Mercers' inventory of 1433 specified "ij paire Aungell Wynges with Iren in þe endes" and two trumpets for the Last Judgment. There are also listings in this inventory for puppet angels, one of which had a banner of "laton & a crosse of Iren in his hede giltid"; four "smaller Aungels gilted" with the instruments of the Passion and nine "smaler Aungels payntid rede to renne aboute in þe heuen" (apparently activated by a cord) were also included.[96] Puppet angels, one of which was missing a wing, were still listed in the Mercers' inventory of 1526.[97] The dramatic records also reveal some details of costuming. The Coventry Cappers' accounts specify the washing of "angelles albes" in 1543—probably the same costumes that are called "surplisses" in the Protestant 1570's.[98] And the Weavers of Coventry arranged for the mending of "two angeles crownes" in 1577.[99] The 1464 pageant at London bridge at the time of the coronation of Elizabeth Woodville used "nine hundred peacock's feathers for making the angels' wings."[100]

That the angels were intended to be ecstatically happy creatures—in contrast to the dissatisfied Lucifer and the angels who first followed and then fell with him—is demonstrated by close examination of extant examples in the visual arts. It is no surprise, therefore, to encounter two dancing angels—both of them bare-footed and wearing albs—in the south choir aisle of Christ Church Cathedral in Oxford; below one of the angels is a minstrel playing a fidel with an arched bow.[101] In the Digby *Mary Magdalene*, during the final years of the Magdalen's life, she is taken up "into þe clowddys" by angels where she is fed heavenly food on a daily basis.[102] All of heaven bursts into a song of praise as she is carried into the clouds, and she shows her gratitude to God for satisfying her hunger, in addition noting that the "melody of angyllys" has shown her "gle and game" (ll. 2031–38). For persons living in the late Middle Ages, the angelic messengers and ministers of God were signs of hope in their earthly pilgrimage, as the dedication of more than seven hundred churches to St. Michael the Archangel and All Angels demonstrates.[103]

Liturgical plays on two topics treat the earthly pilgrimage which will culminate in the sight and enjoyment of God. The first topic, which finds expression in several plays from the Continent, is the Emmaus story that was dramatized in the *Peregrinus* drama.[104] The version from Beauvais Cathedral presents the two disciples burning in desire to see again the face of Jesus whom they believe to have been taken away from them.[105] Yet as they are joined on the road to Emmaus by the risen Christ, they do not recognize him until at last he blesses the bread at their meal—an act that suggests the Eucharist through which Jesus is made our contemporary each time that Mass is said. Finally, even the apostle St. Thomas ("Doubting Thomas") must acknowledge the reality of the Resurrection when Christ appears to him and to the others. The play is thus on one level about living as pilgrims who desire to anchor their lives in eternity and in order to do so must overcome their doubts. Such laying aside of doubt and the kindling of hope, especially through the Sacraments of the Church, is ultimately essential if the journey of life is to reach its terminus in bliss.

The second topic is the parable of the Wise and Foolish Virgins from *Matthew* 25, a chapter that otherwise focuses on the end of history and the Second Coming of Christ. The unique liturgical play in this case is the eleventh-century bilingual *Sponsus* from St. Martial at Limoges.[106] The theme of this drama is the vigilance required of the Christian—the initial line of the drama warns, "*uigilate, uirgines!*"—which, if relaxed, will lead to a terrible fate: the Foolish Virgins, having gone to sleep and allowed their lamps to be extinguished, are in the end received by demons and thrown into hell. The most moving lines are the despairing refrains sung by these Virgins in the vernacular: "Dolentas, chaitiuas, trop i auem dormit!" ("Unhappy, despairing, too long have we slept"). On the other hand, the Wise Virgins, who faithfully wait for the Bridegroom even though they do not know the hour when he will come, will be allowed to enter into the celestial marriage banquet through the doorway—a doorway which also recalls the metaphor presented in *Apocalypse* 3.20. The Wise Virgins are the ones who have let Christ into their hearts and have kept the flame of their love for him alive, and they are the ones who will be invited to

share in the heavenly feast. They are the ones who will be invited
to sup with the Bridegroom and to experience the supreme joy of
heaven, while the others will be rejected. The scene at the doorway
is represented, for example, in a miniature in the *Rossano Gospels*[107] and in sculpture of c.1180 at Basel;[108] in both cases the Wise
and Foolish Virgins are separated by a door, with the Foolish on
the outside at the left. The *Rossano Gospels* show Christ, to the
right of the door and facing it, gesturing his denial of the request
that the ineligible ones might enter; on his side of the door flowers
are growing in a garden setting, on the other side is barrenness. In
the sculpture at Basel, Christ is shown above, enthroned with an
open book and a vexillum. On his left is St. Paul, and at his right
are St. Peter and other saints. The Wise Virgins represent all who
will see God and heaven, which is also the abode of the saints,
while the Foolish Virgins are those will be denied a sight of bliss.

The suggestion of eroticism in the depiction of the love of the
Wise Virgins for Christ in the *Sponsus* is not an accident.[109]
Drawing on the *Song of Songs* which Bernard of Clairvaux in the
next century would focus upon as providing a model for human
feeling toward God, the play suggests that the Wise Virgins are in
fact to be regarded in terms of the *Sponsa* while Jesus is to be seen
as the *Sponsus*—Bride and Bridegroom, like the two crowned
figures seated side by side in a manuscript at Munich in the
Bayerische Staatsbibliothek, MS. lat. 4450, fol. 1^v.[110] Eschatological
hope is emotionally rich; in the drawing in the Munich manuscript,
the Sponsus has his right arm around the Sponsa, who looks at him
with longing. The experience of the soul in heaven is one of
ecstasy of being with God, though it stops short of the mystical
union of Plotinus' Neoplatonism.[111]

At the Last Judgment, the souls of the righteous and of those
who have completed penance in Purgatory will be joined with their
resurrected bodies. Separated by St. Michael from the eternally
wicked who are consigned to hell, they will be invited to ascend to
the gate of heaven, usually depicted, as in the wall painting in the
Guild Chapel in Stratford-upon-Avon, above and at Christ's right—
that is, at the viewer's left.[112] This wall painting was placed in the
conventional location over the chancel arch so that members of the
congregation would gaze past the representation of the Last Judgment when looking from the nave in the direction of the high altar
located in the east, the direction in which the Second Coming was

expected.[113] Since the chancel with its reserved sacrament was identified with heaven and the nave was seen to symbolize the region of this world in which one was on pilgrimage to the other, such paintings suggested the idea that one must pass the final Judgment before entering into bliss. The depiction was designed both as a warning and a sign of hope, with the damned stripped of their clothing and the saved being not yet dressed in the white clothing that they will receive in heaven. No hypocrisy, dishonesty, or self-deception will be tolerated. Sometimes escorted by angels in their upward movement from the open graves, they were traditionally met at the gate of heaven by its gatekeeper, St. Peter, recognizable because he invariably held a pair of keys (or, elsewhere, a single key) as his symbol. In the York cycle this scene at the end of the last pageant dissolves into the music of angels. In the Towneley manuscript play collection, the music is identified as the *Te Deum.*

The significance of the *Te Deum* in this position will be realized when it is recalled that a portion of this canticle had been sung in the York play of the *Creation and Fall of Lucifer* at the beginning of that cycle by the angelic host as their first act following their creation. In the N-town play collection, an abbreviated form of the item is sung by the newly-created angels in heaven: "*Tibi omnes angeli, tibi celi et uniuerse potestates, tibi cherubyn et seraphyn incessabili voce proclamant: Sanctus, Sanctus, Sanctus, Dominus Deus Sabaoth.*"[114] A pageant in Cheapside for the welcoming of Catherine of Aragon included "the Father of Heven" and "many angels" who held "scriptours of *te Deum,* and *tibi omnes* &c."[115] The singing of the *Te Deum* was also represented in the visual arts and is implied in the *Te Deum* panels carved in alabaster showing the nine orders of angels, the apostles, the prophets, and "white-robed throng of martyrs" praising the Lord of Hosts.[116] A group of painted glass panels formerly in the York church of St. Michael, Coney Street, and now in York Minster also provides illustration of the *Te Deum.* Particularly relevant to the first pageant in the York cycle is the panel illustrating God as Creator with compasses—iconography that in itself is a reflection of the idea of God as Master Builder which was espoused by the School of Chartres. In the York glass God has a gold face, reflecting the practice of painting faces with gilt or wearing gilt masks when playing the role of the deity in plays. At Coventry the Cappers' accounts mention

"godes hede," and the Smiths' gilt wig may have involved a mask
as well.[117] The 1433 York Mercers' inventory specifically identifies
"a verserne gilted" for Jesus in the Doomsday play.[118] The Last
Judgment, of course, is the event that will represent the closing of
the book of history, whereupon all those who have merited salvation will join in the eternal songs of praise in heaven itself.

The condition of those who have received salvation is described
by Aquinas in terms of the Gifts of the Blessed, given as a dowry
that is received by the bride.[119] This imagery is appropriate
because, as implied in the *Sponsus*, the soul/Church is the bride
who is received into mystical marriage upon being taken up into
glory. Aquinas also reflects the belief in specific beatitudes, first
set forth by St. Anselm in a sermon;[120] these beatitudes, fourteen
in number, appear in sculpture on the left portal of the north porch
at Chartres Cathedral where Security, Health, Majesty, Friendship,
Concord, Strength, Agility, Honor, and Liberty are identified, while
the rest—Knowledge, Beauty, Pleasure, Joy, and Longevity—have
also been recognized. Each of these statues is a crowned queen
with a nimbus, and together they represent both the beautified soul
and the condition of bliss. Mâle has written:

> They have an air of nobility and freedom. Their unbound hair flows to
> their shoulders; their full robes fall in straight folds and mold the pure
> lines of their noble bodies. In one hand they hold a scepter, the other rests
> lightly on a large shield decorated with an emblem. Each has her own
> blazon. Liberty wears two crowns to recall that sovereigns are freer than
> other men. Honor has a double miter on her shield, because the miter is
> the highest symbol of honor. . . . On her shield, Longevity has the eagle,
> which in old age grows young again in the heat of the sun; for emblem
> Wisdom has the griffin which knows where hidden treasures lie. Certain
> attributes of the beatitudes are less erudite: Agility carries three arrows,
> Strength has a lion, Concord and Friendship have doves, Health has fish,
> Security has a fortified castle, and Beauty has roses.[121]

The contrast with the instability, pain, helplessness, joylessness,
ugliness, and demeaning treatment by sadistic devils in hell will be
obvious to all who are familiar with the iconography of that other
place—the place of eternal punishment forever hidden from the
face of God.

To be in heaven is to be always in God's presence much more
immediately than is possible on this earth, where we "see through
a glass in a dark manner [i.e., by way of enigmatic reflections in

a mirror]; but then [in the luminescence of bliss] face to face" (*I Corinthians* 13.12; cf. *Apocalypse* 22.4). The power of this image is somewhat diluted by mistranslation and our experience with modern mirrors, which are large in size and relatively non-distorting in reflecting images. The Greek word (*esoptron*) used by St. Paul signified a metal mirror, normally a small implement not guaranteed to reflect with accuracy.[122] In the late Middle Ages, images illustrating God the Father or Trinity could thus only be regarded as pale and distorted reflections, useful mainly as devotional channels to the actual deity who exists outside of time. In earlier centuries, God the Father was not illustrated in sacred art, though the Second Person, through whom the deity had revealed himself, was pictured in catacomb art as early as the third and fourth centuries—but not as the Crucified One, a subject which first appeared at the beginning of the fifth century (the earliest example perhaps is an ivory Crucifixion in the British Museum[123]). In heaven, however, there would be no need for images of either God or the saints.

Nevertheless, for the time being the medieval Church understood its obligation to replicate within earthly limits the glory of heaven in its churches and cathedrals. Suger at the Abbey of St.-Denis and the architects of glass-walled Gothic structures elsewhere attempted to create gloriously luminescent buildings that would provide appropriate settings for the Office and Mass; as acoustically wonderful sanctuaries, redolent with the odor of incense, they provided enclosed space where the harmony of the voices and instruments would, as noted above, join with the harmony of heaven. David O'Connor has commented on York Minster as modeled on heaven—that is, as the heavenly Jerusalem descended to earth to glorify God here just as he is offered praise in that heavenly place.[124] It is a connection that was also made in the liturgy of the consecration of churches, where the description of the New Jerusalem in the *Apocalypse* 21.2–5 was used as a lesson, the gradual noted that the house of God is the gate to heaven, and the sequence affirmed that earth and heaven are joined in worship.[125] Sacred space within the walls of a building was to resound with the heavenly song, which in turn would unite temporal experience with eternity in the perfect harmony of its music.

The richness that struck the eye upon entering such churches as Suger's St.-Denis or York Minster may have offended the ascetic minded—Wycliffites and Protestants were not alone in arguing that the wealth of the Church diverted money from assistance to the poor—but the gilt in image and decoration and the jeweled windows were seen by others as providing an appropriately rich setting for worship of the Master Builder of the universe. In the *Apocalypse*, heaven is described in as incredibly brilliant, enlightened by God himself, and of "pure gold, like to clear glass" (21.18, 23; 22.5). The profusion of jewels in heaven additionally added to the image of brilliance; its twelve gates are each made of a massive pearl, and even the streets are of "pure gold, as it were transparent glass" (21.21). This is a place of aristocratic splendor—indeed, it is in fact the court of heaven, where the ceremonial thoroughly and appropriately outshines in splendor any earthly rituals of emperor worship.[126]

Yet heaven is not a sterile place, for, watered by the "river of water of life, clear as crystal, proceeding from the throne of God," the tree of life will flourish in it as a symbol of fruitfulness (*Apocalypse* 22.1). In contrast to the dead tree of vices—destined for the everlasting bonfire, and in some cases pictured with the axe to its trunk—the iconographic motif of the tree of virtues was associated with life and was hence shown as bearing all manner of fruit of goodness.[127] So heaven itself from a very early date was depicted as a place where flowers covered the ground—e.g., at S. Vitale, Ravenna.[128] In Fra Angelico's *Last Judgment* at San Marco, Florence, those who receive salvation dance hand in hand through a garden rich with flowers and shrubs as they pass in a circle up to the gate of heaven; the scene is in contrast to the stark picture of desolation at the Judge's left hand where there is no living vegetation, only anguish and gnashing of teeth as the damned are herded off to their doom.[129] The garden setting is reminiscent of the *Song of Songs*, which provided the source of the *Sponsus-Sponsa* imagery for Christus-Ecclesia, and also looks back to the prophecy of Jeremiah: "And they shall come, and give praise in mount Sion: and they shall flow together to the good things of the Lord, . . . and their soul shall be as a watered garden, and they shall be hungry no more" (*Jeremias* 31.12).

The heavenly Jerusalem is also a city with walls and gates, which are always open since it is never night, though unlike the earthly Jerusalem there is no temple therein (*Apocalypse* 21.22, 25). The words of the psalmist are taken to refer analogically to the pilgrimage of the individual to heaven and also anagogically to the concluding place in the earthly journey:

> I rejoiced at the things that were said to me: We shall go into the house of the Lord.
> Our feet were standing in thy courts, O Jerusalem.
> Jerusalem, which is built as a city, which is compact together.
> For thither the tribes go up, the tribes of the Lord: the testimony of Israel, to praise the name of the Lord. (Psalm 121.1–4)

While the earth is a place which is no continuing city—in St. Augustine's terminology, it is the place of captivity, Babylon—the men and women who live here in the earthly city also have the opportunity of living simultaneously in the heavenly Jerusalem which they will see only at the end of the earthly pilgrimage.[130] The description of this city in the *Apocalypse* seems perhaps confusing because of the liturgical arrangement of the centrally located throne of God (before which seven lamps are burning), the altar of the Lamb, the seats of the twenty-four crowned elders in white robes, the choirs of angels, virgins, martyrs, and the multitude of men and women—all of which seems indicative of an architectural rather than a municipal setting.[131] Artists, however, like the illuminator of the *Liber Floridus* (Ghent University Library, MS. 92, fol. 95ʳ) in the early twelfth century, translated the description of the walled city of heaven into a schematic and symbolic municipal architecture that would seem reasonably familiar to people of his time.[132]

Specific architectural features which point to the idea of heaven as a city, however, had appeared in c.400 in the catacombs of SS. Pietro and Marcellino where the Christ and Lamb are shown in the city of paradise.[133] In the early fifth-century mosaic of Christ in Majesty at the Church of S. Pudenziana at Rome (fig. 21), he appears with the disciples in front of a wall punctuated by doors and behind which are numerous buildings.[134] Late medieval Last Judgment wall paintings like the previously cited example in the Guild Chapel at Stratford-upon-Avon set forth the walled city as an idealized fifteenth-century municipality with a gate for the saved to enter—a gate probably very like a miniaturized replica of one of the entrances to the city in nearby Coventry.[135] Crenellated walls guard the city, and upon them angel musicians play musical instruments. In the background are towers and other structures. In the

Guild Chapel wall painting, the city is set off to the right side of the Judge. At St. Thomas of Canterbury at Salisbury the walled city extends across the entire top of the chancel arch which contains the restored wall painting. Placed across the entrance to the chancel of the church and in a location where they could be seen by all the lay persons in the nave, such wall paintings emphasized the ultimate destination of worshippers when they would be taken into the heavenly city of the Creator and ruler of the universe.[136]

In the church at Östra Vemmerlöv in the province of Skåne in southern Sweden, a painted ceiling contrasts the terrors of the damned—i.e., those who, watched over by St. Michael with an upraised sword, are being caught by devils and herded into hell—with the joys of the blessed, who are about to enter the heavenly city (figs. 4–5). St. Peter, whose key is opening the gate to bliss, takes the hand of the pope who is the first of those who have merited salvation—a grouping which includes the whole Christian community, rich and poor, young and of mature age, cleric and lay. Protecting the smallest, who are nude, is the Virgin Mary. The procession is accompanied by angel musicians, who play fidel and lute, while more angel musicians are seen in the windows of the heavenly city—a sign that in that place all will experience very great aesthetic pleasure.

The heavenly city is a place where, as we have seen, the *Te Deum* and other canticles and songs of praise and joy will resound at all times, for in the eternal light cast by God there will be no periods of darkness or sorrow. The architecture of the place is to be imagined in terms of perfect harmony as it was understood by the music theorists of the Middle Ages. Indeed, heaven is a location outside of time where perfect harmoniousness exists. Those who formed and developed the iconography of heaven were certain that, as the *Te Deum* promises, Christ came into the world and accepted crucifixion so that "the kingdom of heaven" would be "opened to all believers." The final words of this canticle perhaps are the most significant: "Come then, Lord, and help your people, bought with the price of your own blood, and bring us with your saints to glory everlasting."

NOTES

[1] "Letter on Certain Questions Concerning Eschatology," *The Pope Teaches*, July 1979, p. 334. See also the discussion of this letter in Colleen McDannell and Bernhard Lang, *Heaven: A History* (New Haven: Yale Univ. Press 1988), pp. 322–23.

[2] Karl Rahner, "Eschatology," in *Sacramentum Mundi*, ed. Karl Rahner (New York: Herder and Herder, 1968), II, 244.

[3] Paul Tillich, *Systematic Theology* (Chicago: Univ. of Chicago Press, 1963), III, 403.

[4] See Luba Eleen, *The Illustration of the Pauline Epistles in French and English Bibles of the Twelfth and Thirteenth Centuries* (Oxford: Clarendon Press, 1982), figs. 264–65.

[5] André Grabar, *Christian Iconography: A Study of Its Origins*, Bollingen Ser., 35, Pt. 10 (Princeton: Princeton Univ. Press, 1968), fig. 106.

[6] Ibid., fig. 322.

[7] See also my discussion of orientation in space in "Space and Time in Medieval Drama: Meditations on Orientation in the Early Theater," in *Word, Picture, and Spectacle*, ed. Clifford Davidson, Early Drama, Art, and Music, Monograph Ser., 5 (Kalamazoo: Medieval Institute Publications, 1984), pp. 39–46.

[8] Clifford Davidson and David E. O'Connor, *York Art: A Subject List of Extant and Lost Art Including Items Relevant to Early Drama*, Early Drama, Art, and Music, Reference Ser., 1 (Kalamazoo: Medieval Institute Publications, 1978), pp. 1–2, fig. 2.

[9] The first line of the first play, spoken by Deus, is *"Ego sum Alpha et O: vita, via, veritas, primus et nouissimus"*; see *The York Plays*, ed. Richard Beadle (London: Edward Arnold, 1982), p. 49. Subsequent references to the York cycle are to this edition.

[10] Clifford Davidson and Jennifer Alexander, *The Early Art of Coventry, Stratford-upon-Avon, Warwick, and Other Sites in Warwickshire*, Early Drama, Art, and Music, Reference Ser., 4 (Kalamazoo: Medieval Institute Publications, 1985), pp. 37, 69–71; George Scharf, Jr., "Observations on a Picture in Gloucester Cathedral and Some Other Representations, of the Last Judgment," *Archaeologia*, 36 (1855), Pl. XXXVI, fig. 1; Clifford Davidson, *The Guild Chapel Wall Paintings at Stratford-upon-Avon* (New York: AMS Press, 1988), fig. 17. The Holy Trinity wall painting is now hidden behind layers of grime and varnish; see Jennifer

Alexander, "Coventry Holy Trinity Doom Painting," *EDAM Newsletter*, 11 (1989), 37; restoration is planned.

[11] See F. K. Flynn, "The Mural Painting in the Church of Saints Peter and Paul, Chaldon, Surrey," *Surrey Archaeological Collections*, 72 (1980), 127–56; E. W. Tristram, *English Wall Painting: The Twelfth Century* (London: Oxford Univ. Press, 1944), pp. 36–39, 108; *The Iconography of Hell*, ed. Clifford Davidson and Thomas H. Seiler, Early Drama, Art, and Music, Monograph Ser., 17 (Kalamazoo: Medieval Institute Publications, 1992), p. 55, fig. 20; and, for John Climacus, see John Rupert Martin, *The Illustration of the Heavenly Ladder of John Climacus*, Studies in Manuscript Illumination, 5 (Princeton: Princeton Univ. Press, 1954), pp. 5–15, figs. 66–67.

[12] See Meyer Schapiro, "The Image of the Disappearing Christ: The Ascension in English Art Around the Year 1000," in *Late Antique, Early Christian and Mediaeval Art: Selected Papers* (New York: George Braziller, 1979), pp. 267–87.

[13] See C. M. Kaufmann, *Romanesque Manuscripts, 1066–1190*, Survey of Manuscripts Illuminated in the British Isles, 3 (London: Harvey Miller, 1975), No. 95, fig. 14.

[14] Schapiro, "The Image of the Disappearing Christ," pp. 273, 277, fig. 7. In an earlier example prior to the introduction of this iconography, in the *Benedictional of St. Ethelwold*, fol. 64ᵛ, he rises upward in full figure holding a cross (Elzbieta Temple, *Anglo-Saxon Manuscripts, 900–1066*, Survey of Manuscripts Illuminated in the British Isles, 2 [London: Harvey Miller, 1976], No. 23).

[15] Francis Cheetham, *English Medieval Alabasters* (Oxford: Phaidon-Christie's, 1984), Nos. 215–21.

[16] Knud Banning, *Kalkmalerierne i Skånes, Hallands, og Blekinges Kirker 1100–1600* (Copenhagen: G. E. C. Gad, 1985), pp. 82–83.

[17] *The Chester Mystery Cycle*, ed. R. M. Lumiansky and David Mills, EETS, s.s. 3 (London, 1974), I, 373–76. Subsequent citations to the Chester cycle are to this edition.

[18] *York*, ed. Alexandra F. Johnston and Margaret Rogerson, Records of Early English Drama (Toronto: Univ. of Toronto Press, 1979), I, 55.

[19] See Karl Young, *The Drama of the Medieval Church* (Oxford: Clarendon Press, 1933), I, 483–89.

[20] Ulla Haastrup, "Medieval Props in the Liturgical Drama," *Hafnia*, No. 11 (1987), pp. 151–52, summarizing the text reported in Neil C. Brooks, "Eine liturgisch-dramatische Himmelfahrtsfeier," *Zeitschrift für deutsches Altertum und*

deutsche Litteratur, 62 (1925), 91–96. The text is also edited by Young, *The Drama of the Medieval Church*, I, 484–88. Quotations in my text are from Haastrup's English translation.

[21] When King Henry VII visited York in 1486, he was treated to a pageant of the Assumption at Stonegate and Swinegate which, following the ascension of Mary into heaven to the accompaniment of angels' song, concluded in a similar effect: "yer schall it snaw by craft tobe made of waffrons in maner of Snaw" (*York*, ed. Johnston and Rogerson, I, 142).

[22] Haastrup, "Medieval Props," figs. 19–20.

[23] Ibid., figs. 26–27.

[24] Ibid., p. 163, fig. 29. Haastrup also cites a "companion-piece" at the Church of St. Mary in Gdansk.

[25] Young, *The Drama of the Medieval Church*, I, Pl. XI.

[26] *The Staging of Religious Drama in the Later Middle Ages: Texts and Documents in English Translation*, ed. Peter Meredith and John E. Tailby, Early Drama, Art, and Music, Monograph Ser., 4 (Medieval Institute Publications, 1983), p. 246.

[27] Ibid., pp. 246–47.

[28] [Philippe de Marnix,] *The Bee Hiue of the Romishe Churche*, trans. George Gilpen the elder (London, 1580), fol. 207^r (STC 17,446). For the Ascension trope—*Quem cernitis ascendisse super astra, o christicole?*—see *The Winchester Troper*, ed. W. H. Frere, Henry Bradshaw Soc., 8 (1894; rpt. New York: AMS Press, 1973), p. 110. Similar tropes are found on the Continent; see Young, *The Drama of the Medieval Church*, I, 196–97.

[29] See also Edward S. Prior and Arthur Gardner, *An Account of Medieval Figure-Sculpture in England* (Cambridge: Cambridge Univ. Press, 1912), p. 519.

[30] Davidson and Alexander, *The Early Art of Coventry*, pp. 28–30.

[31] *Inventory of the Historical Monuments of the City of York* (London: Royal Commission on the Historical Monuments of England, 1962–), III, 6, Pls. 43, 96–97.

[32] *Acts* 2.3. For the ceremony at St. Paul's, see William Lambarde, *Dictionarium Angliae Topographicum et Historicum* (London, 1730), pp. 459–60, and below, pp. 118–19. This practice also comes under attack in *The Bee Hiue of the Romishe Churche*, fols. 206^v–207^r, which reports the use of "rosin and gunpowder,

with wilde fire" for the Holy Spirit. For an example of a mosaic that depicts the descent of tongues of fire from the top of a dome (where heaven is represented) upon the disciples, see Otto Demas, *The Mosaic Decoration of San Marco, Venice*, ed. Herbert L. Kessler (Chicago: Univ. of Chicago Press, 1988), Pl. 13.

[33] Lambarde, *Dictionarium*, p. 459.

[34] See E. G. Cuthbert F. Atchley, *A History of the Use of Incense in Divine Worship* (London: Longmans, Green, 1909), p. 112.

[35] *Records of Plays and Players in Lincolnshire*, ed. Stanley Kahrl, Collections, 8 (Oxford: Malone Soc., 1974 [for 1969]), p. 27.

[36] Ibid., pp. 32–33 and *passim*.

[37] See J. Francesc Massip, "The Cloud: A Medieval Aerial Device, Its Origins, and Its Use in Spain Today," *Early Drama, Art, and Music Review*, 16, No. 2 (1994), 65–77.

[38] Davidson and O'Connor, *York Art*, p. 109, fig. 32.

[39] See, for an important example of the Last Judgment, Adrian Wilson and Joyce Lancaster Wilson, *A Medieval Mirror: Speculum humanae salvationis, 1324–1500* (Berkeley and Los Angeles: Univ. of California Press, 1984), p. 198, and, for an example of the particular judgment at which Our Lady bears her breast in a plea to her Son for mercy for an individual, see the Yorkshire Carthusian Miscellany (British Library MS. Add. 37,049, fol. 19ʳ). For an application of this motif in drama, see Stephen K. Wright, "Iconographic Contexts of the Swedish *De uno peccatore qui promeruit gratiam*," *Comparative Drama*, 27 (1993), 12–13.

[40] Mary Phillips Perry, "On the Psychostasis in Christian Art," *Burlington Magazine*, 22 (1912–13), 104.

[41] *The Apocryphal New Testament*, trans. M. R. James (1924; rpt. Oxford: Clarendon Press, 1980), pp. 31–32.

[42] Clifford Davidson, "Stage Properties and Iconography in Early English Drama," *Mediaevalia*, 15 (1993), fig. 2. For an example in which the soul is instead taken away by a devil, see the wall painting at Sæby, Denmark; illustrated by Niels M. Saxtorph, *Danmarks Kalkmalerier* (Copenhagen: Politikens Forlag, 1986), p. 192.

[43] *Apocryphal New Testament*, trans. James, p. 531.

[44] E. A. Gee, "The Roofs of All Saints, North Street, York," *York Historian*, 3 (1980), 3.

[45] Davidson and O'Connor, *York Art*, p. 112; *Inventory of the Historical Monuments in the City of York*, III, Pl. 43.

[46] E. W. Tristram, *English Wall Painting of the Fourteenth Century* (London: Routledge and Kegan Paul, 1955), pp. 251–52, fig. 56a.

[47] Kaufmann, *Romanesque Manuscripts*, No. 48.

[48] T. S. R. Boase, *Death in the Middle Ages* (London: Thames and Hudson, 1972), fig. 39.

[49] Emile Mâle, *Religious Art in France: The Thirteenth Century*, trans. Marthiel Mathews, Bollingen Ser., 90, Pt. 4 (Princeton: Princeton Univ. Press, 1984), figs. 251–52.

[50] *Inventory of the Historical Monuments in the City of York*, V, 20, Pl. 30.

[51] Peter Brown, *The Cult of the Saints: Its Rise and Function in Latin Christianity* (Chicago: Univ. of Chicago Press, 1981), pp. 33–34 and *passim*.

[52] G. G. Willis, *Further Essays in Early Roman Liturgy* (London: SPCK, 1968), p. 147.

[53] One of the most spectacular is perhaps the curing of Matilda of Cologne; see Madeline Harrison Caviness, *The Early Stained Glass of Canterbury Cathedral* (Princeton: Princeton Univ. Press, 1977), p. 94, figs. 209–11.

[54] *The Fabric Rolls of York Minster*, ed. James Raine, Surtees Soc., 35 (Durham, 1859), p. 220.

[55] *Breviarium ad usum insignis ecclesie Eboracensis*, II, Surtees Soc., 75 (Durham, 1883), pp. 388–90.

[56] Davidson and O'Connor, *York Art*, p. 155.

[57] Pilgrimage as a liminoid phenomenon is sensibly described from the standpoint of a Catholic anthropologist by Victor Turner; see Victor Turner and Edith Turner, *Image and Pilgrimage in Christian Culture* (New York: Columbia Univ. Press, 1978).

[58] George Herbert, *Works*, ed. F. E. Hutchinson (1945; Oxford: Clarendon Press, 1945), pp. 77–78.

[59] See *Speculum Sacerdotale*, ed. Edward H. Weatherly, EETS, o.s. 200 (London: Oxford Univ. Press, 1936), p. 1.

[60] *Concerning Widowhood*, in Ambrose, *Select Works and Letters*, trans. H. de Romestin *et al.*, Select Library of Nicene and Post-Nicene Fathers, 10 (rpt. Grand Rapids: Eerdmans, 1955), p. 400 (ix.55).

[61] *Speculum Sacerdotale*, ed. Weatherly, p. 1.

[62] Abelard considered the music of the spheres to be reference to "heavenly habitations" of saints and angels where they "in the ineffable sweetness of harmonic modulation offer eternal praise to God" (*Theologia Christiana* I.5, in *Opera*, ed. V. Cousin [1859; rpt. Hildesheim: Georg Olms, 1970], II, 384, as quoted by Otto von Simson, *The Gothic Cathedral: Origins of Gothic Architecture and the Medieval Concept of Order*, Bollingen Ser., 48 [New York: Pantheon, 1956], p. 37).

[63] Pamela Sheingorn, "The Te Deum Altarpiece and the Iconography of Praise," in *Early Tudor England*, ed. Daniel Williams (Woodbridge: D. S. Brewer, 1989), p. 179; see also Josef A. Jungmann, *The Mass of the Roman Rite* (New York: Benziger, 1955), II, 128, 135, and, for commentary on the *Trisagion* beginning "Sanctus, sanctus, sanctus" quoted in the *Apocalypse*, Lucetta Mowry, "Revelation 4–5 and Early Christian Liturgical Usage," *Journal of Biblical Literature*, 71 (1952), 77–78. An interesting aspect of heavenly iconography introduced into the chancel of earthly churches in the Middle Ages is described by Richard H. Randall, Jr., "Thirteenth Century Altar Angels," *Record of the Art Museum, Princeton University*, 18 (1959), 2–16. In the *Apocalypse of St. Paul* the heavenly song, led by David, is the *Alleluia*, which is the model for ecclesiastical song below: "as it is performed in heaven, so also is it upon earth" (*The Apocryphal New Testament*, trans. James, p. 541).

[64] Sheingorn, "The Te Deum Altarpiece," Pl. 4.

[65] *The Lay Folks Mass Book*, ed. Thomas Frederick Simmons, EETS, o.s. 71 (London, 1879), p. 28; the passage is noted by Sheingorn, "The Te Deum Altarpiece," p. 181.

[66] C. Clifford Flanigan, "The Apocalypse and the Medieval Liturgy," in *The Apocalypse in the Middle Ages*, ed. Richard K. Emmerson and Bernard McGinn (Ithaca: Cornell Univ. Press, 1992), p. 347; see also *The Winchester Troper*, ed. Walter Howard Frere, *The Winchester Troper* (1894; rpt. New York: AMS Press, n.d.), p. 65.

[67] Flanigan, "The Apocalypse and the Medieval Liturgy," p. 345.

[68] John Lydgate, *The Minor Poems*, Pt. 1, ed. Henry Noble MacCracken, EETS, e.s. 107 (London, 1911), p. 100.

[69] *Testamenta Eboracensia*, IV, ed. James Raine, Surtees Soc., 53 (Durham:

Andrews, 1969), 209, as quoted in translation by Miri Rubin, *Corpus Christi: The Eucharist in Late Medieval Culture* (Cambridge: Cambridge Univ. Press, 1991), p. 62; however, the words within brackets, omitted in Rubin's translation, have been supplied here.

[70] While angels are frequently mentioned in biblical literature, sources for the other angelic orders are: *Ephesians* 1.21 (principalities, powers, virtues, dominions), *Colossians* 1.16 (thrones, dominations, principalities, powers), *Ezechiel* 10 (cherubims), *Isaias* 6.2 (seraphims); *Jude* 1.9 (Michael the archangel), and *1 Thessalonians* 4.15 ("the voice of an archangel").

[71] See Hilary Wayment, *The Stained Glass of the Church of St. Mary, Fairford, Gloucestershire* (London: Society of Antiquaries, 1984), p. 56, Pl. XXII; compare the encircling angels, which are not differentiated by order, in Fra Angelico's *Last Judgment* in the Museo San Marco, Florence. Another iconographic motif in which the angels praise the Virgin Mary appears in an illumination by Jean Fouquet, who has illustrated the orders of angels in blue and gold encircling the Trinity (in three separate persons) with Mary enthroned at their right hand; the saints are seated in ranks at the right and left, while others stand in attendance. See Claude Schaefer, *The Hours of Etienne Chevalier [of] Jean Fouquet* (New York: Braziller, 1971), Pl. 27. See also the iconography of Christ in Majesty surrounded by a circle of unidentified angels at the Allerheilig Kapelle in Regensburg and at Hersfeld (Otto Demus, *Romanesque Mural Painting* [London: Thames and Hudson, 1970], figs. 44, 51); this design is used in both cases to decorate a dome.

[72] Cesare Gnudi, *Giotto* (Milan: Aldo Martello, 1958), Pl. 124; Philip Hendy, *The National Gallery, London*, 4th ed. (London: Thames and Hudson, 1971), p. 85.

[73] Hartmann Schedel, *Liber Chronicarum* (Nuremberg, 1493), fol. 5^v.

[74] Jacobus de Voragine, *Legenda aurea*, trans. William Caxton (Westminster: Wynkyn de Worde, 1493), fol. 283^r–283^v; for a comparison of the different orders presented by Pseudo-Dionysius/Aquinas, Gregory, and Bernard, see C. A. Patrides, "The Orders of the Angels," in *Premises and Motifs in Renaissance Thought and Literature* (Princeton: Princeton Univ. Press, 1982), p. 13.

[75] *Legenda aurea*, trans. Caxton, fol. 283^r–283^v.

[76] Reinhold Hammerstein, *Die Musik der Engel* (1962; rpt. Bern: Francke Verlag, 1990), fig. 65.

[77] See Patrides, *Premises and Motifs*, pp. 10–14; James Collins, *The Thomistic Philosophy of the Angels* (Washington: Catholic Univ. of America Press, 1947), pp. 96–97, 154–55.

[78] Hildegard of Bingen, *Scivias*, ed. Adelgundis Führkötter and Angela Carlevaris, Corpus Christianorum, Continuatio Mediaevalis, 43–43A (Turnhout: Brepols, 1978), Pt. 1, pp. 100–08, Pl. 8; for an English translation, see *Scivias*, trans. Columba Hart and Jane Bishop (New York: Paulist Press, 1990), pp. 137–43.

[79] *The Creacion of the World: A Critical Edition and Translation*, ed. and trans. Paula Neuss (New York: Garland, 1983), p. 7; subsequent quotations in my text are from Neuss' edition.

[80] See the convenient chart in Patrides, *Premises and Motifs*, pp. 13–14.

[81] See *Batman vppon Bartholome, his Booke De Proprietatibus Rerum* (London, 1582), fols. 5^v–10^v, and *On the Properties of Things: John Trevisa's Translation of Bartholomæus Anglicanus De Proprietatibus Rerum* (Oxford: Clarendon Press, 1975), I, 67–84.

[82] *Coventry*, ed. R. W. Ingram, Records of Early English Drama (Toronto: Univ. of Toronto Press, 1981), p. 107.

[83] Davidson and Alexander, *The Early Art*, pp. 15, 17; Bernard Rackham, "The Glass Paintings of Coventry and Its Neighborhood," *Walpole Society*, 19 (1931), 97–98, Pl. XVI. Technically, angels with six wings ought to denote cherubim; see *Isaias* 6.2.

[84] Mary Dormer Harris, *The Story of Coventry* (London: Dent, 1911), p. 329. For an extant set of angel musicians on another roof at Coventry—at St. Mary's Hall—see Davidson and Alexander, *Early Art*, p. 17, figs. 62–65. In this case the location is the great hall rather than an ecclesiastical space, however.

[85] Christopher Woodforde, *The Norwich School of Glass-Painting* (London: Oxford Univ. Press, 1950), pp. 129–37; E. Gee, "The Painted Glass of All Saints Church, North Street, York," *Archaeologia*, 102 (1969), 170–74, Pl. XXXI; *Inventory of the Historical Monuments in the City of York*, III, 9; Gordon McN. Rushforth, *Mediaeval Christian Imagery* (Oxford: Clarendon Press, 1936), pp. 204–16. Further examples are listed by Rushforth (ibid., p. 305n).

[86] George Warner, *The Queen Mary Psalter* (London: British Museum, 1912), p. 31, Pl. 300.

[87] Philip Chatwin, "The Decoration of the Beauchamp Chapel, with Special Reference to the Sculptures," *Archaeologia*, 77 (1928), 313–34, Pls. LVIII–LXII.

[88] Charles F. Hardy, "The Music in the Painted Glass of the Windows in the Beauchamp Chapel at Warwick," *Archaeologia*, 61 (1909), 583–614.

[89] Jeremy Montagu, *The World of Medieval and Renaissance Musical Instruments* (London: David and Charles, 1976), Pls. 45, 47, 55, 58. On the Beauchamp Chapel windows, see also below, p. 190.

[90] See, for example, *The Apocalypse: A Series of Seventy-Seven Miniatures from an English Apocalypse Illuminated in York, c. 1270*, Sotheby's Sale Catalogue, 25 April 1983, Pl. 32.

[91] See the list of instruments in Davidson and Alexander, *The Early Art*, pp. 84, 86, and William Bentley, "Notes on Musical Instruments figured in Windows of the Beauchamp Chapel, Warwick," *Transactions of the Birmingham Archaeological Society*, 53 (1931), 167–72.

[92] Feathered angels in the visual arts were believed by a number of art historians (e.g., Prior and Gardner, *An Account of Medieval Figure-Sculpture*, p. 516) to be derived from theatrical practice; for sceptical assessments, see M. D. Anderson, *Drama and Imagery in Medieval English Churches* (Cambridge: Cambridge Univ. Press, 1963), p. 168, and Rhoda-Gale Pollack, "Angelic Imagery in the English Mystery Cycles," *Theatre Notebook*, 29 (1975), 134. For Bartholomeus Anglicanus angels are "Truely . . . paynted feathered and winged: for that they are of contrary cause and cleane from all earthlye cogitation" (*Batman vppon Bartholome*, fol. 4^v).

[93] Davidson and Alexander, *The Early Art*, pp. 83–84. The emblems held by various orders of angels can only be described as flexible; Woodforde has described their iconography in Norfolk churches as characterized by "a surprising diversity of representation and detail" (*The Norwich School*, pp. 129–30). St. Michael is usually recognizable by his sword or, in the case of the psychostasis which appears less frequently, his scales, and Gabriel is known, for example, through his position in the iconography of the Annunciation, where this archangel usually appears with a wand or scepter. In the sculptures at the Beauchamp Chapel, Warwick (see Chatwin, "The Decoration of the Beauchamp Chapel," p. 325, Pls. LIX [2], LXI [3]), and in Great Malvern glass, Virtues carry chrisom—in the latter in a box with its lid held open (see Rushforth, *Mediaeval Christian Imagery*, pp. 213–14, fig. 102). But another angel from the same order at Warwick is seen holding a censer and incense boat, while at St. Neot's Church a censer is held (Gordon McN. Rushforth, "The Windows of the Church of St. Neot, Cornwall," *Exeter Diocesan Architectural and Ecclesiological Society*, 15 [1937], 159). Elsewhere, in the parish church of Barton Turf, the censer is given to the seraphim (Woodforde, *The Norwich School*, p. 131). Since cherubim are associated with the knowledge of God, they are most often depicted holding books, and at Exeter Cathedral they are illustrated with doctors' caps, which are black—headgear, however, similar to that worn by Dominations at the Beauchamp Chapel (Woodforde, *The Norwich School*, p. 133). At Great Malvern angels are depicted as holding scrolls, while also in the glass in this church each of the various orders is depicted adorned with a specific jewel (see Rushforth, *Mediaeval Christian*

Imagery, pp. 206–16, figs. 98–104); for the origin of the association linking angelic orders and jewels, see Gregory the Great, *Forty Gospel Homilies*, trans. David Hurst (Kalamazoo: Cistercian Publications, 1990), p. 286.

[94] Emil Schneweis, *Angels and Demons According to Lactantius* (Washington: Catholic Univ. of America Press, 1944), p. 51.

[95] *Coventry*, ed. Ingram, pp. 468, 471.

[96] *York*, ed. Johnston and Rogerson, I, 55–56.

[97] Ibid., I, 242.

[98] *Coventry*, ed. Ingram, pp. 163, 261, 267, 283.

[99] Ibid., p. 285.

[100] Glynne Wickham, *Early English Stages, 1300 to 1660* (London: Routledge and Kegan Paul, 1959), I, 326; for comment on the purpose of the peacocks' feathers for "making such wings as 'full of eyes' in Ezekiel's description of the Cherubim," see Anderson, *Drama and Imagery*, p. 169.

[101] Tristram, *English Wall Painting of the Fourteenth Century*, p. 232, figs. 26–27, 52.

[102] *The Late Medieval Religious Plays of Bodleian MSS Digby 133 and E Museo 160*, ed. Donald C. Baker, John L. Murphy, and Louis B. Hall, EETS, o.s. 283 (Oxford, 1982), p. 91 (l. 2025).

[103] Frances Arnold-Forster, *Studies in Church Dedications, or England's Patron Saints* (London: Skeffington and Son, 1899), I, 37–39; see also Francis Bond, *Dedications and Patron Saints of English Churches* (London: Oxford Univ. Press, 1914), pp. 36–40.

[104] Young, *The Drama of the Medieval Church*, I, 451–83.

[105] See F. C. Gardiner, *Pilgrimage of Desire: A Study of Theme and Genre in Medieval Literature* (Leiden: Brill, 1971), pp. 116–28. The Rouen play is explicit about wanting to see the stranger's face, which is hidden from them in that play. For the Society for Old Music production of the Beauvais *Peregrinus* presented at Viterbo, Italy, for the 1983 colloquium of the Société pour l'Etude du Théâtre Médiévale for which I was dramatic director, I chose not to have the Stranger's face hidden for practical and acoustical reasons; the actors playing the disciples simply appeared not to recognize Jesus in the Stranger because of their firm belief that he was dead. The effect can still be very startling when the moment of recognition comes to them.

[106] The Latin text is printed by Young, *The Drama of the Medieval Church*, II, 362–64. Performing editions, which include the music and translations, have been provided by William L. Smoldon, *Sponsus: An Eleventh-Century Mystère* (London: Oxford Univ. Press, n.d.), and Fletcher Collins, Jr., *Medieval Church Music-Dramas: A Repertory of Complete Plays* (Charlottesville: Univ. Press of Virginia, 1976), pp. 259–79. Quotations in my text are from Smoldon's translation.

[107] Arthur Haseloff, *Codex Purpureus Rossanensis* (Berlin: Giesecke and Devrient, 1898), pp. 95–96, Pl. IV.

[108] Gertrud Schiller, *Ikonographie der christlichen Kunst* (Gütersloh: Gerd Mohn, 1971), III, fig. 648. For other examples, see Clifford Davidson, "On the Uses of Iconographic Study: The Example of the *Sponsus* from St. Martial of Limoges," in *Drama in the Middle Ages*, ed. Clifford Davidson, C. J. Gianakaris, and John H. Stroupe (New York: AMS Press, 1982), pp. 43–62.

[109] See ibid., pp. 46–47, 50–52.

[110] McDannell and Lang, *Heaven*, Pl. 8.

[111] See Tillich, *Systematic Theology*, p. 411.

[112] For the Last Judgment, see especially David Bevington et al., *Homo, Memento Finis: The Iconography of Just Judgment in Medieval Art and Drama*, Early Drama, Art, and Music, Monograph Ser., 6 (Kalamazoo: Medieval Institute Publications, 1985); for the Stratford-upon-Avon wall painting, see Davidson, *The Guild Chapel Wall Paintings*, fig. 17.

[113] See M. D. Anderson, *The Imagery of British Churches* (London: John Murray, 1955), p. 68, and Davidson, "Space and Time in Medieval Drama," p. 44.

[114] *The N-town Play: Cotton MS Vespasian D.8*, ed. Stephen Spector, EETS, s.s. 11 (Oxford, 1991), p. 22 (I.339 *s.d.*). For other uses of the *Te Deum* in the mystery cycles, see JoAnna Dutka, *Music in the English Mystery Plays*, Early Drama, Art, and Music, Reference Ser., 2 (Kalamazoo: Medieval Institute Publications, 1980), pp. 42–43. The *Te Deum* is also sung by the priest and "clerkys, wyth woycys cler" at the conclusion of the Digby *Mary Magdalene* (l. 2138). As the canticle sung at the end of Matins, the *Te Deum* also commonly appeared at the conclusion of the church music-dramas when they were presented in that liturgical position.

[115] *The Receyt of the Ladie Kateryne*, ed. Gordon Kipling, EETS, 296 (Oxford: Oxford Univ. Press, 1990), p. 26.

[116] For a listing of extant alabaster Te Deum panels, see Sheingorn, "The Te Deum Altarpiece," pp. 172–74; see also Prior and Gardner, *An Account of*

Medieval Figure-Sculpture in England, pp. 494–95, fig. 570.

[117] *Coventry*, ed. Ingram, pp. 74, 240.

[118] *York*, ed. Johnston and Rogerson, I, 55.

[119] St. Thomas Aquinas, *Summa Theologica*, trans. Fathers of the English Dominican Province (New York: Benziger, 1948), III, 2974–80 (Supplement, Q. 95).

[120] Mâle, *Religious Art in France*, pp. 386, 498 (n. 116).

[121] Ibid., pp. 386–88, figs. 253–54.

[122] For this information I am indebted to my colleague Otto Gründler.

[123] Ernst Kitzinger, *Early Medieval Art in the British Museum*, 2nd ed. (London: Trustees of the British Museum, 1955), p. 21, Pl. 7.

[124] David O'Connor, "York and the Heavenly Jerusalem," in *Medieval Europe 1992*, Art and Symbolism, 7 (York: York Archaeological Trust, 1992), p. 71.

[125] See, for example, *Pontificale Lanaletense*, ed. G. H. Doble, Henry Bradshaw Soc., 74 (London: Harrison and Sons, 1937), pp. 25–26.

[126] Grabar, *Christian Iconography*, p. 43; Mowry, "Revelation 4–5 and Early Christian Liturgical Usage," pp. 81, 83.

[127] Lucy Freeman Sandler, *The Psalter of Robert de Lisle* (London: Harvey Miller and Oxford Univ. Press, 1983), Pls. 8–9; Lambert of St. Omer, *Liber Floridus*, ed. Alberto Derolez (Ghent: Story-Scientia, 1968), pp. 462–63 (fols. 231^v–232^r); see also Adolf Katzenellenbogen, *Allegories of the Virtues and Vices in Mediaeval Art*, trans. Alan J. P. Crick (1939; rpt. New York : W. W. Norton, 1964), pp. 65–66, figs. 64–67.

[128] Grabar, *Christian Iconography*, fig. 106.

[129] See Wilhelm Hausenstein, *Fra Angelico* (Munich: Kurt Wolff, 1923), Pl. 34.

[130] See *Enarrationes in Psalmos* LI.4, 6, as quoted in *An Augustine Synthesis*, ed. Erich Przywara (New York: Harper and Brothers, 1958), pp. 271–72.

[131] McDannell and Lang, *Heaven*, pp. 42–44.

[132] Lambert of St. Omer, *Liber Floridus*, ed. Derolez, p. 131 (fol. 65^r). The

twelve towers of the celestial paradise are given labels associating them with the twelve apostles and with precious stones. The accompanying text is the opening of 2 *Paralipomenon*.

[133] Schiller, *Ikonographie der christlichen Kunst*, III, fig. 634.

[134] See also pp. 146–47, below.

[135] Davidson, *The Guild Chapel Wall Paintings*, fig. 17.

[136] This placement for Last Judgment wall paintings is not unique to England; see Jerzy Domasłowski, Alicja Karłowska-Kamzowa, Marian Kornecki, and Helena Małkiewiczówna, *Gotyckie malarstwo ścienne w Polsce*, Uniwersytet im. Adama Mickiewicza w Poznaniu, Ser. Historia Sztuki, 17 (Poznań: Adam Mickiewicz Univ. Press, 1984), fig. 200, for a fifteenth-century wall painting over the chancel arch at Gdansk which shows the city of heaven at the bottom left and hell like a castle keep at the right.

The Bread of Heaven: Foretaste or Foresight?

Ann Eljenholm Nichols

"This is the bread that came down from heaven. Not as your fathers did eat manna, and are dead. He that eateth this bread, shall live for ever."—*John* 6.59

There is no better way to begin a discussion of the bread of heaven than with this passage drawn from the exegesis of the Johannine metaphor: "Ego sum panis vitae" ("I am the bread of life").[1] The discourse provides the explication for one of the key Old Testament types of the Eucharist, the manna in the desert, and it also provides the gospel for the feast of Corpus Christi. The texts for that feast, designed to be sung over the twenty-four hours of the liturgical day, are replete with references to food and drink. The first antiphon for vespers sets the theme, calling to mind Melchisedech's gift of bread and wine, a second major type of the Eucharist, and the last antiphon moves to the reality of the type. The Lord *satiaties us with the fat of wheat*: "frumenti adipe saciat nos dominus." The theme of wheat and bread weaves in and out of the canonical hours of the feast like a leitmotif: "pane suavissimo," "panis vivus et vitalis," "Panis angelicus," "panis hominum," "panis cælicus," "Panem cæli dedit eis. Panem angelorum manducavit homo."[2]

In a single article it is impossible to do more than sample the rich feast of texts, so I propose to deal with only three phrases, which were singled out by manuscript illustration. The first is "Cibavit eos ex adipe frumenti," the opening text of the introit of the Mass, but which is first used as the versicle in two nocturns as well as in terce, the hour immediately preceding Mass, and sext, the hour immediately following. The text is also closely related to the vespers antiphon already cited. The second and third phrases

40

are similarly related: *bread of angels* (*panem angelorem*) and *bread from heaven* (*panem cæli*), the two marvelously conflated as "swettest manna aungyll mete," in Nicholas Love's translation of Henry Suso's prayer.[3] I will argue that these texts can usefully contribute to our understanding of the iconography of heaven, and that, contrary to what they seem to say, the texts do not focus on the Eucharist as bread to be eaten, on bread as a foretaste of heaven (*praegustatum*, to use the phrase from the popular elevation prayer *Ave verum corpus*[4]), but instead on bread to be seen. I will further argue that the devotional gaze incorporated into the illustrations for these texts as well as in representations of the Eucharist in other media reflects more than pious demeanor—that it actually prefigures the beatific vision.

My focus is on English materials, though I will from time to time draw parallels from Continental sources. The corpus is small, and so the generalizations are necessarily tentative, but if this paper serves any purpose beyond that of a textual/visual exercise, it may be to suggest a corrective to the generally critical assessment of what Édouard Dumoutet described as a liturgical paradigm shift, a realignment of the axis of the canon from communion to consecration.[5] Liturgists as well as social historians have been critical of this shift, as were the Reformers, who, as J. Wickham Legg once phrased it, "made themselves merry" over the elevation. It may be, however, as Gary Macy noted ten years ago in his key study of the Eucharist in the early scholastic period, and, as Eamon Duffy more recently has argued in *The Stripping of the Altars*, that we have for too long allowed the Reformers to define the terms of debate.[6]

As the feast of Corpus Christi was slowly included in new breviaries and missals,[7] illustration typically appeared at the beginnings of the respective offices historiating the initials of the opening word of the first antiphon for vespers—"Sacerdos in eternum Christus dominus secundum ordinem melchisedech panem et vinum optulit"—or the introit—"Cibavit eos ex adipe frumenti."[8] In the Longleat Breviary (1316–22), which may well claim the earliest English illuminations of the feast, both offices are illustrated with marginal miniatures. The *Temporale* is illustrated by a consecration scene (fol. 81ᵛ). The officiating priest, inclining at a lateral altar, holds the Host in his left hand and blesses it with his right. A veiled chalice stands on the altar. There is another ton-sured figure at the left, and three figures kneel with hands joined in prayer. The gesture of the priest identifies the rite as one of the prayers immediately preceding the actual words of consecration. In the Mass section (fol. 193ᵛ) the miniature depicts communion. Two tonsured clerics hold the extended houseling cloth, while a third at the far right holds the houseling cup. The officiating priest gives a Host to the first of the four kneeling communicants, who touches the cloth. Modeled in three-quarters profile, the communicant gazes at the priest. His head is tipped slightly back, and his mouth is partially open.[9] These iconographic details of the communion rite remain static for the next two hundred years in English illustration. They are found, for example, in the historiation of *cibavit* (fig. 6) in a late fourteenth-century Sarum missal (Oxford, Trinity College, MS. D.8).[10] There the communion scene (fol. 158ᵛ) takes place outside of Mass, as was commonly the case for the laity. A tonsured cleric in an alb stands with his back to the altar as he communicates one of four men who kneel before him. It seems par-ticularly appropriate that a text focusing on food, specifically a word like *cibavit* ("he fed"), should be illuminated by eucharistic feeding.

The feast of Corpus Christi in English manuscripts, however, was not typically illustrated by communion. The elevation is used in the well-known Carmelite Missal, illuminated at the turn of the fifteenth century. It is paired with the Last Supper in a two-register historiation of *cibavit*, a case where a communion scene would seem more in keeping with the *cibum turbae duodenae* pictured above.[11] In the less well known East Anglian Ranworth Antiphonal the elevation also figures, in this case historiating the S of *Sacerdos*. Miri Rubin, in a passage that relies heavily on Continen-tal illustration, notes that the elevation was the favored subject in the earliest manuscripts. This is not to say that communion never illustrates the feast, but Rubin provides only two illustrations out of a total of nineteen. Both are texts of Italian provenance.[12]

A number of reasons have been posited for the preference for elevation scenes—the ready availability of elevation patterns (artistic habit undoubtedly played a role in the genesis of Corpus Christi iconography), a sacerdotal focus (particularly when *sacer-dos* is the word being historiated), or the theological focus of the elevation as announcement of the real presence (certainly a central theme in the Corpus Christi liturgy).[13] But there is, I believe, another reason for the seemingly curious decoration of the word *cibavit* with the elevation of the Mass, and that reason should be sought not in the pattern books of artists nor in the tomes of theologians, but instead in the traditional commentaries on the psalms from which this text and others in the Corpus Christi liturgy were drawn. The Corpus Christi introit is taken from Psalm 80 (in the Sarum breviary appointed to be said or sung every Friday at Matins): "Et cibauit illos ex adipe frumenti: & de petra melle saturauit eos." Richard Rolle translates and glosses as follows: "And he fede thaim of the grese of whete: and of the hony stane he thaim fild. That is, he fed thaim with the body of crist. and gastly vndirstandynge, and of huny that ran of the stane, that is, of wisdome that is swete till the hert, he fild thaim. . . ."[14] The food dematerializes into "gastly vndirstandynge" and "wisdome." Similar dematerialization occurs with "Gustate & videte quoniam suauis est dominus: beatus vir qui sperat in eo" (Ps. 33), which Rolle translates and glosses as, "'Swelighis and sees for soft is lord; blisful man that hopis in him.' Swelighis the swetnes of his luf and swa sees, that is, undirestandis, that god is soft mete, and diletabile til the saule. . . . he that hopis in him wham he swalighis sall be blisful in endles life. . . ."[15] Even here where the Lord is described as "soft mete," even where words like "fede" and "swallows" intensify the physical meaning of eating, eating is glossed as understanding. This dematerialization has a long history in psalm commentary and was particularly influential in the Laon-Victorine theology of the Eucharist.[16]

"Bread from heaven," the manna in the desert, is subject to the same spiritualization, in this case evidenced in typological illustration as well as in psalm commentary. Verses from Psalm 77, used as versicle and respond in the first and third nocturns, recapitulate the miracle of the Old Law. In Rolle's commentary we read, "Et mandauit nubibus desuper: & ianuas celi aperuit. Et pluit illis manna ad manducandum: & panem celi dedit eis. Panem angelorum manducauit homo: cibaria misit eis in habundancia" ("And he bad til the cloudis abouen; and the ȝates of heuen he oppynd. And he rayned til thaim manna for to ete; and brede of heuen he til thaim gaf. Brede of aungels man ete; fode he sent till thaim in haboundance").[17] The Last Supper page of the *Biblia Pauperum* pairs this gift of bread from heaven with the encounter between Abraham and Melchisedech as types of the Eucharist, but although the texts for this page are rich in references to food and feeding, the pictures do not represent the act of eating. Melchisedech holds a chalice in his right hand, lifting up in his left a Host on which Abraham gazes, his right hand raised in a gesture that is typical of elevation scenes.[18] The Israelites gather but do not eat the manna. Traditional cloud bands delineate the heavens, and Host-shaped manna falls from among the bands to a large plate held by one man with upturned face, into the cloak of a second who also gazes to heaven, and to the ground, where it is collected by two men in the foreground. An Israelite in the background looks up to heaven with both hands outstretched. This gaze towards heaven from which the bread rains down and the raised hands are standard features of the iconography of the manna in the desert.[19] As the eleventh-century sequence *Ave, praeclara maris stella* so aptly noted, "Therefore, the true manna, once prefigured to Moses, is now . . . given to the true Israelites, the children of the true Abraham, *for their admiring beholding*" (italics mine).[20] The bread from heaven is for beholding, not for eating. The beholding is visually emphasized by the verticality of the *Biblia Pauperum* Last Supper page, a feature that characterizes the relatively uniform iconography of the manna in the desert found elsewhere, for example, in the *Speculum Humanae Salvationis*.[21]

The spiritualization of the manna text in Psalm 77 is rooted in mainstream commentary. "What is the bread of heaven?" asks the *Glossa Ordinaria*. "None other than Christ by which the heavenly ones, that is, the angels, are restored with his contemplation." In Rolle's gloss we read, "Brede of aungels is crist. for in his sight thai hafe that thaim list. and him etis man in the sacrament and in luf. . . ."[22] The key word here is *sight*. In this complex metaphor, the tenor is the sight of Christ, but the vehicle, bread, operates on two different levels, earthly and heavenly. What is sacramental bread for the faithful on earth (the bread from heaven) is vision in heaven (the bread of angels). Sight also works on two levels, for the eyes of the flesh perceive only an elevated Host, whereas the eye of the soul perceives Christ and so has a fore-sight of the eternal vision. A Middle English free translation of *Lauda Sion* makes the relationship between the sight of God and the food of heaven, between tenor and vehicle, even more explicit:

> Þy face, wiþ loue to seen in syȝt,
> In lond of lyf, þou vs lede.
> Among þy seyntes in heuene on hyȝt,
> At þat feste of life, god, vs fede!
> Soþfast brede, god of myȝt,
> Ihesus herde, þou vs hede! [23]

In heaven humankind will feed on the sight of God's face, on the bread of angels. Since the bread of angels is their sight of the Second Person of the Trinity, and since the Eucharist at the elevation of the Mass is the bread of angels, it follows that the sight of the Eucharist in some way prefigures that ultimate vision.[24] It is, therefore, possible to conclude that the focus on vision in the illustrations of Corpus Christi texts is not anomalous but perfectly in keeping with a centuries-old interpretation that links temporal sight with eschatological vision.[25]

Vision is also central in the iconography of communion. The communicants in the illumination of *Cibavit* in Trinity College MS. D.8 (fig. 6) are typical. They are rendered in profile, with the result that we see their open eyes staring ahead. The priest holds the Host just at the open mouth of the communicant to the left, who raises his chin at an angle. He both sees the Host and prepares to eat it as well.[26] This double focus on the Eucharist as Host to be seen and bread to be consumed is characteristic of communion iconography in a wide range of media both in England and on the Continent, and was in use for at least two hundred years. Rubin reproduces an early fourteenth-century example, and a classic example of this iconography from the middle of the same century exists in a fresco at Santa Maria Incoronata (Naples) by Roberto d'Odorisio. In this scene, which is part of a seven-sacrament composition, a group of lay communicants fix their eyes on the priest, who places the Host into the mouth of the foremost of the group.[27] Again the rendering of the figure in profile means that the angle of the chin and open eyes are a prominent feature of the iconography. The cartoonists at the Exeter workshop that made seven-sacrament windows for Doddiscombsleigh and Crudwell in the last quarter of the fifteenth century incorporate the same iconography into viaticum scenes (figs. 7–8). At Doddiscombsleigh the communicant also has his eyes open and chin tilted, the better to see the extended Host, and his mouth open to receive the sacred species, which the priest is about to place on his tongue. Similarly at Crudwell, *moriens'* eyes are open, and we can just see a Host at his open mouth. The same iconography can be seen in the sixteenth-century Eucharist window at Hoogstraten, where a group of male communicants to the right fix their eyes on the bishop, who holds the Host about to give it to the foremost man whose lips are slightly parted.[28] To rephrase the psalm text "Gustate and videte," in the iconography of communion the communicant sees and then tastes, *manducatio per visum et per gustum*.

In the iconography of the elevation, it is sight alone that is featured, *manducatio per visum*. In a full page miniature from a Latin-English book of hours (fig. 9) opposite a prayer for a happy death, the priest raises a large white Host, while the patron kneeling on the cushion holds out both hands in one of the three typical elevation gestures.[29] The layman is in demiprofile, so again his eyes are visible. As in communion iconography, the chin is tilted up as he raises his eyes to the elevated Host. Thus the iconography of communion and elevation are identical in their emphasis on vision, a uniformity that may well reflect a connection between the elevation and non-sacramental communion, traditionally known as spiritual communion. Though sacramental communion in England was generally restricted for the laity to Easter and for religious to a limited number of feasts, all could communicate daily in spiritual communion.[30] The theological nature of spiritual communion was a matter of dispute,[31] but vernacular texts make it clear that the people believed it equivalent to sacramental communion and so reflect the position taken by Thomas Aquinas, who held that desire produced the reception of the *res* (the reality) of the sacrament.[32] Except for a priest, *panem nostrum quotidianum* necessarily meant spiritual communion, and the phrase was so interpreted in commentaries on the *Pater noster*: "And gyue vs suche faythe, & charyte, and deuocyon in our soules that therby we may receyue euery day the brede of thy holy sacramente of the aulter, that is lorde Iesu thy selfe . . . though we receyue yt not euery day *with our bodely mouthes*."[33]

Caroline Walker Bynum has noted that continental female mystics fell into ecstasy not at the moment of sacramental communion but rather at the elevation, a fact that supports the localization of spiritual communion at that point of the Mass.[34] The iconography of the elevation as represented in the lovely seven-sacrament window at Doddiscombsleigh (fig. 10) also suggests this localization, for not only do we see the rapt gaze of all the participants, layfolk as well as acolytes, but the male figure in profile (upper left) also has his lips parted like *moriens* in the viaticum scene of the same window (fig. 7). The evidence in English texts, however, is not so simple to interpret. In a remarkable illustrated Anglo-French missalette, *Ceo qe vous deuez fere e penser a chascon point de la Messe* (1310–20), spiritual communion is correlated explicitly in word and image with the communion rite. There is no miniature of communion proper, but the prayer for the third *Agnus Dei* refers to spiritual communion in imagery that is strongly nutritive. Jesus provides the sacrament to nourish us and incorporate us in himself as members of their head ("pur nous nourir e encorporer a lui meismes come membres a lor chief"). Following a prayer directed to the good shepherd ("pasce agnos tuos pasce oues tuas"), the text directs the readers to believe that one may be totally united with the sacrament through spiritual communion ("Creez purvoir e esperez qe vous soiez espiritalment comunie tout ne receiuez vous veablement le sacrement"), and the reader is also directed during the communion antiphon to give thanks for the sacrament received ("Pur graces rendre a la trinite e pur le sacrement qe nous est done").[35] The illumination that accompanies the third *Agnus Dei* shows the congregation in the same posture as in the earlier elevation miniature: they look up and raise their hands in traditional levation gestures. The only difference is that a dove descends from a bust of Christ in a nebuly, not to the priest holding the broken Host preparatory for his communion but instead to the laity, whose spiritual union with Christ is effected by the power of the Holy Ghost.

Spiritual communion is also handled at the time of ritual communion in that remarkable work written for the women at Syon, *The Myroure of Oure Ladye*. It is again handled at the *Agnus Dei*, the last sung text before communion proper.

And for asmoche as they that ar presente & here masse may receyue our
lorde spiritually at euery masse, like as the preste receyueth hym in the
sacramente, therfor in tyme of *Agnus dei*, & whyle the preste vsyth
[communicates], ye oughte to dyspose you ful dylygently & deuoutly,
and with grete feruoure & gostly desyre, to stretche oute your loue &
deuocion reuerently to our lorde, that ye lese not so grete a gostly fruyte
& be not pryued of the swetnes of that heuenly feaste, with whyche ye
may be fed at eche masse that ye here, if ye wil desyrously set youre
harte thereto.[36]

However, when we turn to other Mass texts designed for lay use,
the evidence shifts to support the contention that the faithful communicated spiritually when they looked upon the elevated Host. To
judge from these vernacular texts, it would seem that the communion
rite proper had disappeared altogether.[37] In the *Lay Folks Mass Book*,
following an elaborate section on the rite of the pax, the text moves
immediately to the priest's ablutions; the communion rite is ignored.[38] In *The Manner and Mede of the Mass*, although the text
does refer to the priest's communion, it does so only perfunctorily:
"Whon he haþ vsed [communicated], he walkeþ riht/ To Laua-
torie."[39] Similarly, in *Merita Missae*, though there is a reference to
the priest's commmunion, the text turns immediately to the medes,
the prayers connected with the benefits of hearing Mass. This text is
of particular interest because it explicitly connects spiritual communion with the *sight* of the priest being houseled.

And whan he is houȝelyed with that oste,
Pray than to the holy goste

. . .

And ȝef ye be in cheryte,
Ȝe be hoslyd as welle as he:
His loue and hys moche myght
Ȝevythe youe houȝyll *in that syght.*[40]

Since the congregation could not *see* the priest consume the Host
because his back was turned to the people, there were obvious
psychological reasons for the gravitation of spiritual communion
from the communion rite to the ritual when the sight of the body
of Christ was dramatized with bell and candle. Vernacular levation
prayers also make it clear that it was at the dramatic moment of the
elevation that the faithful communicated spiritually. Sometimes the

reference is explicit, as in the beautiful prayer ascribed to John Audelay: "Hayle! graunt me grace goostely/ To ressayue þi blessid body/ In parfyte loue and charite,/ Þat is here present."[41] Sometimes the evidence is implicit in the references to food, as in the acclamation "Welcome be þou, soule fode."[42] Lydgate's long prayer in *The Interpretation and Virtues of the Mass*, designed, he says, as an alternative to other levation prayers, begins, "Hayle, holy Iesu our healthe our goostly foode," and the phrases roll on majestically, "spirytuall Manna, brede contemplatyf," "of Aungellys thow art foode,/ Repaste to pylgryms in theyr pylgremage,/ Celestiall brede to chyldren than byn goode."[43] Certainly, texts like these stand at odds with Reformation castigations of "elevation mania."

Since sight was psychologically central in the act of spiritual communion, it is hardly surprising that it figures so prominently in vernacular directions for how one should behave at the elevation. In the Anglo-Norman missalette, the cue line for the elevation reads, "quant vous *verrez* leuer le corps nostre segnor" (italics mine here and in the next five quotations).[44] In *Merita Missae* one is enjoined to pray to "be wordy to see that *syght*,/ That schalle be in hys handis lyght."[45] John Audelay's *De salutacione corporis Ihesu Christi* begins "When þou *scyst* þe sacrement,"[46] and in *De meritis misse* he notes, "Þen glad mai ȝe be/ ȝour Saueour so to *se*."[47] Sight figures in levation prayers, where the phrase "In forme of brede as y the *se*" is commonplace, and also in one of the promises attached to the "Fifteen Oes" in books of hours, which promised that those who recited the prayers should before death *see* and receive Christ's body.[48] All this may be laboring the obvious, but if we are to understand properly the iconography of the bread of angels, it is crucial to recognize that sight was intimately connected with the act of spiritual communion.

This recognition also enables us to come to terms with the one of the medes of the Mass, which have been so generally criticized as superstitious. The particular mede I wish to address promises final communion (viaticum) as a reward for merely seeing the elevation. In one variant, however, the mede takes the form of a statement rather than a promise: "þat day · þou hast god se · ȝif þou be ded · þe same day, þou schalt be founden/ I þe say,/ Houseled [with viaticum] · as þou hed be [sacramentally]."[49] That is, if one dies without viaticum, but has seen the elevation the same day, that sight substitutes for viaticum. The same substitution is stated by Audelay: "When þou His bode ast y-seyne, / 3if þou dey þat ilke day. / Þou schalt be found in þe fay / As þou houseld hadust bene."[50] Texts like the ones quoted do not say "the day you see bread" but "the day you see *God*"—that is, the Eucharist is perceived with the eyes of faith. This "mede" certainly is not mere superstition, for if the viewer is "in cheryte" such an act qualifies as spiritual communion. Whatever the theological dubiety of the medes as a whole, there is nothing superstitious about substituting spiritual for sacramental communion. The substitution, in other words, should not be dismissed as grossly mechanical. Indeed, it may be post-Reformation interpretation that is mechanical, and that what has been labeled a popular fixation on the sight of the elevated Host needs to be reexamined in a more sympathetic light.[51]

Contemporary theories of vision help to shed more than a little light on the subject. Sight, an act of sensation by which an individual perceives a separate object, was, according to Aristotle and Alhazen after him, accomplished through intromission, the passive sense receiving the species of the sensible body being perceived. The exact nature of species varied from one theorist to another, but it was generally accepted that something issued from the sensible body and affected the medium between the object and the eye.[52] The term most commonly used to explain this "something" was *ray*. Rays, according to the classic formulation in Alhazen, issue in all directions from an object and strike the eye, but it is only the perpendicular ray that enters the eye since it is strong enough to weaken oblique or refracted rays.[53] The visual pyramid thus had its base at the object viewed and its apex at the center of the cornea.[54]

The depiction of rays of light around sacred objects must in some way reflect the pervasiveness of this psychology of sight. Light rays are integral to a late Eucharist composition that represents the bread of angels in a communion scene. The composition occupies the central third of a seven-sacrament illumination preserved at the Bruges Convent of the Potterie, and probably was commissioned originally for the sisters there. Fine lines radiate in all directions from a central crucifix. Immediately below the crucifix is a massive monstrance containing a large Host. The monstrance is held up by two angels dressed in albs and standing on an altar dressed for Mass, a literal representation of the "bread of angels," which commonly illustrates Corpus Christi texts.[55] The open missal stands to the left, and the chalice rests on a corporal directly below the monstrance. The exact moment of the service is communion. The priest stands with his back to the altar, and a nun kneels before an extended houseling cloth held by two deacons kneeling at either side. The priest and nun are on the same axis as crucifix, elevated Host, and chalice. The nun has already received communion, for no Host is depicted on the paten held in the priest's left hand, nor does he raise the Host in his right, a common feature of communion iconography. Instead the priest holds his right hand in a gesture of blessing. The delineation of the rays is not geometrically precise, but the central ray proceeds from the feet of Christ through the elevated Host to the paten held by the priest and ends at the head of the kneeling nun. It is thus a perpendicular ray that links the image of the salvific act, the reenactment of that act in the sacrifice of the Mass, and the communion of the nun. She has eaten, an act that is not depicted, but in the act of eating sees—and it is the act of sight that is the visual focus of this composition.

David Lindberg has commented that we know next to nothing about how visual theory affected theology because the material is scattered in so many different sorts of texts that it is difficult to identify or study.[56] Nonetheless, we do know that the Aristotelian theory of intromission was largely unchallenged in the fourteenth and fifteenth centuries.[57] Such a theory requires a reassessment of the ready criticism that has been vented against "elevation mania." For if real physical contact is effected through vision, if the sight of the elevated Host is also a moment of intense spiritual experience, if to gaze "With all your myght," to use Lydgate's phrase,[58] can actually effect union with Christ, then we must allow that even the phrase "devotional gaze" is too pallid to describe the spiritual experience depicted. Certainly, artists were at pains to depict the intensity of liturgical gaze. Whether lay people at Mass (fig. 10) or an acolyte assisting at a deathbed communion (fig. 7), these men and women, the artists seem to be saying, are united through sight and grace with the Second Person of the Blessed Trinity. In this intense spiritual vision, one in which the eyes of the mind move beyond the accidents of sense, the worshippers have in some very real sense a preview of heaven when the blessed see the essence of God intuitively face to face.[59] Since this is so, the intense gaze of the faithful directed to the consecrated Host, whether in the iconography of the elevation or of communion, should be added to our list of images of heaven.

Rolle makes the same point in a gloss on another Corpus Christi text reminiscent of the *cibavit* introit: "Qui pacem ponit fines ecclesie frumenti ex adipe saciat nos dominus": "That sett thin endis pes; and of the grese of whete he fillys the. . . . that pes is fyllynge of the brede of aungels. that syght of the trinyte sall be till vs fulnes of ioy. . . ."[60] Since the filling bread of angels is the "syght of the trinyte," it is but a short step to the belief that the sight of the bread of angels in its sacramental form, the vision of the Eucharist, is a preview of the beatific vision of heaven. From the prospective of eternity, the Eucharist is not only a pledge of future glory ("futuræ gloriæ nobis pignus datur"),[61] it is also itself a type of what is to come, a point made by the postcommunion of the Corpus Christi Mass: "Fac nos, quæsumus, Domine divinitatis tuæ sempiterna fruitione repleri, quam pretiosi corporis et sanguinis tui temporalis perceptio praefigurat" ("Make us, O Lord, we beseech you, to be filled with the everlasting fruition of your divinity, which the temporal reception of your precious body and blood prefigures").[62] To be filled with eternal fruition of the Lord's divinity is nothing else than to experience the vision of the Trinity, to use Rolle's phrase "when thou sees god in his fairhed."[63]

References to the Trinity are not restricted to the relatively elite world of the Latin liturgy and psalm commentaries. The Trinity is sometimes invoked in levation prayers: "Hayle, Almyghty God in Trinyte"; and the index to the poems of the *Vernon Manuscript* entitles one prayer "Sixe salutacions to þe trinity in tyme of the eleuacioun of godies body."[64] One fourteenth-century poem to the Trinity concludes with the prayer, "On þe to se þat swete siht,/ Fadur & sone & holigost. Amen."[65] And Lydgate provides a variant of a typical Host miracle, in which the vision is not the Christ child or Image of Pity, but instead the Trinity.

> Þis hoolly Thomas, called of Algwyne,
> By hie myracle þat sawghe persones three
> An ooste ful round, a sunne about it shune,

Joyned in oon by parfyte vnytee,
A gloryous liknesse of þe Trynitee.[66]

There is also iconographic support for connecting the act of sacramental communion with the vision of the Trinity. In the *Sherborne Missal* the feast of Corpus Christi is illustrated by two acolytes in surplices holding a communion cloth for a kneeling communicant, who extends his hands as if in adoration, while a priest holds a paten in his left hand and an unusually large Host in the other. Above are the Trinity, the Father and Son with a Tau cross and orb between them, and the Holy Ghost descending with a Host in his beak. Predictably, the communicant is modeled in profile, his head is tilted back slightly, and he gazes at the Host. The priest offers the sacrament (the sacramental species), while the Holy Ghost offers the bread of heaven—here both foretaste and foresight of the Trinity.[67]

The theology suggested by this unusual communion scene is clarified in three medallions at the top of the Whit Wednesday page, an octave Mass that repeated the gospel used for Corpus Christi.[68] The medallion to the left reads "sacramentalis" both above and below a miniature of the elevation of the Mass. The one to the right reads "eternalis" above and below a scene of an angel in an ermine tippet. The central medalion reads "panem nostram quotidianum da nobis hodie," and in that scene a man kneels with his folded hands extended while a large Host is extended to him by the hand of God. The communicant's head is again tilted, his mouth open to eat, his eyes open to see. The sacramental bread raised at the elevation and consumed at communion prefigures the bread from heaven, the eternal vision enjoyed by the angels.

The bread from heaven as sacrament, as we have already seen, was particularly valued at the last moment of life. As one author explained, the sacrament "is also called viaticum . a . via . for . . . it is ȝouen to hem þat be goynge þe pilgrymage in extremis."[69] To be able to receive viaticum was something the faithful prayed for at every elevation, that "housel be my last brede,"[70] and in addition to the viaticum mede, final shrift and housel are also the objects of petition in a wide range of prayers: "O mercyful Iesu! graunt only of þi grace,/ In sowle and body ffull consolacyoun,/ By shryfft and hoosill or I hens pace."[71] This intimate connection between the Eucharist and the final moment of life already existed in early levation prayers,[72] and Lydgate uses viaticum as a leitmotif in the long prayer attached to *The Interpretation and Virtues of the Mass* as an alternative to customary levation prayers. Each octave concludes with a prayer to receive "hosyll and schryft" or a reference only to viaticum, e.g., "Graunt, or I dy, Cryst, for thy passyon,/ I may receue thys brede sent downe from heuene."[73] The final stanza of the elevation hymn *Adoro te* with its wordplay on *velatum/ revelatum* connects the sight of Eucharist with the unveiled vision of God's glory: "Jesu, quem velatum nunc aspicio,/ Oro fiat illud quod tan sitio;/ Ut revelata cernens facie, Visu sim beatus tuae gloriae" ("Jesus, as I look on your veiled presence, I pray that what I long for so ardently may come about, and that I may see your face unveiled and be happy in the vision of your glory").[74] It is vision in the iconography of the elevation, vision in the iconography of communion and viaticum that connects the communicant (sacramentally or non-sacramentally) with the vision of God's face in eternity. In viaticum scenes like the one at Doddiscombsleigh, it is the intense gaze of *moriens* that creates the emotional tone of the composition, for it is a gaze into eternity. The bread of angels made food for wayfarers ("panis angelorum/ Factus cibus viatorium")[75] now will provide a safe journey through the mouth of death and into the heavenly kingdom, where man's sight will no longer be defective but will be made to see the Good, the Beatific, in the land of the living: "Tu nos bona fac videre/ In terra viventium."[76]

Appendix: *Medes*

The much maligned merits of the Mass have recently been handled with some sympathy in Eamon Duffy's treatment of the importance of the liturgy in the everyday lives of the people.[77] I have already addressed the viaticum mede, and would like also to look briefly at a mede that deals specifically with sight, the promise that blindness will not occur on the day one sees the Eucharist. This mede has characteristically been lumped together with superstitious promises of enough to eat ("He xal hys fode [enjoy] þat day/ Suffesantly I dar wel say") or protection from sudden death, but it would be well to consider whether the sight promise should be interpreted literally. Medieval men and women had good reason to fear sudden death, but sudden blindness was hardly a daily threat. On the other hand, one did regularly pray at the levation to be preserved from sin, and the notion of spiritual blindness was scarcely an arcane concept.[78] For example, a Middle Dutch communion prayer facing an illumination of a nun receiving communion asks that one who is blind may be led to the light of eternal salvation.[79] The composition conforms to the norms already described. The nun is in three quarters profile, her eyes open as she looks at the Host extended by the priest. If we look only at the treatment of the Crucifixion in popular medieval drama, the juxtaposition of physical/spiritual blindness is commonplace. In the Chester play of the Passion, where sight is a leitmotif, Christ prays for those that "be blynd and may not see/ howe fowle they donne amys."[80] The Jews are sighted but blind to Christ's identity; Longinus is blind but given sight for his "trespas"; and the pagan Centurion perceives the enormity of the trespass: "I am ashamed, verely,/ this vncooth sight to see."[81] In the Towneley Play of the Crucifixion, Longinus calls out, "Ere was I blynde, now may I se."[82] In visual representations Longinus points to his eyes, and the centurion raises his hand in the gesture recommended in Mass books at the time of the elevation.[83] In the N-Town Passion play Longinus repeats the word "see" three times in as many lines: "O good Lord, how may þis be,/ Þat I may se so bryth now?/ Þis thretty wyntyr I myth not se/ And now I may se . . . ," and the centurion proclaims Christ's true nature: "In trewth, now I knowe with ful opyn syght/ That Goddys dere sone is naylid on tre . . ./ quod vere Filius Dei erat iste."[84] The centurion's words are translated in levation prayers: "Hayle! þi gloryous Godhede hit may not be sene,/ Hayle! with no freelte of flesly ʒene;/ Hayle! I beleue truly in þis brede that ʒe bene,/ Verey God and mon."[85] If spiritually blind, one sees only bread, but with the sight of faith one sees beneath the accidental veil to the reality. If the senses are frail ("si sensus deficit"), faith will suffice ("sola fides sufficit"). It does not seem to be stretching a point too far to argue that one of the rewards of faith-filled sight of the Eucharist is protection from the defects of spiritual blindness: "Praestet fides supplementum sensuum defectui."[86]

NOTES

[1] For a discussion of the *ego eimi* metaphors in *John*, see Raymond E. Brown, *The Gospel According to John I–XII*, Anchor Bible (Garden City: Doubleday, 1966), pp. 533–38; for the internal structure of the discourse, see ibid., pp. 272–80, 284–94.

[2] I am here concerned with the "mature" text of the liturgy; for the complex history of competing liturgical texts, a good place to begin is L. M. J. Delaissé, "A la Recherche des Origines de l'Office du Corpus Christi dans les Manuscrits Liturgiques," *Scriptorium*, 4 (1950), 220–39. Primary citations for the hours texts are from *Breviarum ad usum insignis ecclesie Sarum*, ed. Francis Proctor and Christopher Wordsworth (Cambridge: Cambridge Univ. Press, 1882), I, mlxi–

mlxxviii, hereafter cited as *Sarum Breviary*. These texts have been cross checked with *Breviarium ad usum insignis ecclesie Eboracensis*, ed. Stephen W. Lawley, Surtees Society, 71, 75 (Durham, 1880–83), I, 529–32, hereafter cited as *York Breviary*. For the Sarum Missal, see *Missale ad usum insignis et praeclarae ecclesiae Sarum*, ed. Francis H. Dickinson (Bruntisland, 1861–83), hereafter cited as *Sarum Missal*.

[3] As Elizabeth Zeeman has pointed out, this phrase combines the *dulcimus* of the Latin original with *angels mete* from an earlier Middle English translation of the prayer ("Two Middle English Versions of a Prayer to the Sacrament," *Archiv für das Studium der neueren Sprachen und Literaturen*, 194 [1957–58], 115, 117). This stanza was copied into a late fifteenth-century book of hours; cited in Eamon Duffy, *The Stripping of the Altars* (New Haven: Yale Univ. Press, 1992), p. 120. One of the many subjects that must be ignored in this brief study is the savor of sweetness. The classic treatment of eating and savoring, particularly in the eucharistic piety of medieval women, is Caroline Walker Bynum's *Holy Feast and Holy Fast* (Berkeley and Los Angeles: Univ. of California Press, 1987).

[4] *Horae Eboracenses: The Prymer or Hours of the Blessed Virgin Mary*, ed. Christopher Wordsworth, Surtees Society, 132 (Durham: Andrews, 1920), p. 70. The prayer is also found in Sarum primers, Latin as well as English; see Edgar E. Hoskins, *Horae Beatae Mariae Virginis; or Sarum and York Primers with Kindred Books and Primers of the Reformed Roman Use* (London: Longmans, Green, 1901), pp. 111, 165. The prayer is included in Joseph Connelly, *Hymns of the Roman Liturgy* (Westminster, Maryland: Newman Press, 1957), p. 130. This convenient volume should be supplemented by *Repertorium Hymnologicum*, ed. Ulysse Chevalier (Louvain, 1897).

[5] Dumoutet does not, of course, use the term "paradigm shift": "l'axe du canon semble se déplacer de la communion vers la consécration, qui devient désormais, grâce à l'élévation, une sort de point culminant vers qui tout converge: plus exactement, c'est l'élévation elle-même qui risque de passer, dans l'opinion des fidèles, pour le véritable sommet du sacrifice, et son rite le plus essentiel" ("Aux Origines des Saluts du Saint-Sacrement," *Revue Apologetique*, 52 [1931], 411).

[6] Gary Macy, *The Theologies of the Eucharist in the Early Scholastic Period* (Oxford: Clarendon Press, 1984); Duffy, *The Stripping of the Altars, passim*.

[7] The feast was extended to the universal Church in 1264 and first recognized in England c.1318. See Miri Rubin, *Corpus Christi: The Eucharist in Late Medieval Culture* (Cambridge: Cambridge Univ. Press, 1991), pp. 176–84, 196–204, for the chronology of the adoption of the feast.

[8] *Sarum Breviary*, I, mlxi; *York Breviary*, I, 529. Rubin, in her encyclopedic *Corpus Christi*, p. 204n and Pl. 9, notes the occasional illustration of the collect, for which see also G. de Boom, "Le Culte de l'Eucharistie d'après la Miniature du Moyen Age," in *Studia Eucharistica DCC[i] Anni a Condito Festo Sanctissimi Corporis Christi 1246–1946* (Antwerp: De Nederlandsche Boekhandel, 1946), p. 330. De Boom notes an early use of the Last Supper to illustrate communion prayers (ibid., pp. 326–27). Rubin provides the best single collection of illustrations, continental as well as insular. Unfortunately, we do not yet have the necessary research tools for a systematic analysis of English Corpus Christi illustrations. Lucy Freeman Sandler's corpus of 150 manusucripts includes only five missals and four breviaries (no index entry for *cibavit*); see her *Gothic Manuscripts 1285–1385*, A Survey of Manuscripts Illuminated in the British Isles, 5 (London: Harvey Miller and Oxford Univ. Press, 1986), 2 vols. Although the forthcoming publication of the sixth volume of the Survey of Manuscripts Illuminated in the British Isles will enlarge our understanding of fifteenth-century iconography, it too will be limited to the best representative manuscripts.

[9] Longleat House, Marquess of Bath MS. 10, fol. 193[v]; Sandler, *Gothic Manuscripts*, No. 52. I am grateful to Kate Harris for providing me a detailed description of these two illuminations. Both occupy lower margins, the consecration scene measuring 29x32 mm, the communion scene 25x46mm. For the dating and history of the manuscript, see Lucy Freeman Sandler, "An Early Fourteenth-Century English Breviary at Longleat," *Journal of the Warburg and Courtauld Institutes*, 39 (1976), 1–20, where the miniature at fol. 193[v] is misidentified as the consecration of the Host.

[10] Sandler, *Gothic Manuscripts*, No. 144. For a fifteenth-century example of the Last Supper depicted as a communion scene in a column miniature immediately above *cibauit*, see Édouard Dumoutet, *Le Christ selon la Chair et la Vie Liturgique au Moyen-Age* (Paris: Beauchesne, 1932), fig. 10.

[11] Margaret Rickert, *The Reconstructed Carmelite Missal* (Chicago: Univ. of Chicago Press, 1951), Pl. B. Paschal Kallenberg, *Fontes Liturgiae Carmelitanae*, Textus et Studia Historica Carmelitana, 5 (Rome: Institutum Carmelitanum, 1962), cites only three Carmelite historiations for *cibavit*: the *Carmelite Missal* elevation (p. 129), communion (p. 231), and procession (p. 146); for summary and discussion, see Ann Eljenholm Nichols, *Seeable Signs* (Woodbridge: Boydell and Brewer, 1994).

[12] The exposition and procession of the Host are beyond the scope of this article. All the evidence suggests that this subject became by far the most popular illustration for the feast of Corpus Christi. Rubin reproduces three such *cibavit* historiations, ranging from c.1430 to c.1470: a procession (p. 253, fig. 12), a

tabernacle on a feretory (p. 254, fig. 13), and two angels holding a monstrance (p. 295, fig. 17). The latter is a literal representation of "the bread of angels," an image that in late seven-sacrament art replaces the more traditional elevation and communion scenes as a representation of the Eucharist; for detailed discussion, see my *Seeable Signs*.

[13] V. L. Kennedy convincingly argues that Dumoutet oversimplified historical issues when he proposed that the elevation was instituted primarily for devotional purposes. Although he does not discount devotional influence, he demonstrates that the institution of the elevation of the Host immediately after the words of institution were spoken marked an important theological resolution in the schools ("The Moment of Consecration and the Elevation of the Host," *Mediaeval Studies*, 6 [1944], 121–50). The theology behind the elevation of the Mass is beyond the focus of this article, as is a suitable bibliography for the Eucharist, for which see Rubin, *Corpus Christi*, pp. 369–419. Essential works include: Peter Browe's magisterial work, in particular *Die Verehrung der Eucharistie im Mittelalter* (Munich: Max Hueber, 1933); Joseph A. Jungmann, *The Mass of the Roman Rite* (New York: Benziger Brothers, 1951–55), especially for the history of the elevation; and Édouard Dumoutet, *Le Désir de Voir l'Hostie et les origines de la dévotion au saint-sacrement* (Paris: Beauchesne, 1926).

[14] Richard Rolle, *The Psalter or Psalms of David and Certain Canticles*, ed. H. R. Bramley (Oxford: Clarendon Press, 1884), p. 300. Rolle's psalm translations and glosses were widely used and hence were formative in English religious development; they also epitomize traditional interpretations of the psalms, for he relied heavily on the *catena* of Peter Lombard. For the English Psalter, see *English Writings of Richard Rolle Hermit of Hampole*, ed. Hope Emily Allen (Oxford: Clarendon Press, 1931), pp. 1–4; for the Middle English manuscripts, see Dorothy Everett, "The Middle English Prose Psalter of Richard Rolle of Hampole," *Modern Language Review*, 17 (1922), 217–27.

[15] Rolle, *The Psalter*, p. 119.

[16] Macy, *The Theologies of the Eucharist*, pp. 93–97 and *passim*.

[17] Rolle, *The Psalter*, p. 281.

[18] Although Abraham typically stands, in a fragment of a Seven Sacrament tapestry (Burrell Collection, Glasgow) he kneels on one knee while gazing at the extended Host and chalice, a posture more typical of elevation scenes. For the reconstruction of the fragmentary tapestry, see William Wells, "The Seven Sacraments Tapestry—A New Discovery," *Burlington Magazine*, 101 (1959), 97–105, fig. 16.

[19] Avril Henry, *Biblia Pauperum: A Facsimile and Edition* (Ithaca: Cornell Univ. Press, 1987), pp. 81, 83. Henry comments on the effective use of the vertical axis in the blocks. For an example of the manna from heaven in an early sixteenth century Flemish altarpiece with painted wings, see Catheline Périer-d'Ieteren, *Les volets peints des retables bruxellois conservés en Suède et le rayonnement de Colyn de Coter* (Stockholm: Almqvist & Wicksell, 1984), fig. E.60.

Unconsecrated Hosts (obols/obleys) feature as bread from heaven in English paraliturgy, plays, and pageants. In the N-Town plays Mary is fed with "aungelys mete" (9.247–48), and the stage directions specify that the angel *"bryngyth manna in a cowpe of gold lyke to confeccyons"* (l. 245 *s.d.*). Stephen Spector glosses 'confeccyons' as "prepared dishes or delicacies," but the noun is derived from the verb meaning to consecrate, so it is clearly a synonym for "oble," the word used in the stage directions for the Last Supper (27.372, *s.d.*); see *The N-Town Play: Cotton MS Vespasian D.8*, ed. Stephen Spector, EETS, s.s. 11–12 (Oxford: Oxford Univ. Press, 1991). For attempts to legislate against the inappropriate use of unconsecrated bread, see Peter Browe, "Der Kommunionersatz im Mittelalter," *Ephemerides Liturgicae*, 48 (1934), 534–48.

[20] "Hinc manna verum/ Israelitis/ veris, veri Abrahae filiis,/ *admirantibus*/ quondam Moysi/ quod typus figurabat, iam nunc/ abducto velo/ datur perspici" (quoted with translation in Siegfried Wenzel, *Preachers, Poets, and the Early English Lyric* [Princeton: Princeton Univ. Press, 1986], pp. 22, 24; italics mine). The same point is found in the *Glossa Ordinaria*: *"Manna quid est hoc?* quia hic cibus *admirando* [italics mine] requiritur, et esse corpus Christi scitur" (*Patrologia Latina*, CXIII, 970).

[21] The treatment of Abraham and Melchisedech and the manna is esssentially the same in *Speculum Humanae Salvationis*, the manna being contrasted with the Eucharist, whose delight "is noght felt . . . in etyng,/ Bot Crist and hevenly thinges thenking and contemplyng" (*The Mirour of Mans Saluacioune: A Middle English Translation of Speculum Humanae Salvationis*, ed. Avril Henry [Philadelphia: Univ. of Pennsylvania Press, 1987], p. 103 [ll. 1837–38]; see illustrations, pp. 102, 104).

[22] *"Panis coeli.* Non aliter, quam Christus, de quo coelestes, id est angeli, reficiuntur ejus contemplatione . . ." (*Glossa Ordinaria, in Patrologia Latina*, CXIII, 970; Rolle, *The Psalter*, p. 281). This verse from Psalm 77 occurs in the first nocturn at the conclusion of Psalm 15, whose final verse reads "adimplebis me laetitia cum vultu tuo" ("thou shalt fill me with joy with thy countenance"). Hope Emily Allen noted that Rolle identified the bread of angels with the angelic chorus in the *Incendium* and that here he adds "the reference to *luf*, where a more conventional writer would have left the Sacrament as the unique act of communion with Christ" (Rolle, *English Writings*, p. 141). On the contrary, Rolle is referring to two kinds of communion, sacramental and spiritual—the latter realized not through the reception of the consecrated Host but through the desire of love.

[23] *Twenty-Six Political and Other Poems*, ed. J. Kail, EETS, o.s. 124 (1904; rpt. New York: Kraus, 1973), pp. 106–07. Although Aquinas does not use the metalanguage of modern criticism, his theological distinctions nicely explicate the tenor and vehicle: "This sacrament holds Christ himself, not in his proper guise but under the external appearance of the sacrament. So there are two ways of feeding on him spiritually [defined in the preceding article as eating Christ's body and also receiving the effect of the sacrament]. First under his own appearance, and thus the angels live on Christ himself spiritually by being united to him in clear vision and enjoyment of perfect charity: this is the bread we look for in heaven [et hoc modo angeli manducant spiritualiter ipsum Christum inquantum ei uniuntur fruitione caritatis perfectae, et visione manifesta (quem panem expectamus in patria)]. . . . The other way of feeding on Christ spiritually is under the sacramental species. . . . This is not the case with angels" (St. Thomas Aquinas, *Summa Theologica*, Blackfriars Edition (New York: McGraw Hill, 1964), LIX, 36–37 (III, Q. 80, a. 2); hereafter *ST*. The translator in this case, Thomas Gilby, cautions against equating this spiritual eating with spiritual communion; see n. 32, below.

[24] The elevation consistently represents the sacrament of the Eucharist in the English seven-sacrament baptismal font reliefs, though the use there reflects sacramental theology, the moment of transubstantiation, rather than eschatological vision.

[25] Rolle also uses the bread of angels metaphor in one of his English lyrics, where the focus in on the sight of the suffering Christ: "Demed he was to hyng, þe faire aungels foode," and "aungels brede was dampned to dede, to safe oure sauls sare" (*English Writings*, pp. 42–43 [ll. 33, 44]; see also William E. Rogers, *Image and Abstraction: Six Middle English Religious Lyrics*, Anglistica, 18 [Copenhagen: Rosenkilde and Bagger, 1972], pp. 67–81).

[26] Other fourteenth-century English examples can be found in the *Queen Mary Psalter* (see George Warner, *Queen Mary's Psalter* [London: British Museum, 1912], Pl. 221) and in the entry for *Communio siue communicacio* in the encyclopedia *Omne Bonum* (British Library, MS. Royal 6.E.VI, fol. 337ᵛ; Sandler, *Gothic Manuscripts*, No. 124). In the latter the illustration for *Eukaristia* shows a priest extending a veiled ciborium to a man lying ill in bed (MS. Royal 6.E.VII, fol. 70ʳ). There is no emphasis on sight or eating because the illuminator is illustrating a text that concerns the need for the priest to have the Eucharist always *ready* for sick calls. This is another of the many instances of the care with which this remarkable work was illustrated.

[27] Rubin, *Corpus Christi*, Pl. 2; the column miniature follows the Magnificat antiphon, which includes the words "pane suavissimo de celo." Ferdinando Bologna, *I Pittori alla Corte Angioina di Napoli 1266–1414* (Rome: Ugo Bozzi, 1969), chap. VII, fig. 18 (detail).

[28] For Doddiscombsleigh and Crudwell viaticum scenes, see Gordon McN. Rushforth, "Seven Sacrament Composition in English Medieval Art," *Antiquaries Journal*, 9 (1929), 84–89, Pls. iv, vi, and Painton Cowen, *A Guide to Stained Glass in Britain* (London: M. Joseph, 1985), pp. 95–96. The Exeter workshop productions are discussed at length by Chris Brooks and David Evans, *The Great East Window of Exeter Cathedral* (Exeter: Univ. of Exeter, 1988). For a reproduction of the Hoogstraten scene, see de Boom, "Le Culte de l'Eucharistie," Pl. 20.

[29] Bibliothèque royale Albert Ier MS. IV. 1095; see Bibliothèque royale de Belgique, *Cinq Années d'Aquisitions, 1974–78* (Brussels, 1979), pp. 61–62, where the folio is incorrectly cited as 41^{v}. I am grateful to Kathleen Scott for calling this illumination to my attention. For the typical elevation gestures, see n. 83, below.

[30] For the frequency of communion in the Lowlands, see Jacques Toussaert, *Le sentiment religieux en Flandre à la fin du Moyen-Âge* (Paris: Librairie Plon, 1963), pp. 169–83. The *Ancrene Riwle* cites fifteen times a year, and once a month seems to have been a norm in the twelfth century (*The English Text of the Ancrene Riwle Edited from Cotton Ms. Nero A. XIV*, ed. Mabel Day, EETS, o.s. 225 [London, 1952], p. 188). The passages cited are substantially the same in the other manuscripts; see *Ancrene Wisse*, ed. J. R. R. Tolkien, EETS, o.s. 249 (London, 1962); *The English Text of the Ancrene Riwle*, ed. Frances M. Mack, EETS, o.s. 252 (London, 1963); and *The French Text of the Ancrene Riwle*, ed. J. A. Herbert, EETS, o.s. 219 (1944; rpt. London, 1967). For bibliography see Charlotte d'Evelyn, "Instructions for Religious," in *A Manual of the Writings in Middle English*, gen. ed. J. Burke Severs (New Haven: Connecticut Academy of Arts and Sciences, 1970), II, 650–54.

[31] For the early period, see Macy, *The Theologies of the Eucharist*, pp. 93–105. See also R. H. Schlette, *Die Lehre von der geistlichen Kommunion bei Bonaventura, Albert dem Grossen, und Thomas von Aquin* (Munich, 1959), and Peter Browe, "Die Kommunionandacht im Altertum und Mittelalter," *Jahrbuch für Liturgiewissenschaft*, 13 (1933), 45–64.

[32] Aquinas draws a parallel with baptism, which can be received either in reality or in desire ("uno modo et re et voto," *ST* III, Q. 68, a. 2): "Dictum est autem supra quod res alicujus sacramenti haberi potest ante perceptionem sacramenti, ex ipso voto sacramenti percipiendi" ("We said earlier that the thing signified by a sacrament may already be possessed before the sacrament is received by reason of one's desiring the sacrament" [*ST*, III. Q. 73. a. 3; Blackfriars Edition, LVIII, 10–11]).

[33] *The Myroure of Oure Ladye*, ed. John Henry Blunt, EETS, e.s. 19 (1873; rpt. New York: Kraus, 1981), p. 75; italics mine.

[34] Caroline Walker Bynum, "Women Mystics and Eucharistic Devotion in the Thirteenth Century," *Women's Studies*, 11 (1984), 184–87.

[35] Francis Wormald, "Some Pictures of the Mass in an English XIVth Century Manuscript," *Walpole Society*, 41 (1966–68), 42–43, Pl. 41. The text, which occupies four folios, identifies the key moments of the Mass with twelve miniatures; text and miniatures are printed in ibid., pp. 40–43, figs. 37–42; for reproductions of the first two *Agnus Dei* illuminations see also Sandler, *Gothic Manuscripts*, I, fig. 145, and commentary, No. 58.

[36] *The Myroure of Oure Ladye*, ed. Blunt, p. 331.

[37] Virginia Reinburg, in her recent study of a group of French Mass books produced for the laity, notes that lay communion is never mentioned, whereas the elevation is given a prominent focus ("Liturgy and the Laity in Late Medieval and Reformation France," *Sixteenth Century Journal*, 23 [1992], 526–47, esp. 541n). The situation is not so clear-cut in England. Both the elevation and communion are treated in the Anglo-Norman missalette, while in *The Myrour of Oure Ladye* there is no entry for the elevation but extensive treatment of communion. On the other hand, Reinburg's generalization seems to be valid for English texts designed for a less elite audience. She also goes on to argue that there were parallel rituals in the Mass—sacerdotal ones, and ones that belonged more properly to the laity, among them the reception of holy bread and wine at the end of the Mass, the latter a point that has also been convincingly argued by John Bossy, "The Mass as a Social Institution 1200–1700," *Past and Present*, No. 100 (1983), pp. 29–61. Audelay evidently treated the rite as sacramental, for in the concluding section of *De meritis misse*, where he rehearses the medes, he allows this ceremony to substitute for viaticum: "And oche a day þi masse þou here,/ And take hale bred and hale watere/ Out of þe prestis hond,/ Seche grace God haþ ȝif þe,/ ȝif þat þou dey sodenly,/ Fore þi housil hit schal þe stond" (*The Poems of John Audelay*, ed. Ella Keats Whiting, EETS [1931; rpt. New York: Kraus, 1988], No. 9 [ll. 390–95]).

[38] *The Lay Folks Mass Book*, ed. Thomas Frederick Simmons, EETS, o.s. 71 (London: N. Trübner, 1879), pp. 48–55. The standard description for this and the other vernacular Mass books is Robert R. Raymo, "Works of Religious and Philosophical Instruction," in *A Manual of the Writings in Middle English 1050–1500* (New Haven: Connecticut Academy of Arts and Sciences, 1986), VII, esp. 2350–51. Since the *Lay Folks Mass Book* was originally a translation of a French original composed in the middle of the twelfth century, it is instructive to compare it with the genuine missalette copied in the first quarter of the fourteenth (see above, n. 35).

[39] In *The Lay Folks Mass Book*, ed. Simmons, p. 145, and *The Minor Poems of the Vernon MS.*, ed. F. J. Furnivall, EETS, o.s. 117 (1901; rpt. New York:

Kraus, 1987), Pt. 2, pp. 493–511, where it is given the Index title *How to Hear Mass*; see Raymo, "Works of Religious and Philosophical Instruction," pp. 2351–52. The work is typically described as a rough paraphrase of the *Lay Folks Mass Book*. The relation deserves further study. The all too similar titles of a handful of vernacular works concerned with the Mass and its benefits make them easy to confuse.

[40] In *Lay Folks Mass Book*, ed. Simmons, pp. 148–54 (ll. 123–24, 127–30; italics mine); Raymo, "Works of Religious and Philosophical Instruction," pp. 2352–53, misascribed to Lydgate. *Merita missae* (so cited in Simmons, but spelled *misse* in Raymo) should not be confused with John Audelay's *De meritis misse* (*The Poems*, ed. Whiting, No. 9).

[41] Ibid., No. 8 (*De salutacione corporis Ihesu Christi*, ll. 51–54).

[42] Rossell Hope Robbins, "Levation Prayers in Middle English Verse," *Modern Philology*, 40 (1942–43), 138. For levation prayers, see also Rubin, *Corpus Christi*, pp. 155–63; Duffy, *The Stripping of the Altars*, pp. 117–21; and Loretta McGarry, *The Holy Eucharist in Middle English Homiletic and Devotional Verse* (Washington, D.C.: Catholic University of America, 1936), pp. 215–34.

[43] *The Interpretion and Virtues of the Mass*, in John Lydgate, *The Minor Poems*, ed. Henry Noble MacCracken, EETS, e.s. 107 (1911; rpt. London, 1961), I, 101 (l. 321), 103 (ll. 377–79). This work should not be confused with the *Virtues of the Mass*, for which see Raymo, "Works of Religious and Philosophical Instruction," Sec. 202.

[44] Wormald, "Some Pictures of the Mass," p. 41.

[45] *Lay Folks Mass Book*, ed. Simmons, p. 150 (ll. 71–72).

[46] Audelay, *Poems*, No. 8 (l. 1).

[47] Ibid., No. 9 (ll. 84–85). According to Raymo ("Works of Religious and Philosophical Instruction," pp. 2352–53), *De meritis misse* is an abridgement of *The Manner and Mede of the Mass*, but although many passages are parallel (see Whiting's comparative table in Audelay, *Poems*, p. 235), there is no attempt to follow the original in sequence of rituals. Audelay's poem, which he calls a sermon (p. 79 [l. 408]), deserves to be studied in its own right.

[48] John Myrc [Mirk], *Instructions for Parish Priests*, rev. ed., ed. E. Peacock and F. J. Furnivall, EETS, o.s. 31 (1902; rpt. New York: Kraus, 1973), pp. 9–10 (l. 291). Rubin (*Corpus Christi*, p. 162) cites an example from Cambridge Univ. Library MS. Ii.6.2, fol. 98ᵛ. The phrase is also used in prayers designed to be said

before the Image of Pity. The prayer connected with an image of the wounded Christ in the Yorkshire Carthusian Religious Miscellany reads, "Beholde and see"—that is, look and understand (British Library MS. Add. 37,049, fol. 20ᶠ). Dumoutet's thesis (*Le Christ selon la Chair*) that devotion to the elevated Host developed from devotion to the cross is supported by a long tradition in Middle English verse, for which see variants of *My Leman on the Rood* (*Lyrics of the XIIIth Century*, ed. Carleton Brown [Oxford: Clarendon Press, 1932], Nos. 34–37, and *Religious Lyrics of the XIVth Century*, ed. Carleton Brown, 2nd ed., rev. G. V. Smithers [Oxford: Clarendon Press, 1952], Nos. 1–4, 15). Later lyrics also end with prayers for the beatific vision: "Þerfore, lord, þou rewe on me/ And helpe me sone, þat I may see/ Þe fererhed of þi face/ With angelys þat byn bryȝt & clere" (*Religious Lyrics of the XVth Century*, ed. Carleton Brown [Oxford: Clarendon Press, 1939], No. 68). For the "Fifteen Oes," see the masterful analysis by Duffy, *The Stripping of the Altars*, pp. 249–56.

[49] *A Treatise on the Manner and Mede of the Mass*, in *The Lay Folks Mass Book*, ed. Simmons, p. 131. See Raymo, "Works of Religious and Philosophical Instruction," pp. 2354–55, for textual citations for the medes. His comments are typical of their almost universal condemnation: "They are of no literary merit and tastelessly exploit the simple piety of the laity" (p. 2354). See also the comments in Simmons, *The Lay Folks Mass Book*, pp. 366–71.

[50] Audelay, *Poems*, No. 9 (ll. 57–59); cf. "ȝyf he se þis body in bred, . . ./ And ȝyf he happe þat day to deyȝe,/ He stant for houselyd, I ȝow seye" in one manuscript of Lydgate's *The Interpretation and Virtues of the Mass* (Simmons, ed., *The Lay Folks Mass Book*, pp. 367–68). With this should be compared the version in John Lydgate, *Minor Poems*, ed. Henry Noble MacCracken, EETS, e.s. 107 (London, 1911), p. 115, cited as spurious. In both versions the medes are ascribed to St. Augustine's vision.

[51] Although beyond the scope of this article, Wycliffite opposition needs to be taken into account in any discussion of the elevation. J. I. Catto has argued that Wyclif, like Hus and Janov, was essentially conservative in maintaining that communion, not the elevation, was the climax of the Mass ("John Wyclif and the Cult of the Eucharist," in *The Bible in the Medieval World: Essays in Memory of Beryl Smalley*, ed. Katherine Walsh and Diana Wood, Studies in Church History, Subsidia 4 [Oxford: Basil Blackwell, 1985], pp. 269–86).

[52] "Aristotle, like Plato, solves the problem of vision by arguing that the eye and external media become parts of a homogeneous chain capable of transmitting motions (in the broadest sense) to the intellect of the observer" (David C. Lindberg, *Theories of Vision from Al-Kindi to Kepler* [Chicago: Univ. of Chicago Press, 1976], p. 9). For a discussion of Roger Bacon's position, see ibid., pp. 114–16, and *Roger Bacon's Philosophy of Nature; A Critical Edition with English*

Translation and Notes, of De multiplicatione specierum and De speculis comburentibus (Oxford: Clarendon Press, 1983).

[53] Lindberg, *Theories of Vision*, p. 109.

[54] For geometric diagrams from Henry of Langenstein, see ibid., pp. 125–29, figs. 15–18.

[55] Nichols, *Seeable Signs*, fig. 15. Rubin reproduces an historiated *cibavit* from a fifteenth century Sarum missal (*Corpus Christi*, fig. 17); two demi-kneeling angels support a massive monstrance between them. This literal representation seems to have been particularly popular with Corpus Christi guilds, so much so that it affected the iconography of the Eucharist in Continental seven-sacrament compositions. The Eucharist is so represented in the painted altarpiece at Aarschot, which includes a text from the Corpus Christi liturgy. The carved font cover at the Stephansdom in Vienna also bears a particularly fine example. For further discussion, see *Seeable Signs*, chap. 4.

[56] Lindberg, *Theories of Vision*, pp. 139–42.

[57] Ibid, pp. 116, 145; see also Clifford Davidson, "The Anti-Visual Prejudice," in *Iconoclasm vs. Art and Drama*, ed. Clifford Davidson and Ann Eljenholm Nichols, Early Drama, Art, and Music, Monograph Ser., 11 (Kalamazoo: Medieval Institute Publications, 1989), pp. 33–46.

[58] Lydgate, *Minor Poems*, p. 101 (l. 313).

[59] The nature of the Beatific Vision was officially defined in a dogmatic constitution promulgated in 1336 by Benedict XII. The souls of the just, before they are reunited with their bodies, see the divine essence by intuitive vision face to face without the medium of any creature: "vident divinam essentiam visione intuitiva et etiam faciali, nulla mediante creatura . . ." (Henricus Denzinger, *Enchiridion Symbolorum* [Friburg: Herder, 1937], p. 230). Aquinas addresses this question in terms of *glory* in an article entitled "Whether the attaining of heaven is an effect of this sacrament" (*ST* III, Q. 79, a. 2): "Utrum effectus hujus sacramenti sit adeptio gloriae." Since grace is the seed of glory ("Gratia nihil aliud est, quam quaedam inchoatio gloriae in nobis" [ST II–II, Q. 24, a. 3, ad. 2]), since grace is bestowed in the sacrament (III, Q. 79, a. 1), and since eternal life is the life of glory, the attaining of glory (the vision of the Trinity) is an effect of the Eucharist.

[60] Vespers antiphon for Corpus Christi (*Sarum Breviary*, I, mlxi; *York Breviary*, I, 529); Rolle, *Psalter*, p. 486.

[61] *Magnificat* antiphon at second vespers (*Sarum Breviary*, I, mlxxvi; *York*

Breviary, I, 539).

[62] *Sarum Missal*, p. 460. See Bernard Capelle, "Les Oraisons de la Messe du Saint Sacrement," in *Travaux Liturgiques de Doctrine et d'Histoire*, III (Louvain: Centre Liturgiques, Abbaye du Mont César, 1976), 242–51. For the manuscript history of *Adoro te*, see André Wilmart, "La tradition Littéraire et Textuelle de 'L'Adoro Te Devote'," *Recherches de théologie ancienne et médiévale* (1920), pp. 21–40.

[63] Rolle, *Psalter*, p. 446 (commentary on Ps. 127): "'beatus es & bene tibi erit.' . . . thou art blisful now in hope. & then shal be wel til the. when thou sees god in his fairhed."

[64] Robbins, "Levation Prayers," p. 136; *Minor Poems of the Vernon MS.*, ed. Carl Horstmann, EETS, o.s. 98 (1892; rpt. London, 1987), Pt. 1, p. 24 (Prayer vii). For the relationship between the Trinity and liturgical prayer, see F. Cabrol, "Le Culte de la Trinité dans la Liturgie et l'Institution de la Fête de la Trinité," *Ephemerides Liturgicae*, 45 (1931), 270–78.

[65] *Religious Lyrics of the XIVth Century*, ed. Brown, No. 93 (ll. 103–04).

[66] *A Procession of Corpus Christi*, in Lydgate, *Minor Poems*, p. 42 (ll. 209–13).

[67] J. A. Herbert, *The Sherborne Missal* (Oxford: Roxburghe Club, 1920), Pl. XXVIIa.

[68] Ibid., Pl. XVIII.

[69] Bodleian Library, MS. Engl. the.c.57, fol. 24.

[70] Robbins, "Levation Prayers," p. 138; compare the formulaic prayer recommended by Mirk: "Schryfte & howsele, lord, thou graunte me bo,/ Er that I schale hennes go" (*Instructions*, p. 10).

[71] Lydgate's translation of *The Fifteen OOes of Christ* (*Minor Poems*, p. 244 [ll. 190–92]); for other examples, see Duffy, *The Stripping of the Altars*, pp. 318–19.

[72] *Adoro te devote*, *Anima Christi*, and *Ave verum*; see Dumoutet, "Origines," pp. 424–25.

[73] Lydgate, *Minor Poems*, pp. 103 (ll. 375–76) and 101 (ll. 327–28). It is not surprising that vernacular levation prayers concern spiritual communion since, as

Dumoutet established sixty years ago, Latin prayers originally said at communion gravitated to the elevation. The *Ancrene Riwle* provides an early English example. The prayer recommended to be said before the reserved sacrament and before communion—"hwon þe preost halt hit up ette messe. ꝺ biure þe confiteor hwon ȝe schulen beon ihuseled" is a variation of the *Five Aves* (*Ancrene Riwle Edited from Cotton MS. Nero A.XIV*, p. 7). A later section on the Mass recommends the classic levation prayer *Ecce [Ave] salus mundi*, to which are attached the *Five Aves* (pp. 13–14), a classic example of the attachment of a communion prayer to the older, simpler levation prayer. The *Ecce salus mundi* was particularly popular in French sources. Dumoutet (pp. 412–13) cites nine occurrences of the prayer in its simplest form in *Horae* in the Bibliothèque Nationale and notes that it was subject to a number of variant accretions. The five *aves*, which begin "Ave Jesu Christi, verbum Patris," with a sixth attached, are also standard features in Sarum and York primers; see Edgar Hoskins, *Horae Beatae Mariae Virginis*, p. 111, and *Horae Eboracenses*, Surtees Society, 132 (London, 1920), pp. 70–71.

[74] Connelly, *Hymns*, p. 130. For the textual history of this prayer, see André Wilmart, "La Tradition Littéraire et Textuelle," pp. 21–40. The *velatum/revelatum* contrast is commonplace. It occurs, for example, in the 1539 *Directorium Divinorum Officiorum* with the directions for the priest's communion: "Postea submissa voce, vel potius mente postulet ab eo, dicens, Domine Iesu christe da mihi . . . vt sicut te velatum videmus, te reuelatum videre, et in eternum cum omnibus electis tuis laudare mereamur" (quoted by J. Wickam Legg, *Tracts on the Mass*, Henry Bradshaw Society, 27 [London: Harrison and Sons, 1904], p. 211).

[75] From the Corpus Christi sequence *Lauda Sion*, in *Sarum Missal*, ed. Dickinson, pp. 459–58; see also *Repertorium Hymnologicum*, No. 10,222, and Connelly, *Hymns*, p. 128 (ll. 63–64).

[76] *Lauda Sion* (in Connelly, *Hymns*; ll. 73–75), a text also used as an antiphon in the Hours of the Dead. An interesting pair of Italian panel paintings by Bernardo Daddi represents a typical viaticum scene with (1) *moriens* looking at the Host and then (2) the closing of *moriens'* eyes (Lionello Venturi, *Pitture Italiane in America* [Milan: Ulrico Hoepli, 1931], Pls. XXXII–XXXIII). For the relationship between the final journey of death and the Eucharist, see Frederick S. Paxton, *Christianizing Death: The Creation of a Ritual Process in Early Medieval Europe* (Ithaca: Cornell Univ. Press, 1990), pp. 43–44, 121–22, 202.

[77] Duffy, *The Stripping of the Altars*, esp. pp. 95–102.

[78] The Sarum Hours include an English prayer attributed to St. Bernard (whose name is also connected to the medes) which begins: "Illuminate mine eyes to the end I never sleep in darkness" (Hoskins, *Horae Beatae Mariae Virginis*, p. 166. This is not to argue that the blindness mede was not taken literally by some,

but rather that abuse is often better documented than original use.

[79] The phrase "blint to tten lichte der eiviger salicheit" parallels a series of traditional phrases, the doctor of life, the fountain of mercy, the king of glory; Amsterdam, Vrije Universiteit, MS. XV 05502, fols. 126^v–127^r. The manuscript, dated 1495–1505, contains the Passion of Christ arranged according to the canonical hours. The facing pages are framed with six small sacrament scenes. I wish to thank Sister Helen Rolfson for help with the Middle Dutch text.

[80] *The Chester Mystery Cycle*, ed. R. M. Lumiansky and David Mills, EETS, s.s. 3 (London: Oxford Univ. Press, 1974), p. 317 (XVIA.299–300).

[81] Ibid., p. 481 (Appendix Ic; XVIA.7–8). These events, common to the three synoptic gospels, are linked in the Vulgate by verbs of seeing; both *Mark* (15.39) and *Luke* (23.47) use the identical phrase: "Videns autem centurio." For the standard "elevation" gesture of the centurion, see Francis Cheetham, *English Medieval Alabasters* (Oxford: Phaidon-Christie, 1984), Nos. 172–76, 179–80.

[82] *The Towneley Plays*, ed. George England, EETS, e.s. 71, (1897; rpt. London, 1966), p. 276 (XXIII.600).

[83] For manuscript illustrations, see Nigel Morgan, *Early Gothic Manuscripts, 1250–1285*, A Survey of Manuscripts Illuminated in the British Isles, 4 (London: Harvey Miller, 1988), II, figs. 20, 140, 250, 303; Sandler, *Gothic Manuscripts*, I, figs. 249, 402. For the directive, see Audelay: "When þat þai knele to þe sacreyng,/ Knelis adoune fore one þyng,/ And hold vp ȝour hond" (*Poems*, p. 68 [ll. 78–80]). *The Lay Folks Mass Book* cites both hands (pp. 38–39). Three principal gestures appear in illustrations: one hand raised (typically as in fig. 10, but not solely a gesture of an acolyte); both hands raised (see fig. 10) or what Gerhart Ladner has called the younger gesture of prayer, both hands pressed palm to palm ("The Gestures of Prayer in Papal Iconography of the Thirteenth and Early Fourteenth Centuries," in *Didascaliae: Studies in Honor of Anselm M. Albareda*, ed. Sesto Prete [New York: Bernard M. Rosenthal, 1961], pp. 245–75). The first and the third gestures are both depicted in the Anglo-French *Ceo qe vous deuez fere e penser* and the illumination for Corpus Christi in Rickert, *Carmelite Missal*, Pl. B.

[84] *N-Town Play*, pp. 341 (34.101–04) and 337 (34.1–2, 3).

[85] Audelay, *De salutacione corporis Ihesu Christi* (*Poems*, No. 8 [ll. 15–18]).

[86] *Pange lingua*, in *Sarum Breviary*, I, mlxiv, and *York Breviary*, I, mlxiv. See also *Repertorium Hymnologicum*, No. 14,467, and Connelly, p. 120. This hymn is sung at matins in the Sarum rite, at vespers in the York, *sacris solemnis* alternating in the respective hours.

The Garden of Paradise

J. T. Rhodes and Clifford Davidson

In their closed position, the top panels of the Ghent Altarpiece of Jan van Eyck in the Vijd Chapel of St. Bavo's Cathedral, Ghent, show the Annunciation with the archangel Gabriel at the left and the Virgin with the dove of the Holy Spirit above her head at the right. Between them, through the windows of the spacious room which separates the figures, the viewer is able to see the palaces and buildings of the city of Jerusalem—the earthly city which foreshadows the heavenly Jerusalem where the souls of the righteous shall be united with God. When the panels of the Altarpiece are moved to the open position, the previously hidden interior reveals the mysteries of heaven. Below the throne of Christ as celebrant in the celestial liturgy (at his left and right Mary and John the Baptist appear with books like deacon and subdeacon in the rite, while angel musicians fill side panels) is the scene of the adoration of the Lamb by the prophets, saints, virgins, and angels.[1] The heavenly city now appears in the background, but the immediate setting is a garden in which are placed the altar and a fountain. Vegetation is profusely evident, and flowers abound on the ground everywhere. This panel is a reminder that heaven was not visualized as a place of sterility but, like the Garden of Eden before the Fall, as a site of growth and fruitfulness.

In contrast to hell where nothing grows and only pain and death prevail—a *locus* where the pleasant fragrances of garden flowers are exchanged for the fetid odors of decaying flesh and excrement—heaven was commonly visualized as vivified by the living waters flowing from the fountain of grace. Here those who have been martyred for their faith and all others who have received the gift of life are engaged in praising the source of all fruitfulness. So too in several miniatures in a fifteenth-century manuscript of the *Livre de la Vigne nostre Seigneur* in the Bodleian Library (MS.

Douce 134) the heavenly court engages in adoration of God,[2] and paradise itself is presented in another miniature as a green wooded region populated with animals (fol. clxv[r]). The fruitfulness of heaven should not be surprising when we consider the depiction of the Tree of Vices and the Tree of Virtues in a manuscript such as the *Liber Floridus* or the *Robert de Lisle Psalter*.[3] In contrast to the barrenness of the former, the latter is laden with green leaves and various kinds of fruit. The source of this fruitfulness is Christ, as Gilbert of Hoyland explained: "He is indeed the field really full and fertile, the field which the Father has blessed." The Church "knows no other field than his; any other she considers a desert, an alkaline wasteland."[4]

Dom Jean Leclercq calls attention to a popular poem, Peter Damian's *De gloria paradisi* (*On the Glory of Paradise*), which expresses the longing of the spiritually thirsty soul for the fountain of life. The exiled soul experiences intense desire for the recovery of the joys of paradise. Leclercq explicates: "All the most beautiful things, the most pleasing to the senses, to be found in the Scripture are called upon to give an idea of this total happiness: fruits, flowers, Springtime, sunlit meadows, the glory of the Saints, the splendor of the Lamb, the recovered harmony between flesh and spirit, health, inexhausible youth, understanding and mutual love among the elect, unalterable union—nothing is lacking of all that a Christian could desire to receive from God upon entering the heavenly joys."[5] Further, satiety never breeds boredom, for the joy of heaven is utterly complete and totally satisfying.[6]

Leclercq cites another text, the twelfth-century *Epithalamium Christi virginum alternantium* (*Epithalamium between Christ and the Virgins*) tentatively attributed to a monk of Hirsau, which likewise gives a description of heavenly joy in terms of garden imagery: "flowers and perfume, enchantment for the senses and the spirit, such is the setting where love is to bloom."[7] The suggestiveness of the garden setting, which carried with it rich associations of both the pleasures of secular love and the garden of Eden before the Fall, had clearly established it also as an appropriate image of the heavenly paradise—a location implied much later in a woodcut chosen for the edition of Vincent of Beauvais' *Myrrour of the Worlde* printed by Laurence Andrewe in c.1529. Here the heavenly paradise is depicted as delineated by high stone walls and is the source of four streams; within are two angels.[8]

The end of the successful pilgrimage of life therefore will be reminiscent of the beginning of the race when our first parents were placed in the Garden of Eden, a place of joy and pleasure and orderly fertility that stands in contrast to the anarchy that came afterward. On the wings of the Ghent Altarpiece (in open position) stand Adam and Eve, while above Eve we see the murder of Abel by Cain, who is using the jawbone of an ass to commit the crime.[9] The murder of Cain is a primary symbol of the lapsarian condition brought about by the Fall and endemic in the human race after the expulsion from the Garden. Subsequent desire for a return to the original state of innocence is thus, not surprisingly, translated into a longing for a heavenly bliss that is a reflection and amplification of the primordial Garden, for it is a commonplace, following St. Augustine, that the the Fall was a happy mischance (*felix culpa*) which eventually will place humankind in a better state than experienced initially at the very beginning of time before the Expulsion.

The Garden of Eden is described in *Genesis* 2.8–10 as being "planted" by God, who thereby created "a paradise of pleasure from the beginning"; he then "brought forth of the ground all manner of trees, fair to behold, and pleasant to eat of." In the garden were the tree of life and the tree of the knowledge of good and evil, and there was a "river" which "went out of the place of pleasure [*loco voluptas*] to water paradise"—a river diverted into four streams. Medieval depictions illustrated the place as surrounded by a wall and containing at least the tree with the forbidden fruit and often a fountain from which water flows. Often too the moment of subversion of the race—Eve's act of tasting the fruit offered by the serpent, which usually appears with the head of a woman,[10] or her subsequent act of tempting Adam to eat thereof—provided the focus for illustrations. Eden thus was the *locus* of temptation, disobedience, and sin against God, with the result that its human inhabitants would be thrust out at the Expulsion. The ambiguity of Eden hence stands in contrast to the eternal garden of heaven which will, we are assured, resound with joy forever.

The recovery of paradise was seen as an avenue of escape from the hostile world of thorns and thistles, hard work (symbolized by the spade and spindle held by the postlapsarian Adam and Eve respectively), pain, strife, exploitation, death, and destruction. The lost paradise also stood for the perfection of God's creation—a place quite different from the harsh realities of this world. In the woodcut depicting the Fall and Expulsion in the *Nuremberg Chronicle*, Adam and Eve are shown being forced out of the lush vegetation of the garden—vegetation watered by a flowing fountain—onto a barren, dry, stony path.[11] In Scripture the paradise of the Lord became a simile for a desirable place to live (*Genesis* 13.10), while the prophets drew upon its features as a way of discussing the messianic vision: the Lord will have pity of Sion, "and he will make her desert as a place of pleasure, and her wilderness as the garden of the Lord" (*Isaias* 51.3). The infertile, drought-stricken lands of the desert stand in contrast to the messianic future with its blossoming, well-watered lands where God's people will enjoy peace and plenty—when, in effect, they will return to the promised land, the paradise that had been lost by disobedience in primordial time.[12]

It is a commonplace that medieval monasteries were regarded not only as a place of preparation for eternal life but also as physically modeled on the idea of heaven.[13] Thus the design and horticulture of the abbey may be described as eschatologically oriented. The location (Ely comes to mind) might be in the midst of swamplands, an island devoted to "Divine Wisdom" and chastity which also might be regarded as "an image of heaven; it makes one think already of heaven."[14] The monastic cloister garden is hence not only a reflection of the perfection of the Garden of Eden, but also more importantly a visual and physical symbol of the garden to which the soul wishes to return at the end of this life.

Such a return to paradise is indeed suggested in *Apocalypse* 22, a text of immense importance since it makes a direct connection between the garden of Eden and the place of joy in the hereafter. In his vision of the heavenly city St. John saw not only the "river of water of life, clear as crystal," flowing from God's throne and the Lamb, but also "the tree of life, bearing twelve fruits, yielding its fruits every month, and the leaves of the tree were for the healing of the nations" (22.1–2). Transplanted from Eden, the tree of life is the symbol of plentitude and of all that is attractive in the heavenly abode where all shall see God's face and join in adoration of him. In this place "night shall be no more" (22.5), and fruitfulness shall reign forever with the saints. The passage is likely influenced by *Jeremias* 31.1–14, which promises a return to a land of plenty: "their soul shall be *as a watered garden*, and they shall be hungry no more" (12; italics added).

While heaven is to be much superior to the first paradise located in the Garden of Eden, in the later Middle Ages the difference seems to have been thought to be a matter of degree rather than kind.[15] Hence the manner of visualizing the Garden of Eden in both the drama and the visual arts is of prime importance for the present investigation. The description in the stage direction of the Anglo-Norman *Adam* is well known: "Let paradise be constructed in a prominently high place; let curtains and silken hangings be placed around it at such a height that those persons who will be in paradise can be seen from the shoulders upwards; let sweet-smelling flowers and foliage be planted; within let there be various trees, and fruits hanging on them, so that the place may seem as delightful as possible. . . ."[16] At Mons the fruit that was specified included "withered and fresh apples, also cherries," newly purchased for the trees.[17] The earthly paradise described for the Paris *Resurrection* was even more elaborate:

> The outside of the walls of this Paradise should be white. And within there should be trees, some in blossom, others laden with fruit of different kinds such as cherries, plums, apples, pears, almonds, oranges, figs, pomegranates, and grapes. Other trees green, such as rose trees, flowers, rosemary, and marjoram. And they should be such a height as to be visible above the wall all over the playing area. And therein should be a fountain that will divide into four streams.[18]

And at Norwich the Grocers' guild decorated the tree within the garden with every kind of "frutes plesant,"[19] which are listed in 1557 in the guild's account book: "Orenges, fyges, allmondes dates Reysens, preunes, and aples to garnyshe the trie with." There also were payments "for collerd thryd to bynd yeflowers" and for "6. oz of perfume." In the next year there were further expenses for various spices and for gilding roses.[20]

Among the Middle English Creation to Doom play collections and cycles, N-town gives indication of the variety of herbs, "flesch, and fysch, and frute of prys," which included "Bothe appel, and pere, and gentyl rys" as well as the spices "pepyr, pyan, and swete lycorys" that Adam might enjoy in the earthly paradise. As Deus announces, "Here is allþinge that þe xulde plese/ All redy made onto thin ese."[21] But it is in the Cornish *Creacion of the World* that perhaps the most interesting dramatic effect is used to reveal the garden to the audience. Here the stage directions demand that

"Paradice be fynelye made, with two fayre trees in yt; and an appell upon the Tree, and som other frute one the other. A fowntayne in Paradice, and fyne flowres in yt paynted." The garden is ready to be shown to the audience, however, only when God announces that he "will make Paradise,/ a place delicious beyond anything./ Behold it made for my pleasure!" Adam is now *"putt . . . into Paradice,"* and God says, "Plenty of flowers of every kind/ see grown in this place!" The latter is a cue for flowers to appear in the garden. After the creation of Eve, the stage direction specifies: *"Lett fyshe of dyvers sortys apeare, and serten beastys, as oxen, kyne, shepe and such like."* These too are pointed out to Adam by God.[22]

The shape of the Garden of Eden probably varied with the theatrical circumstances, but we at least have one example of a diagram that shows its location and design within a larger play with multiple sets. Renward Cysat's plan for the Lucerne Passion Play of 1583 (first day) in the town square encloses the Garden of Eden inside palings immediately before the Haus zur Sonne, which appropriately housed the heaven scene "high up" with room for the Father Eternal and, immediately underneath, a choir of seven angels. At the very top of the building was an opening used by the operator of the Holy Ghost.[23] The orientation of the Garden of Eden in this location is to the east. There is a single tree within this garden, and a rectangle on the ground signifies a trapdoor or hiding place, apparently for Eve prior to the time of her creation. To one side of this garden is space for a second garden, Mary Magdalene's, which is described as "not walled in or enclosed like a stand, but simply an enclosure with laths, and low; also hung round with carpets."[24] On the second day, the Garden of Eden becomes transformed into the Mount of Olives for the capture of Jesus at the Betrayal.[25]

In the visual arts in the late Middle Ages, the Garden of Eden appears as a place of pleasure that sometimes is very similar to gardens that depict secular scenes, including scenes associated with courtly love.[26] In illustrations of the biblical *Genesis* garden we may expect to see a wall or enclosure, a fountain, and a tree as well as, when necessary to identify the location for the viewer, depiction of the events that took place in the garden: the creation of Adam and Eve, their temptation, the Fall, and their expulsion through the gate, an act enforced by an angel with a sword. Such representations were to be viewed by the privileged few in luxury illuminated manuscripts such as the well-known *Très Riches Heures* of the Duke of Berry or the *Bedford Hours*.

The illustration in the *Très Riches Heures* includes the entire narrative from Eve's encounter with the serpent through the Expulsion in a single miniature, which depicts the earthly paradise as round and womblike, an enclosed garden surrounded by a wall, and set in the sea like an island. The vegetation is varied, with shrubs, trees, and flowers in evidence.[27] In the center of the garden is a fountain which dominates the scene, and at the right is the gate through which Adam and Eve, who are clutching fig leaves over their genitals as they step over rocky terrain on the path outside the enclosure that will lead to their new earthly home, are forced to leave by the angel. The pictorial narrative in the *Bedford Hours* is even more extensive, including the fate of Adam and Eve after the Expulsion and as well as the sacrifice of Cain and Abel and the latter's murder (fig. 11). In this example there is a wall of stone in the foreground with a gate and a slender tower from the base of which water streams forth—water originating in a fountain even more elaborate than the one that appears in the *Très Riches Heures*. The garden itself is encircled by a fence of wattle.[28] Both these illuminations suggest an aristocratic setting and a place of pleasure but include a representation of the Fall, thus providing an explanation of humankind's exile from a state of perfect happiness. The scene of Seth returning to Eden to obtain the "oil of mercy" for Adam is not shown, but this episode, which directly connects the tree of the earthly paradise with the wood of the cross (made according to the legend from a tree grown from seeds from the tree of knowledge), is illustrated, for example, in the *Hours of Catherine of Cleves*.[29] The cross, in turn, will appear as one of the symbols of the Passion often displayed in Last Judgment scenes, linking the beginning of the race in the Garden of Eden to the last day of its history. The presence of supposed relics of the cross (all supposedly from the cross discovered by St. Helen) throughout Western Europe also provided a connection not only to events at the center of history when a new beginning was made through the sacrifice of Christ, but also to the tree from which the cross was made—a tree grown from seeds from the earthly paradise in order to play a role in opening the gate to the heavenly paradise for the descendants of Adam and Eve. To underline this point the artist who created the illustration in the Caedmon manuscript of Anglo-Saxon poetry (MS. Junius XI) had placed a cross on the tree in the Garden of Eden.[30] Gertrud Schiller calls attention to the Preface of the Holy Cross, which is used from from Passion Sunday to Maundy Thursday as well as for the feasts of the Holy Cross and the Precious Blood: "By thy ordinance the salvation of mankind was accomplished on the wood of the Cross, so that life might rise again there where death had its beginning, and that he who conquered through a tree should on a tree himself be conquered. . . ."[31]

In the manuscript illumination in the *Holkham Bible Picture Book* which shows God with the newly created Adam and Eve in the garden, the trees are laden with apples, pears, cherries, acorns, and flowers. Birds are poised in each tree, and the central position is given to the pelican in her piety piercing its breast so that its young ones might live—a symbol of the crucifixion.[32] Here and in the next illumination illustrating the Fall, the walls enclosing the garden are illustrated as quite low and made of flint, a material also used for some East Anglian churches, while after the Fall the walls are symbolically shown as very high—fortifications, guarded at the gate by an angel, that prevent Adam and Eve from returning to paradise.[33] For those living thereafter in the harsh world outside (in the *Holkham Bible Picture Book* Adam is symbolically wounded in the knee as he is expelled from Eden, a reflection of the sermon commonplace that the "deserte" of this world is characterized by the "thornes of synne"[34]), the enclosed garden of paradise must now be sought forward in time rather than in the past; the desire to return to the garden can only be channeled into longing for the heavenly paradise beyond time and history.

A number of scenes of the earthly paradise likewise appear in woodcuts in incunabula, though the subject was not among the most popular ones. An example in an early sixteenth-century Flemish edition of Ludolphus of Saxony's *Vita Jhesu Christi* again shows a profusion of vegetation and animals, a fountain at the center, and a gate—in this instance a gate through which the unfallen Adam and Eve, their hands joined in prayer, are being led into the garden by God. Streams of water flow from four mask-like apertures in the circular wall of the garden and form the rivers of paradise.[35] Woodcuts from English incunabula are generally much less detailed, but sometimes identify the garden location for the Fall through the presence of a few plants.[36] In the woodcut in

Richard Fakes' edition of John Mirk's *Festyuall* (c.1520) a more elaborate narrative scene is depicted, and the garden is grassy and set off by elaborate romanesque stone walls to designate its antiquity.[37]

Even more widely influential than book illustrations, however, were public representations, to be seen not only in the ephemeral dramatic performances described above but also in painted glass and wall paintings in churches and chapels. Again, much of the surviving glass, like that at Great Malvern,[38] St. Neot in Cornwall,[39] York Minster (especially John Thornton's Great East Window of 1405–08),[40] and the chapel at Hengrave Hall in Suffolk (in this instance the scenes of the creation of the birds and of Adam are reminiscent of the woodcuts in the *Nuremberg Chronicle*[41]), was essentially narrative, depicting the garden as the site for the Creation, Fall, and Expulsion in a variable number of lights. M. D. Anderson has argued that some visual representations might reflect dramatic performances,[42] but more recently opinion has tended to be skeptical of this theory. Thornton's glass in the Great East Window at York, which is closely related to new styles of painting being developed in manuscript illumination, is a major artistic and intellectual accomplishment that is designed to be read from the top, where God is shown holding the Book of Creation (open to the words "Ego sum Alph[a] & [Omega]") above the nine orders of angels in paradise, through the events of the Creation, Fall, and early history of the race, and culminating in the events of the *Apocalypse* at the end of history.[43]

The painted glass at Great Malvern presented a garden enclosed by a masonry wall with battlemented towers and, inside, the usual trees, grass, and flowers—signs of vegetative fertility that had been present in earlier times, as in Bodleian Library MS. Junius 11, p. 13, which is dated from the Anglo-Saxon period.[44] Later artists such as Fra Angelico and Giovanni di Paolo, in their well-known paintings of the blessed in paradise, set their figures amidst shady trees and jewel-like flowers and bushes. Fra Angelico's paradise was precisely located in relation to the Last Judgment and in opposition to the torments of the damned.[45] In its present state Giovanni di Paolo's lacks a clear context;[46] had many of his figures not been dressed in religious habits, their intimate embraces might have suggested that this was a secular pleasure garden, more akin to Botticelli's *Primavera* than to a sacred paradise. The garden setting, profoundly important for establishing the context of heavenly joy, nevertheless, as we have seen, could be very ambiguous; without taking into account the context, the place could be either one of religious fulfilment or secular (and usually sexual) achievement or exploitation.[47]

The hermeneutic process by which the Garden of Eden became a visual symbol for the heavenly paradise was based in the practice of typological interpretation.[48] The Crucifixion was located, according to common belief, at the grave of Adam, and, as we have seen, the cross itself was directly grown from seeds of the tree in the Garden of Eden. The tree of life, along with the water of life (often flowing from the fountain in the garden), anagogically signified the paradise to be encountered in eternity, but they also alluded to Christ's sacrifice on the cross and his redemption of his followers. As a previously cited passage from the *Apocalypse* indicates, "the leaves of the tree were for the healing of the nations" (22.2).[49] Typological arrangements of this kind untied history from the past and brought events into a present symbiotic relationship. In the *Biblia Pauperum*, for example, texts and images combined to connect three separate historical events in a rich and allusive way. Hence the Annunciation was flanked by the scenes of Eve with the serpent, holding the fateful apple, and Gideon with his fleece.[50] Elsewhere the Fall was placed with the temptation of Christ, and the creation of Eve from the side of Adam was shown as a prefiguration of the piercing of the side of Jesus on the cross.[51] Block books like the *Biblia Pauperum* and the *Speculum Humanae Salvationis*[52] used compartmentalization much like painted glass, for windows were divided up into panels by mullions.[53] Wall paintings where divisions were less regular and less obtrusive, on the other hand, seem to have tended much more to narrative treatment, as in the case of the twelfth-century series in the Church of St. Botolph at Hardham, Sussex, where the temptation, expulsion, and subsequent life of Adam and Eve are shown.[54] But typology was deeply ingrained in the medieval way of seeing salvation history—an aspect of what Marie-Dominique Chenu has labeled "the symbolist mentality."[55] That way of seeing meant that the juxtaposition of Eve and the Blessed Virgin on either side of the tree in the *Hours of Catherine of Cleves*[56] was understood typologically, the one reversing the sin of the other in bearing the means of salvation;[57] it was not seen as an historically anachronistic image. A single image could imply all of history—its beginning, its ending, and the hereafter.

Although typology and richly symbolic envisioning allowed artists to transcend many of the limitations of representational art, they were still restricted to a more literal medium than writers. Illustrations of Dante's *Purgatorio* or *Paradiso* are unable to contain his vision.[58] The most detailed representations of the heavenly paradise were "seen," not painted on plaster, wood, or parchment, but in visions, which transcended the natural geographical and temporal limitations of the physical world and its literal representation.[59]

English literature is not lacking in descriptions of the ideal landscape of paradise.[60] One of the most developed visions of the garden of paradise was seen by the father in the Middle English poem *Pearl*. The vision opens in the garden where the child Pearl is buried: a grassy plot, a bower, fragrant herbs, yellow, red, and blue flowers, ginger, gillyflowers, gromwell, and peonies. It is in this garden or "erber grene" (l. 38) that he falls into a a trance and enters another, visionary landscape.[61] Its features are representative of other descriptions of the earthly paradise: the high cliffs, the woodlands with their rich crop of fruit and their brilliant, sweet-singing birds, and the jewel-like qualities of the stream and its banks—and everything shimmering in the light. It is noteworthy that the child Pearl is described as a jewel lost in the initial garden and then observed in the state of paradise, for the presence of jewels in the garden of paradise was a recurrent feature.[62] The father first sees his beloved, Pearl, across the stream, which functioned as a boundary of paradise—a paradise seen on the other side of an uncrossable river. The same effect of difficulty or impossibility of access was visualized as characteristic of the earthly paradise, as in the case of the illustration in the *Très Riches Heures*.

Many of these elements also appear in *The Lyfe of saynt Brandon*,[63] which, derived verbatim from the Caxton-de Worde translation of Jacobus de Voragine's *Golden Legend*, combined visions of paradise with a reputedly actual voyage. There is the vision which the holy abbot Beryn described of a voyage that took his son Mervoke to the East, where, after entering a black cloud, the Lord removed the darkness to show the travelers a fair island shining with light "as bryght as the sonne" and filled with "Ioy and myrth ynough." Everywhere there were fair herbs and trees "full of fruyte so that it was a gloryous syght and an heuenly Ioy tabyde there." This location was the "paradys terrestre" where "Adam and Eue dwelte in fyrst" but from which they were evicted because of their crime.[64] The voyagers upon their return reported that they had visited the "londe of byheest afore the gates of paradys where as is euer day and neuer nyght"—a location that "is full delectable/ for yet all theyre clothes smelled of that swete and Ioyfull place."[65] Such a clinging fragrance was a significant aspect of the earthly paradise, and of course was regarded as characteristic of the heavenly paradise as well.

Brendan's subsequent voyage to various islands seems to bring him into contact with representations of various degrees of paradise. These islands include one with green pastures with enormous, very white sheep and constant summer, and another was filled with "floures herbes and trees" where there was also "a full fayre well" and beside it a tree with singing birds which "sange so meryly that it was an heuenly noyse to here."[66] (These birds were fallen angels whose trespass was little, and hence they served God in song and sang all the divine hours.) On yet another island there were twenty-four monks who were miraculously provided with fair white bread and necessary roots and herbs. In their church, where light was provided by seven tapers which had been lit by no human hand and which never diminished as they burned, the monks constantly served God. It was always fair weather there, and none of the monks had experienced illness since they arrived on the island eighty years ago.

The final island was "the fayrest countree eestwarde that ony man myght se and was soo cleere and bryght that it was an heuenly syght to beholde." The trees were laden with "rype fruyte" and the herbs with flowers the year around. There was no inclement weather, "ne to hote ne to colde," and it was always daytime. This island lay at the furthest reaches of the earth, since "on that other syde of this water may no man come that is in this lyfe."[67] On his return, Brendan carried with him the fruit of paradise and also "great plente of precyous stones."

The Brendan legend has been cited at some length because it is neither a literary creation nor a doctrinal statement about paradise, but rather a piece of popular hagiography, likely to contain many stock features, which may be compared to the characteristics of paradise enumerated above in the present essay. As such, the legend was intended to affirm in the reader's mind that this voyage was more than merely a physical adventure story.[68] The promise that these paradises provide a model for an individual's post-mortem experience brought these temporally and geographically distant lands close and gave them existential validity. The reality of such lands was thus not confined to the limitations of the present physical world; they were spiritually significant places, and the enjoyment which they promised was analogous to the eternal pleasure of the blessed.

As will have been observed above, one of the most frequent attributes of the garden is its separation from the world around it. In the voyage of St. Brendan, the terrestrial paradise is cut off from present human experience by a wide river or body of water, which is similar to an attribute also cited by Christopher Columbus in support of his theory that he had located the earthly paradise in the West Indies.[69] While the river boundary probably recalls the visions of *Ezechiel* 47 and *Apocalypse* 22.1–2, more often, as we have seen, the immediate boundary of paradise was conceived of as a wall, fence, or hedge. The boundary of the Garden of Eden, however, is not specified in Scripture, though an enclosure is implied in another garden to which we will call attention below: the garden in the *Song of Songs*, which also seems to specify a solid, locked gate (5.2, 6). We have seen that in painted glass at Malvern and in some manuscript illuminations such as the *Holkham Bible Picture Book* the garden is enclosed by a solid masonry wall, and in other instances the space was surrounded by boundaries that were more varied: various kinds of hedges, wattles, and palings were depicted. The Blessed Virgin, the Queen of Heaven, was also pictured in a wide range of garden enclosures from the solid masonry of the Frankfurt paradise garden to the rose bower of Stefan Lochner's Madonna, a line of trees, a wattle enclosure,[70] and fabric hangings.[71] The garden of Gethsemane was sometimes bounded by palings, as we have seen in the Lucerne Passion Play where the fence was reused from the Garden of Eden scene on the day before. The choice of this fencing material seems to have been deliberate and may not implausibly have intended a very oblique reference to the wood of the cross,[72] but more often it and the garden of the Resurrection seem to have been shown bounded by wattle fences.

The garden, set off from the space around it as in the *Genesis* account and in numerous illustrations as well as in the medieval drama, separated sacred space from ordinary space. Even when the boundary is not emphasized as in the paintings of Fra Angelico or the Ghent Altarpiece, the idea of separation is present. Here the separation is a matter of choice by the blessed, since they do not need to be protected from without or to be constrained to stay. The theological view was that they are content with the degree of blessedness that they have been granted, and hence the boundaries of paradise must be "natural" and unrestrictive. Inside these "natural" boundaries there was little sign of artificial cultivation, and so no hint of the labor which inevitably accompanied the creation of ordinary human gardens. The impression given by the constant daylight, the temperate climate, and the profusion of fruit and spices in these examples was of nature made perfect; this was God's work, not the result of human skill and labor. So too would the place which the Father has prepared for the saints and others whom he has adopted as his own in eternity be the work of no human hands.

The other earthly garden that is relevant to the present discussion is that of the *Song of Songs*. This garden is described in great detail, and was identified allegorically with the Beloved, the Sponsa who from Patristic times had been identified with the Church longing for union with Christ, the Bridegroom; thus too it was seen as a symbol for the individual soul.[73] Unlike the terrestrial paradise, it was located near the city and its houses. It was a *hortus conclusus*, a "garden enclosed" (4.12), and entrance to it was by a bolted door (5.6). In it was a fountain, "the well of living waters, which run with a strong stream from Libanus" (4.15). The place was redolent with spices, particularly frankincense and myrrh, which perfumed the garments of all of those who went into it. Its trees included the apple, pomegranate, and "all the trees of Libanus" (4.14). Every fruit was there; among the flowers the lily was especially noticed. Wine, honey, and milk were freely available and contributed to the overall sense of a rich, nurturing, delectable environment—qualities further heightened by the similitudes used to describe the two lovers. If possible this setting was more luxurious than the initial earthly paradise, but the agitation of the lovers, their passionate and yet uncertain love gave it a sense of fragility and instability. The boundary not only enclosed the fragility and beauty of the fertile garden but also defined the lovers themselves. This paradise of pleasure was a human construct, a beautiful artifact, and a setting for human emotions of love, anxiety, and potential disappointment.

Yet it is this paradise garden that was held most appropriately to express the human condition of longing for the eternal state of perfection in eternity, and its iconography indeed contained within it the power to energize the desire for the experience of bliss.[74] The allegorical reading of the *Song of Songs*, forcefully elucidated by the commentary of St. Bernard of Clairvaux, affirmed its eroticism to be a paradigm explaining the relationship between Christ and the *individual* member of the Church (the Bride) who longs for mystical union with the second person of the deity (the Bridegroom). The kiss of the *Song*, for example, is interpreted by Bernard as inherently fertile and as "the uniting of God with man."[75] The language of love and the garden-related iconography of the *Song* thereafter would stimulate a great deal of spiritual writing, including a substantial body of works in Middle English.[76] Its imagery, though much less often illustrated in the visual arts and to our knowledge only presented indirectly on stage in the Macro morality *Wisdom*,[77] was far more influential in devotion, mysticism, and non-dramatic literature.[78]

Ascribed to King Solomon, the *Song of Songs* had long been regarded as a sacred text both in Jewish and early Christian traditions. In the later Middle Ages especially its emotionalism provided a way of imagining the joy and ecstasy of bliss, for its frank eroticism became a powerful source for conceptualizing the way in which the soul needs to be drawn upward in its desire, sometimes, according to Bernard, even against its own will.[79] The surrender to desire is expressed in two remarkable songs by Abbess Hildegard of Bingen, who spoke of Christ as the "sweetest lover" ("dulcissime amator") and "sweetest giver of embraces" ("dulcissime amplexator") and as one to whom her nuns are joined in spiritual marriage eternally.[80] Surrender is even more completely expressed in the Middle English *Quia amore langueo*, a poem which uses the text of the *Song of Songs* to allude to Christ's bleeding side as a wound of love—a combining of the romance mode and courtly love with the sacred eroticism encouraged by St. Bernard.[81] Christ is the Sponsus, the Bridegroom, speaking to the Sponsa, or "spouse": "My swete spouse/ will we goo play;/ apples ben rype in my gardine . . ." (ll. 81–82). He promises the "dere soule" or Sponsa that she will be clothed "in new array" and will dine on milk, honey, and wine (ll. 83–85) and that in heaven's chamber will be the nuptual bed (ll. 101–02).[82] The garden in this case is very like the secular pleasure garden of medieval poets such as the authors of the *Romance of the Rose*,[83] but this place of sensual play is instead a prelude to the paradoxically chaste union of the soul with Wisdom who is Christ.

In the *Rothschild Canticles* described and illustrated by Jeffrey Hamburger, the garden setting of the *Song of Songs* is symbolized at first by trees as the Sponsus joins the Sponsa; in the lower portion of fol. 23[r] he holds a pruning knife and points to the tree, while she is nude with dark skin (see "I am black but beautiful" [*Song of Songs* 1.4], and also, for the Sponsus, the image of Christ the gardener in the *Hortulanus* scene in the Type III *Visitatio Sepulchri* music-drama[84]). Finally, in the lower scene in the illumination in fol. 25[r] they join together in enjoyment of the fruits and flowers which characterize this garden.[85] These illustrations, Hamburger explains, represent the stages of the mystical life[86] which are possible through the cultivation of the soul=garden.[87] The flowers in the garden are virtues, and here in this enclosed space which was said to represent the soul, according to certain of the mystics, God wished to be with his beloved.[88] But in another illumination in the *Rothschild Canticles*, the garden is raised to the eschatological level since Christ as Sponsus, recognizable by his cross nimbus, stands holding the book of life atop the fountain of life from which issue four streams (three are visible) of living water that have presumably vivified the souls of many in bliss, for their faces appear in the water (fol. 34[r]).[89]

The kiss and embrace of the lovers represent the consummation of the love of the Sponsus and Sponsa;[90] these gestures are analogous to the entry into the marriage feast of the five Wise Virgins of the parable in *Matthew* 25—a parable that was transformed into the Provençal music-drama *Sponsus* which promised feasting and joy to those who entered the open door of heaven made available to them by the Bridegroom.[91] And in another iconographic type, the Sponsus and Sponsa seated together on a throne,[92] the configuration of the scene is reminiscent of the Coronation of the Virgin. As in the latter subject, the feminine figure is seated at the right of the Sponsus (i.e., to the viewer's left). This similarity of subject matter is not surprising when we consider that the Sarum liturgy for the offices of the feast of the Assumption of the Virgin included readings from the *Song of Songs*.[93]

In the late Middle Ages, the Virgin Mary—like the Sponsa she typologically represents the Church—also frequently appeared within a garden setting[94] that provides a reflection of the final state of humankind in glory. Further, the garden in this case is intended as a reflection of her own essence as the sinless mother of the Redeemer who was taken up into heaven at her Assumption and thereafter crowned as Queen of Heaven. As Pearsall and Salter felicitously explain, "every Madonna in a garden enclosed by wall, palisade or rose hedge is enclosed in a symbol of her own nature and power—'hortus conclusus soror mea sponsa'."[95] No gate is visible in the garden in which she is placed, or else it is a closed door (*clausa porta*)—a sign of her immaculate conception and perpetual virginity.[96] Appearing in the setting of a paradise garden, which is of the greatest natural beauty, with her infant Son, Mary is the most beautiful of all women.[97] But, as Pearsall and Salter also point out, the minute attention to botanical detail carries a precise spiritual significance: "the detail . . . attends to both botanical and spiritual truth, fusing them in a decorative scheme which appeals powerfully to the senses and, from there, to the mind."[98] The effect was deliberately to create a scene which, in its spiritual dimension, would utilize the specific properties of flowers and birds to provide a proper symbolic atmosphere for a place of utter paradisaical beauty.

What seems to have been ignored is that these images cannot be interpreted other than symbolically. There was no historical moment at which Mary, the Mother of God, appeared with her infant in such a setting. In a wall painting of c.1500 at Århus Cathedral in Denmark, flowers (along with dots which are probably meant to be pearls) are displayed in a circle around a crowned and radiant Virgin holding a scepter and the Child; she is being raised heavenward by angels at her feet—an image that brings together even more aspects of her life within a stylized garden-like setting.[99] The ahistoricity of these images might suggest a visionary landscape, but there was no widely diffused text to accompany them. If we look for parallels, the closest that is available would seem to be not the *pietà*—the scene in which Mary holds the body of her crucified Son—but the *imago pietatis*.[100] Like the Marian paradise garden, this was another ahistorical *summa*. If the enclosed garden symbolized the fruit of the Virgin's womb, and the joys and sorrows that Mother and Son would experience in reversing the sin that had excluded humankind from the paradise of the Garden of Eden, then the Image of Pity represented all the sufferings that Jesus endured in his Passion and death, sufferings which reversed the sin of Adam and brought redemption to the faithful, those obedient to his will. Both depictions also functioned similarly as devotional images in which the eye could look upon the physical features of one who was in heaven and who loved and showed concern for the viewer.[101] The image could serve powerfully to draw a worshipful person toward the place where he or she might enjoy the delights of heaven, understood to be represented in the delightful scene presented in the "Mary Garden."[102]

The formal "Mary Garden" of the kind included in Books of Hours was entirely an artificial construct, a literal realization of the iconography of the *Song of Songs* applied to the Blessed Virgin.[103] In block book illustrations of the *Song* the figures of the Sponsus and Sponsa are depicted as Christ and Mary.[104] Various depictions of symbols derived from the *Song* as applied to Mary were presented in numerous manuscript and block-book versions of the *Speculum Humanae Salvationis*. The Annunciation of Mary was paired with the enclosed garden and the sealed fountain (*Song of Songs* 4.12, 15), and the marriage of the Virgin with the tower of David hung with a thousand shields (4.4).[105] The Middle English text of the *Speculum Humanae Salvationis* explained:

> Of this doghter sometyme sange Salomon mistikly,
> That in hire modere wombe God wold hire seintify,
> For a gardin enclose he lykned hire vntoo,
> And till a seled welle; this the resoune, loo:
> For in hir moders wombe whils this virgine was shette,
> On hire the Haly Gast his speciell blissing yette,
> And merkid hire with the seale of the Haly Trinitee,
> That neuer thing that warre synne shuld haue in hire entree.
> Forsoth, Marye, thowe ert gardin of alle swettenesse,
> And welle of sawles witt, euer flowyng in fulnesse.[106]

Mary Garden illustrations became increasingly common with the popularity of Books of Hours in the late fifteenth and early sixteenth centuries. A typical example is the woodcut (fig. 12) used in a 1535 Sarum *Horae*.[107] Gathered around Mary are her symbols, each depicted and labeled. The labeling emphasizes the symbolic nature of this garden, which cannot be mistaken for a literal construct. Near the top are the sun and a star, "ELECTA VT SOL," "STELLA MARIS"; on either side of Mary are structures identified as "PORTA CELI" and "TVRRIS DAVIDCV" (sic), with "ORTVS CO*N*CLVSVS," and below "CIVITAS DEI"; while "PVTEVS AQVA PV*R*A" balances "FONS ORTORVM," above which is placed a mirror. The margins are formed by an olive tree on one side and a cedar on the other; flowers include the rose, lily, and a blooming rod of Jesse.[108] God the Father looks down from above, wreathed in scrolls with the text "tota pulcra es amica mea et macula non est in te" from *Song of Songs* 4.7. The attempt elsewhere, by the artist of the *Grimani Breviary* (Venice, Biblioteca Nazionale Marciana, fol. 831), to make such a selection of iconographic attributes seem naturalistic was not entirely successful.[109] Yet another example, a design from Brussels dated in the early seventeenth century which represented the Virgin of Montaigu within a garden planted in contemporary style with trees and plants symbolic of her attributes, is very attractive; the Virgin and her Son here are somewhat detached visually from a convincingly realistic garden.[110]

These visual representations presented direct parallels to the Marian verses of James Ryman[111] and John Lydgate.[112] The Marian epithets were later rehearsed in the Litany of Loretto, which, derived from earlier Marian litanies, was authorized for public use in 1587; in his preface to his commentary on it John Sweetnam wrote:

> I haue thought good to entytle this small worke, *The Paradise of delights*, or *the Bl. Virgins garden of Loreto*. And for our better Collection, it will not be amisse to imagine, a priuate Garden, adorned with all kind of delightfull flowers, amidest which the Bl. Virgin vseth to walke. . . . Vnto the gate of this mysticall garden, and Paradise, we must approach with all humility, desiring to be admitted to the pleasant view of those celestiall flowers, whose dainty odours haue filled the whole world with their fragrant smell.[113]

To be sure, terms like 'paradise,' 'garden,' or 'flowers,' 'garlands,' 'nosegays,' and 'posies' were popular for the titles of almost any kind of 'anthology' (i.e., collection of flowers), especially in sixteenth- and seventeenth-century England.[114] English Recusant writers such as Richard Rowlands celebrated the traditional Marian epithets; his *Odes* of 1601 included eight-line verses on twenty-two of them, including *"Hortus conclusus"* which links the Mary Garden with the garden paradise established by God at the beginning of time:

> Moste pleasant garden plot, true *Paradise* of praise,
> Erected in the roome, or *Paradise* of iore,
> But yet that garden far, exceeding sundry wayes,
> As perfect second woorkes, exceed things wrought before:
> All closely wall'd about, inuiolate it stayes,
> No serpent can get in, nor shal for euermore,
> All goodly flowers and frutes, here in perfection grow,
> Vertue on stockes of grace, hath them engraffed so.[115]

But the most extensive, elaborate, and many-layered "Mary Garden" published in English was Henry Hawkins' *Partheneia Sacra: Or The Mysterious and Deliciovs Garden of the Sacred Parthenes; Symbolically Set Forth and Enriched with Pious Devices and Emblemes* (1633).[116] Like the Paradise Garden painting of the Frankfurt Master, Hawkins informed every detail of the garden with a moral and spiritual meaning. But whereas the earlier painting was, in Graham Hough's terminology, incarnational,[117] Hawkins' treatment was unashamedly symbolic and emblematic (see fig. 13).

As every reader of Dante knows, the rose was a flower associated with the heavenly Paradise and with the Blessed Virgin Mary—as well as with secular lovers and pleasure gardens.[118] Rosemary Woolf cites the opinion of St. Ambrose and St. Basil that the roses growing in the Garden of Eden had been unfading and without thorns, as would be the case in the Mary Garden or the heavenly Paradise.[119] The Virgin Mary was herself addressed as a rose or was otherwise associated with this flower. The most famous example is probably the late medieval carol that opens with the lines "Ther is no rose *of* swych vertu/ As is the rose that bare Jhesu;/ Alleluya."[120] In another fifteenth-century example, she is the rosebush and her Son is the blossom,[121] while in a poem which Carleton Brown entitled *Mary, Remember Me at My Last Day*, she is called "Myrroure without spot, rede rose of Ierico,/ Close gardyn of grace. . . ."[122] Elsewhere she was not only identified with the rose but also not surprisingly pictured against a background of roses. With the increased popularity of rosary devotions and their associated confraternities, the *Rosarium*, or rose-garden, took on a wider range of meaning in the last quarter of the fifteenth century. Sixteenth-century German rosary paintings not only were smothered with roses but also were clearly para- disaical.[123] In England there were, however, complicating factors on account of the politicized nature of the image as represented by the Tudor rose, and later Queen Elizabeth would use the title *Rosa Electa* (in her case implying her transcendental right to rule) and would also adapt a number of other traditional religious and Marian epithets.[124] But for our purposes the most elaborate moral, spir- itual, and practical devotional application of the figure of the rose in English was again that provided by Henry Hawkins in his *Par- theneia Sacra*. In his discourse on the rose, he cited St. Bernard to elaborate the idea of Mary as the second Eve:

> O thou *Virgin* (sayth S. *Bernard*) most flourishing *Rod of Iesse*! through whom was recouered in the Branch, what had perished in the Root! *Eua* was a branch of bitternes, *Marie* a branch of eternal sweetnes. An admirable and most profound dispensation of the Diuine Wisedome! that such a *Rod* should grow from such a *Root*; such a *Daughter* from such a *Mother* . . . from so dry a *Thorn*, so flourishing a *Rose*.[125]

The allusion here is to the Tree of Jesse, which is united to the image of the rose. This well-known iconographic motif[126] in- volves a life-giving symbolic tree issuing from the root of the sleeping Jesse, fulfilling Wisdom's prophecy in *Ecclesiasticus* 24.16–23.

The appearance of the Blessed Virgin with her Son at the summit of the Jesse Tree, as in painted glass at Llanrhaeadr-yng- Nghinmeirch, Denbigh (fig. 14), or on a benchend of c.1380 at Chester Cathedral,[127] brought together the Old Testament pro- phetic forerunners of Christ through his Mother. It is of interest that Jesse may be pictured, as at Llanrhaeader, lying in an enclosed garden. In examples in which the entire design is intact, the summit of the aromatic tree or vine is the Virgin, the rose whose existence on earth was only a prelude to her enjoyment of heaven, where she may be called upon by her devotees who wish to have her aid in matters both earthly and heavenly. The symbol of the rose, like the Virgin herself, joins not only past and present but also the present and eternity. In a sense, too, the Tree of Jesse functions in a similar way to link earth and heaven and also to unite the old dispensation (preparatory) with the new dispensation of grace (fulfillment). A comparison indeed may be in order with the cosmological tree found in many of the world's religions and taken up in Christian tradition.[128]

As indicated above, the fertility of the Garden of Eden is related to the presence of water—water arising from a spring and giving moisture to the entire world—which flowed into four streams (*Genesis* 2.6, 10). The ornamental fountain was present in secular gardens, but its symbolic role was much more specific in depictions of paradisaical gardens, both earthly and heavenly. While the biblical valuing of water in the arid Near East may be easily explained, its symbolic significance in subsequent Christian tradition is also important to recognize. Dryness, as the North African St. Augustine of Hippo recognized, was an appropriate metaphor for despair, a condition lacking the water of grace represented by baptism. Prior to his conversion, Augustine in the *Confessions* hence described his life as like a wasteland, and St. Gregory the Great insisted that taking away grace is like drawing the moisture from the soil so that it becomes infertile.[129] In his *Spiritual Espousals*, Jan van Ruysbroek likened the second of the three ways by which Christ comes to the soul to "a living fount of water with three streams."[130] Some two centuries later St. Teresa of Avila used the similitude of a gardener watering his garden by different means to explain the development of the life of prayer: unless it is given moisture through prayer, the garden of the soul cannot be kept fertile.[131]

The fountain, as we have seen, could be a discrete well, as in the paradise garden of the Frankfurt Master,[132] or it could be an elaborate Gothic fountain, as in Bosch's *Garden of Earthly Delights* (left wing), the *Très Riches Heures* of Jean, Duke of Berry, or the *Bedford Hours* (fig. 11).[133] The appearance of such fountains in paintings of the Blessed Virgin suggested a paradisaical garden setting, but it also implied reference to her current heavenly role as influential with regard to the dispensing of grace. Yryö Hirn quotes a relevant passage from St. Bernard: "A pleasure-garden for us is thy most holy womb, O Mary, from which we can pluck manifold flowers of joy every time we think of what wealth of sweetness has thence streamed forth over the world."[134]

Hawkins would prominently place a fountain in the symbolic

Mary Garden (fig. 13) in his *Partheneia Sacra* of 1633 and would draw on many of the scriptural references to this symbolic feature to illustrate the role of the Virgin. In his "Theories" section of the explication, his Marian fountain assumes the proportions of the cosmological tree:

> our glorious *Virgin*, the *Fountain* . . . of liuing waters, as an Aqueduct hath so great a length, as she reaches euen from heauen to the earth; according to that mellifluous *Doctour: Marie* is an Aqueduct, whose top like *Iacob's* ladder, reaches to Heauen. And the breadth of this Aqueduct is such, as she was able to containe the Diuine *Fountain* itself, as the same *S. Bernard* affirmes.[135]

The aqueduct image used here is even more theologically precise than the description of Mary as a fountain elsewhere by Hawkins, for her role included serving as a conduit of grace. However, the more usual figure of the Blessed Virgin was the "sealed fountain" (*fons signatus*) of *Song of Songs* 4.12.

Evelyn Underhill has pointed out that the late medieval iconography of the Fountain of Life involved a summing up of the doctrine of grace, but her analysis only concentrates on the connection with the cult of the precious blood of Christ.[136] This Fountain of Life tradition, which emphasizes the eucharistic element—sometimes, as in the painting in the Prado, by Hosts floating in the water of the basin[137] or otherwise by stressing the healing power of the blood flowing into and out of it[138]—does not adequately explain the fountains which appear in gardens under discussion in the present paper. In the Garden of Eden, the fountain, as in the *Bedford Hours* (fig. 11) and the *Très Riches Heures*, even seems in its central position to eclipse the fateful tree. Instead there is a suggestion of a connection between this item and the fountains of knowledge and fear of the Lord to which the Wisdom writers refer (e.g., in *Proverbs* 13.14, 14.27, 16.22 and *Ecclesiasticus* 21.16), and in this regard they are to be seen as related to the fountain as it will later be described in Cesare Ripa's *Iconologia* where it is associated with penitence.[139] But they are also reminiscent of the elaborate font covers characteristic of East Anglia in the churches at Salle, North Walsham, and Ufford,[140] and they additionally resemble the tabernacles used to reserve the Blessed Sacrament in Northern Europe.[141] Interestingly, in the later Fountain of Life paintings such as the example by Lucas Horenhault discussed by

Underhill or the one by Jean Bellegambe,[142] the vessel resembles a chalice and a font. Thus the fountain is doctrinally and visually associated with the two dominical sacraments, the sources of grace and redemption which have reversed the catastrophe of the Fall and have made possible the restoration of Paradise. Jan van Eyck's Ghent Altarpiece places a fountain in the foreground, visually preceding the altar and the Lamb of sacrifice, as baptism sacramentally precedes the Eucharist and is the necessary condition for entry into the Paradise of the blessed. Jean Daniélou remarks that for Cyril of Alexandria the catechumens about to be baptised "are on the threshold of the royal garden of Paradise, where the marriage [of Christ and his Church, of Sponsus and Sponsa] is to take place."[143]

Gardens in their practical and symbolic aspects continued to be related to—or constrasted with—the original paradise described in *Genesis* well into the seventeenth century. In rather different ways, the garden with paradisaical overtones was discussed and praised by writers Reformed, Protestant, and Catholic, and was featured widely in emblem books such as Henry Peacham's *Minerva Britanna, or a Garden of Heroical Deuices* (1612) and George Wither's *A Collection of Emblemes* (1635). Conversely, John Parkinson's strictly practical book about plant varieties and their cultivation—and about different kinds of gardens—was called *Paradisi in sole, paradisus terrestris* (1629). Its title page was adorned with an illustration of the first paradise garden, containing birds and fish but no animals other than what appears to be a vegetable lamb, which might also be intended to point forward to the redemptive Lamb of God, the *Agnus Dei* invoked as the one who "takes away the sins of the world" following the canon of the Mass in the English medieval rites.[144] Parkinson's Preface notes that herbs and flowers magnify their Creator and afford many good instructions, even as herbs and flowers may perfume a whole house. The scent of Paradise wafting from the garden of the *Song of Songs* might likewise perfume practical gardeners as well as pilgrims and voyagers in search of the earthly paradise. The garden of paradise continued to be more than a symbolic image to seventeenth-century Christians: it was a real place and a hoped for destination where those who have received salvation will persever through all eternity in a place characterized by (in George Herbert's words) "Light, joy, and leisure."[145]

Again, at the center of the original garden of paradise "the tree of knowledge of good and evil" remained a problem to be reckoned with; further, this garden was a location where the relationships between God and humankind, between man and woman which were tested there, had been fatally disrupted by the Fall. Thereafter all things would be changed utterly, and yet the hope of restoring the condition of paradise was a part of the messianic dream. Images of the garden perfected were included in the Old Testament and were taken up by Christian exegetes, writers, and artists. The reversal of the Fall and the recovery of Paradise for Christians began in an enclosed space, the womb of the Blessed Virgin, and was accomplished through and in garden areas: the Garden of Gethsemane and the garden in the place where Jesus had been buried—and where he was mistaken for a gardener by Mary Magdalene (*John* 20.15). This story of salvation was enacted in the great mystery play cycles of England as well as in individual plays such as the Digby *Mary Magdalene*.[146] These scenes were illustrated in private books and in public Church art. The stories were familiar to all Christians at various levels of sophistication. The most rustic would recognize the scenes of the Creation of the world and of humankind, of the Temptation, Fall, and Expulsion from the garden. Representations of Paradise and the joy of the blessed, as opposed to the fate of the damned and the tortures of hell,[147] were easily distinguished in the context of the Last Judgment.

But, as we have seen, there were many more subtle suggestions concerning Paradise available to those who were able to "read" the visual and literary symbolism and who could detect more concealed visual statements. The representation of the Blessed Virgin is a case in point, with many of the Marian titles derived from that most fruitful of scriptural gardens, the garden of the lovers in the *Song of Songs*, a book which exercised a decisive influence on all subsequent images of the terrestrial paradise—or, by extension, the heavenly paradise. On another level, the *Song* also crystallized the dilemma of the garden as a setting: was "the paradise of pleasure" (*Genesis* 2.8) representative of pleasure according to the will of God or of human, sensual, sexual pleasure? Both kinds of gardens existed in profusion in the literature and art of the late Middle Ages and the early modern period. Religious writers needed to be certain that their gardens were properly understood, for the imagery of secular and religious love was shared, garden settings for human and divine love easily confused. For this reason, therefore, the tendency toward more obviously symbolic, even emblematic representations such as the Mary Garden perhaps was generated.

However, a great many visual representations of Paradise are as allusive as the perfumes that clung about all that came out of this location or even about those who simply drew near to it. Pure blue skies, such as those above the Paradise Garden by the Frankfurt Master, and sparkling golden light of the kind that illuminates the paradises of Fra Angelico or Jan van Eyck, suggest the quality of heavenly light and the temperate climate. The sparkling light was often enhanced by jewels, particularly in painted glass and in paintings by van Eyck and others. Might not the heavily jeweled borders of many of the robes and the jeweled crowns to be seen, for example, in the Annunication window (the northwest window, St. John's Chapel) in Ludlow parish church carry overtones of paradise?[148] The presence of patterned carpets of flowers and brightly colored birds also designated Paradise. The golden haloes and green-painted, flower-dotted painted backgrounds to representations of the saints on alabasters and screens are perhaps also faint echoes of Paradise.

The subject of the Paradise Garden is thus complicated by its sources in *Genesis* and other biblical accounts as well as by the literalistic understanding sometimes entertained concerning the terrestrial paradise—a paradise for which voyagers, including Columbus, might continue to search. But the understanding of the garden was much more complex on account of the multifaceted ways in which this place might be interpreted, indeed often operating on several levels at once. On one level the "Mary Garden" was simply an emblem which might describe the Virgin Mary by means of terminology derived from Old Testament types of her; but it was also about grace and how this was mediated. The Fountain of life, so often pictured in the center of the Garden of Eden, might also carry visual reminders of a font or tabernacle for the Sacrament of the Altar, as we have suggested above. The related imagery of the eucharistic Fountain of Life, as pictured in the woodcut on the title page of *The Fountayne or well of lyfe*,[149] or of wells of life, pity, charity, etc., labeled in woodcuts,[150] or on a quarry of glass at Sidmouth, Devon,[151] reinforced the sacramental implications of the fountain in other contexts. In a Flemish painting now at the National Gallery in Prague, the eucharistic fountain is the wine-press of the Passion, flanked by two thieves on Calvary, but the landscape and the ranks of the devout receiving Christ's blood from chalices held by angels suggest that this is Paradise.[152] It is. For the Blessed Virgin and her Son were the new Eve and the new Adam, who reversed the catastrophe that led to the expulsion of humankind from Eden and brought the garden of Paradise within reach of all Christian souls through the sacraments of the Church.

The proper condition of humankind is to be a pilgrim in search of the vision of God and to hope to enjoy the company of his Son and his Mother Mary as well as of all the saints in an eternity which is rich in the fullness of its joy.[153] The present life must pass through an alien land full of thorns and along a rocky way, but its goal must be to return to the blissful pre-lapsarian state. As Alcuin said (in F. C. Gardiner's translation),

> our hope, like an anchor, draws us to the solidity of the celestial fatherland. Then happiness will be perfected, when the sight of love will be full and God will be seen in his glory, who is now loved in our hearts. . . . But let the pilgrimage of this exile be borne patiently until comes the desired presence of the blessed fatherland.[154]

The beginning and end of time were understood to be marked by the garden, in eternity presenting a fertile landscape conducive to joy. The details to be visualized in imagining this place were codified, drawn from the many sources, though as we have seen the iconography is nevertheless flexible and rich. The pilgrimage of hope will terminate at the Garden of Paradise, which will be the fulfillment of every hope and desire, and, as the *Apocalypse* proclaims, "there shall be no curse any more" (22.3). Here, then, the blessed will find themselves translated from the thorny world to a place where only the "flow'rs of grace"[155] and all good things grow—a place safe at last from the ravages of the anti-gardener Satan and from all earthly anxiety.

NOTES

[1] Lotte Brand Philip, *The Ghent Altarpiece and the Art of Jan van Eyck* (Princeton: Princeton Univ. Press, 1971), pp. 61–78, figs. 1–3, 41–42, 62.

[2] Fols. cxliv^r–cxlv^r, clii^r, clviii^v; Otto Pächt and J. J. G. Alexander, *Illustrated Manuscripts in the Bodleian Library*, I: *Dutch, Flemish, French, and Spanish Schools* (Oxford: Clarendon Press, 1966), No. 710.

[3] Lucy Freeman Sandler, *The Psalter of Robert de Lisle* (London: Harvey Miller and Oxford Univ. Press, 1983), Pls. 8–9; Lambert of St. Omer, *Liber Floridus*, ed. Alberto Derolez (Ghent: Story-Scientia, 1968), pp. 462–63 (fols. 232^r–232^v; see also Adolf Katzenellenbogen, *Allegories of the Virtues and Vices in Mediaeval Art*, trans. Alan J. P. Crick [1939; rpt. New York: W. W. Norton, 1964], pp. 65–66, figs. 64–67).

[4] Gilbert of Hoyland, *Sermons on the Song of Songs*, Cistercian Fathers Ser., 14, 20, 26 (Kalamazoo: Cistercian Publications, 1978–79), I, 179.

[5] Jean Leclercq, *The Love of Learning and the Desire for God*, trans. Catharine Misrahi, 2nd ed. (New York: Fordham Univ. Press, 1974), pp. 73–74; for the text of Peter Damian's poem, see *Patrologia Latina*, CXLV, 980–81.

[6] Leclercq, *Love of Learning*, p. 74.

[7] Leclercq, *Love of Learning*, p. 75, citing *Analecta Hymnica*, ed. Guido Maria Dreves (1907; rpt. Johnson Reprint, 1961), L, 499–506.

[8] Edward Hodnett, *English Woodcuts 1480–1535*, 2nd ed. (Oxford: Oxford Univ. Press, 1973), No. 1974. The original intent of the artist, of course, may in this case have been to design a woodcut that represents the barrier defining the earthly paradise.

[9] Philip, *Ghent Altarpiece*, figs. 1, 107–09. Above Adam, who stands at the left, is depicted the sacrifice of Cain and Abel—providing the motive for the murder but also presenting one of the Old Testament types for the sacrifice of Christ on the cross and the Eucharist (ibid., pp. 101–02).

[10] J. K. Bonnell, "The Serpent with a Human Head in Art and in Mystery Play," *American Journal of Archaeology*, 2nd ser., 21 (1917), 255–91. A very good example is presented in the early fifteenth-century painted glass in the East Window of York Minster; in this instance, the body of the serpent is a modern replacement with glass chosen arbitrarily from another source, but otherwise the glass is good (see Clifford Davidson and David O'Connor, *York Art*, Early Drama, Art, and Music, Reference Ser., 1 [Kalamazoo: Medieval Institute Publications, 1978], p. 22).

[11] Hartmann Schedel, *Liber Chronicarum* (Nuremberg, 1493), fol. 7^r; Adrian Wilson, *The Making of the Nuremberg Chronicle* (Amsterdam: Nico Israel, 1976), Pl. 3.

[12] See also Jean Daniélou, *From Shadows to Reality: Studies in the Biblical Typology of the Fathers*, trans. Wulstan Hibberd (London: Burns and Oates, 1960), pp. 22–29.

[13] Paul Meyvaert, "The Medieval Monastic Garden," in *Medieval Gardens*, introd. Elisabeth Blair MacDougall, Dumbarton Oaks Colloquium on the History of Landscape Architecture, 9 (Washington, D.C.: Dumbarton Oaks Research Library, 1986), p. 51.

[14] William of Malmsbury, as quoted by Terry Comito, *The Idea of the Garden in the Renaissance* (New Brunswick, N.J.: Rutgers Univ. Press, 1978), p. 43.

[15] It has been suggested that paradise tended to be pictured as nature perfected in the earlier Christian centuries, when writers and artists were able to draw upon their geographical and cultural contacts with the classical past and the oriental world. Representations of paradise as nature perfected, and particularly in a garden setting, very much returned to fashion by the fifteenth century. In this century, as Anne Winston-Allen has pointed out ("'Minne' in Spiritual Gardens of the Fifteenth Century," unpublished paper read at the International Congress on Medieval Studies, Kalamazoo, May 1990), garden allegories were more popular than at any other time; it is also significant that the majority of the examples shown by John Harvey in his *Mediaeval Gardens* (London: B. T. Batsford, 1981) are from this period.

[16] Translation from David Bevington, *Medieval Drama* (Boston: Houghton Mifflin, 1975), p. 80; for the Old French and Latin text of this play, see the edition of Willem Nooman (Paris: Champion, 1971).

[17] *The Staging of Religious Drama in Europe in the Later Middle Ages: Texts and Documents in Translation*, ed. Peter Meredith and John E. Tailby, Early Drama, Art, and Music, Monograph Ser., 4 (Kalamazoo: Medieval Institute Publications, 1983), p. 93.

[18] Ibid., pp. 92–93.

[19] *Non-Cycle Plays and Fragments*, ed. Norman Davis, EETS, s.s. 1 (London: Oxford Univ. Press, 1970), p. 11 (Norwich Grocers' Play, Prologue B¹, l. 13).

[20] *Norwich 1540–1642*, ed. David Galloway, Records of Early English Drama (Toronto: Univ. of Toronto Press, 1984), pp. 43–44.

[21] *The N-town Play: Cotton MS Vespasian D.8*, ed. Stephen Spector, EETS, s.s. 11 (Oxford: Oxford Univ. Press, 1991), I, 24–25 (Play 2, ll. 20–41).

[22] *The Creacion of the World*, ed. and trans. Paula Neuss (New York: Garland, 1983), pp. 30–33.

[23] *The Staging of Religious Drama*, ed. Meredith and Tailby, p. 83 and diagram inside back cover; A. M. Nagler, *The Medieval Religious Stage: Shapes and Phantoms* (New Haven: Yale Univ. Press, 1976), p. 30.

[24] *The Staging of Religious Drama*, ed. Meredith and Tailby, p. 86. This garden was also used for the Annunciation; see ibid.

[25] Ibid., p. 84.

[26] See the illustrations collected in Frank Crisp, *Medieval Gardens* (1924; rpt. New York: Hacker, 1966), *passim*.

[27] Jean Longnon and Raymond Cazelles, *The Très Riches Heures of Jean, Duke of Berry* (New York: George Braziller, 1969), Pl. 20. Interestingly, the *paradis* illustrated on the Valenciennes stage plan (at stage right, and above a mansion designated as *salle*) is round with God seated on a throne at its center and angels circling around the edge; see A. M. Nagler, *The Medieval Religious Stage* (New Haven: Yale Univ. Press, 1976), p. 85. For the illustration of the Garden of Eden in the painting by Herri met de Bles (c.1480–1550) which is also round, in the Rijksmuseum, Amsterdam, see Derek Pearsall and Elizabeth Salter, *Landscapes and Seasons of the Medieval World* (London: Paul Elek, 1973), fig. 22.

[28] British Library, Add. MS. 18,850, fol. 14; see also Janet Backhouse, *The Bedford Hours* (London: British Library, 1990), fig. 3.

[29] John Plummer, *The Hours of Catherine of Cleves* (New York: George Braziller, 1966), Nos. 79–87. For this legend, see E. C. Quinn, *The Quest of Seth for the Oil of Life* (Chicago: Univ. of Chicago Press, 1962), and also Gertrud Schiller, *Iconography of Christian Art*, trans. Janet Seligman (Greenwich, Conn.: New York Graphic Society, 1972), II, 131–32.

[30] Thomas T. Ohlgren, *Anglo-Saxon Textual Illustration* (Kalamazoo: Medieval Institute Publications, 1992), Pl. 16.5; see also Israel Gollancz, *The Caedmon Manuscript of Anglo-Saxon Biblical Poetry* (Oxford: Oxford Univ. Press, 1927), p. 7.

[31] Schiller, *Iconography of Christian Art*, II, 133–34; translation for convenience from *The Missal in Latin and English* (London: Burns, Oates, and Washbourne, 1957), p. 738.

[32] W. O. Hassall, *The Holkham Bible Picture Book* (London: Dropmore Press, 1954), fol. 3^v, p. 64. In late medieval representations of the Crucifixion in which the cross is a tree, the pelican in its nest sometimes appeared above the figure of the crucified Savior; see Schiller, *Iconography of Christian Art*, II, 136–37, figs. 451, 504.

[33] Hassall, *The Holkham Bible Picture Book*, fols. 3^v–4^v.

[34] *Speculum Sacerdotale*, ed. Edward H. Weatherly, EETS, o.s. 200 (London: Oxford Univ. Press, 1936), pp. 166–67.

[35] Ludolphus of Saxony, *Leeven heeren Ihesu Cristi* (Antwerp, 1503), fol. ix^r; see the reproduction in John Prest, *The Garden of Eden* (New Haven: Yale Univ. Press, 1981), fig. 8, and Crisp, *Medieval Gardens*, I, fig. 116. Crisp also includes a later copy of this illustration (I, fig. 117)

[36] See Hodnett, *English Woodcuts*, Nos. 699, 1444, 1945, 2083, fig. 182.

[37] Ibid., No. 2049, fig. 193.

[38] Gordon McN. Rushforth, *Mediaeval Christian Imagery* (Oxford: Clarendon Press, 1936), pp. 153–58, figs. 63–66.

[39] Gordon McN. Rushforth, "The Windows of the Church of St. Neot, Cornwall," *Exeter Diocesan Architectural and Archaeological Society*, 15 (1937), 154–58.

[40] Davidson and O'Connor, *York Art*, pp. 21–23, figs. 4–5.

[41] Wilson, *The Making of the Nuremberg Chronicle*, pp. 91, 93, 100, Pl. 2.

[42] M. D. Anderson, *Drama and Imagery in English Medieval Churches* (Cambridge: Cambridge Univ. Press, 1963), pp. 141–42. This hypothesis may be attributed to Émile Mâle; see especially his *Religious Art in France: The Late Middle Ages: A Study of Medieval Iconography and Its Sources*, trans. Marthiel Mathews, Bollingen Ser., 90, No. 3 (Princeton: Princeton Univ. Press, 1986), pp. 35–80.

[43] See *Apocalypse* 22.13: "I am Alpha and Omega, the first and the last, the beginning and the end."

[44] Ohlgren, *Anglo-Saxon Textual Illustration*, Pl. 16.10; Gollancz, *Caedmon Manuscript*, p. 13. In this illustration, which shows the scene set off by architectural

columns and arches (the center column is not present), small animals are nibbling at the plants.

[45] Wilhelm Hausenstein, *Fra Angelico* (Munich: Kurt Wolff, 1923), Pl. 34.

[46] John Pope-Hennessy, *Giovanni di Paolo* (London: Chatto and Windus, 1937), pp. 19–23, Pl. VIIIa.

[47] In the visual arts the garden setting is a common signal that a secular love scene is meant; for example, the man and woman standing on each side of a fountain on a fragmentary sixteenth- or seventeenth-century comb in the British Museum (O. M. Dalton, *Catalogue of the Ivory Carvings of the Christian Era in the British Museum* [London: British Museum, 1909], No. 485) cannot be mistaken for characters in sacred art. The *fons amoris* was a frequent image; for an engraving, see Arthur Hind, *Catalogue of Early Italian Engravings* (London: British Museum, 1910), I, 274 (No. E.III.3). In an illumination showing the garden of love in an illustrated *Romance of the Rose* (British Library MS. Egerton 1069, fol. 1^r), water flows from a fountain and through a grated opening in the garden wall much as in illustrations of the Garden of Eden. But the figure looking into the pool in the fountain is Narcissus, and lovers appear (the man at the gate takes the lady's hand in his). See also Helen Phillips, "Gardens of Love and the Garden of the Fall," in *A Walk in the Garden*, ed. Paul Morris and Deborah Sawyer, Journal for the Study of the Old Testament, Suppl. Ser., 136 (Sheffield: Sheffield Academic Press, 1992), pp. 205–19.

[48] For a convenient explanation of typology, see William G. Madsen, *From Shadowy Types to Truth* (New Haven: Yale Univ. Press, 1968). A more detailed study is Daniélou, *From Shadows to Reality*.

[49] See Schiller, *Iconography of Christian Art*, II, 133–34. Schiller also cites the mystics Tauler and Eckhart, who spoke of "the lovely tree of heavenly life."

[50] Avril Henry, *Biblia Pauperum* (Aldershot: Scolar Press, 1987), pp. 48, 50.

[51] Ibid., pp. 65, 67, 97, 99.

[52] Adrian Wilson and Joyce Lancaster Wilson, *A Medieval Mirror: Speculum Humanae Salvationis, 1324–1500* (Berkeley and Los Angeles: Univ. of California Press, 1984), pp. 141–99.

[53] For an example at Fairford, see Hilary Wayment, *The Stained Glass of the Church of St. Mary, Fairford, Gloucestershire*, Occasional Papers, n.s. 5 (London: Society of Antiquaries, 1984), pp. 21–23, Pl. I; here Eve with the serpent is accompanied by Moses and the burning bush, Gideon and his fleece, and Solomon

with the Queen of Sheba.

[54] See Patrick J. Collins, "Narrative Bible Cycles in Medieval Art and Drama," *Comparative Drama*, 9 (1975), 138; E. W. Tristram, *English Medieval Wall Painting: The Twelfth Century* (London: Oxford Univ. Press, 1944), pp. 128–32.

[55] Marie-Dominique Chenu, *Nature, Man, and Society in the Twelfth Century*, trans. and ed. Jerome Taylor and L. K. Little (1968; rpt. Chicago: Univ. of Chicago Press, 1979), pp. 99–145.

[56] Plummer, *Hours of Catherine of Cleves*, Pl. 89.

[57] The name Eva was understood to be reversed in the archangel's greeting at the Annunciation; see, for example, Richard Leighton Greene, *The Early English Carols*, 2nd ed. (Oxford: Clarendon Press, 1977), Nos. 238a–238c; Robert Southwell, *The Poems*, ed. J. H. McDonald and Nancy P. Brown (Oxford: Clarendon Press, 1967), pp. 5, 117. The Eve-Mary comparison, however, dates from the Church Fathers; see Irenaeus, *Against Heresies* V.xix.1.

[58] Pearsall and Salter, *Landscapes and Seasons*, pp. 71–75; Pope-Hennessy, *Giovanni di Paolo*, pp. 6–7.

[59] See Paul Piehler, *The Visionary Landscape* (London: Edward Arnold, 1971), esp. chaps. 5–6, 8. For a useful bibliography, see Eileen Gardiner, *Medieval Visions of Heaven and Hell* (New York: Garland, 1992).

[60] Pearsall and Salter, *Landscapes and Seasons*, pp. 229–43.

[61] *Pearl, Cleanness, Patience, Sir Gawain and the Green Knight*, 2nd ed., ed. A. C. Cawley and J. J. Anderson (London: Dent, 1976).

[62] Perhaps derived from *Genesis* 2.12 and the *Song of Songs* (for the importance of this book, see below), but more likely from the *Apocalypse* and its description of the New Jerusalem (chap. 21).

[63] *The Lyfe of Saynt Brandon* (London: Wynkyn de Worde, [?1520]) (STC 3600).

[64] Ibid., sig. A2^r.

[65] Ibid.

[66] Ibid., sig. A3^r–A3^v.

[67] Ibid., sig. B3^v.

[68] Belief in a physical earthly paradise was not confined to literature or legend, since actual people in fact set out to look for it and returned convinced that they had come close to finding it. See Prest, *The Garden of Eden, passim*; M. M. Lascelles, "Alexander and the Earthly Paradise in Mediaeval English Writings," *Medium Aevum*, 5 (1936), 31–47, 79–104, 173–88; George Boas, *Essays on Primitivism and Related Ideas in the Middle Ages* (1948; New York: Octagon Books, 1978), pp. 154–74; Howard R. Patch, *The Other World According to Descriptions in Medieval Literature* (1950; rpt. New York: Octagon Books, 1970), chap. 5. One of the most comprehensive accounts, presented as travels that had been personally undertaken by the author, was Sir John Mandeville's.

[69] Christopher Columbus, in a report from his third voyage which cited authorities such as Isidore of Seville, the Venerable Bede, Peter Comestor, St. Ambrose, Duns Scotus, and "all the learned theologians" about the location of the terrestrial paradise in the East, concluded that it was very likely located in the islands of the West Indies which he had discovered (Boas, *Essays on Primitivism*, pp. 171–74).

[70] Pearsall and Salter, *Landscapes and Seasons*, figs. 21, 32a, 32b; Giovanni di Paolo's Madonna of Humility, Boston, Museum of Fine Arts.

[71] For the use of hangings for the Garden of Eden in the Anglo-Norman *Adam*, see above.

[72] E.g., Bedford Hours, fol. 208; Durham, Ushaw College, MS. 10, fol. 31^v; N. R. Ker and A. J. Piper, *Mediaeval Manuscripts in British Libraries*, IV (Oxford: Clarendon Press, 1992), 516–19. The fence of palings in Fra Angelico's Annunciation at San Marco is not only a reminder of the Garden of Eden but also a foreshadowing of the Passion and Christ's sacrifice on the cross, which would rectify the Fall; see William Hood, *Fra Angelico at San Marco* (New Haven: Yale Univ. Press, 1993), p. 271, figs. 252, 256.

[73] For the further association of the garden with the Blessed Virgin Mary, see E. Ann Matter, *The Voice of My Beloved: The Song of Songs in Western Medieval Christianity* (Philadelphia: Univ. of Pennsylvania Press, 1990), *passim*, and below.

[74] For a comparison of the literal and allegorical aspects of the garden in the *Song of Songs* with the Garden of Eden, see Francis Landy, *Paradoxes of Paradise: Identity and Difference in the Song of Songs* (Sheffield: Almond Press, 1983), chap. 4.

[75] Bernard of Clairvaux, *On the Song of Songs*, trans. Kilian Walsh, Cistercian Fathers Ser., 4, 7, 31, 40 (Kalamazoo: Cistercian Publications, 1971–80), I, 10.

[76] Wolfgang Riehle, *The Middle English Mystics*, trans. Bernard Standring (London: Routledge and Kegan Paul, 1981), p. 215 (for reference to the garden iconography in *Ayenbite of Inwyt*), chap. 3, and *passim*.

[77] See *The Macro Plays*, ed. Mark Eccles, EETS, 262 (London: Oxford Univ. Press, 1969), pp. 113–52, the protagonist of which is Anima, a figure who initially speaks of Wisdom (Christ) as her "spowse most specyally" (l. 19).

[78] See Wilson and Wilson, *A Medieval Mirror*, pp. 106–07; Stanley Stewart, *The Enclosed Garden* (Madison: Univ. of Wisconsin Press, 1966), figs. 6–8, 21, 32–33. The artistic and devotional significance of the *Song of Songs* is outlined by Jeffrey F. Hamburger, *The Rothschild Canticles* (New Haven: Yale Univ. Press, 1990), chaps. 4–5.

[79] Bernard of Clairvaux, *On the Song of Songs*, II, 11.

[80] Hildegard of Bingen, *Symphonia*, ed. and trans. Barbara Newman (Ithaca: Cornell Univ. Press, 1988), pp. 220–27.

[81] *Political, Religious, and Love Poems*, ed. Frederick J. Furnivall, EETS, o.s. 15 (London, 1866), pp. 180–89; the quotation is from the version in the Cambridge University Library manuscript.

[82] See the discussion of this poem in Rosemary Woolf, *The English Religious Lyric in the Middle Ages* (Oxford: Clarendon Press, 1968), pp. 187–91.

[83] E.g., British Library MS. Harley 4425, a profusely illustrated Flemish manuscript of the *Roman de la Rose* of c.1500; see John Harvey, *Mediaeval Gardens* (London: B. T. Batsford, 1981), figs. 9, 13A, 46, 57, 60–61, 70A, Pls. VIIB, VIII, and John Fleming, "The Garden of the *Roman de la Rose*: Vision of Landscape or Landscape of Vision," in *Medieval Gardens*, introd. MacDougall, pp. 201–34.

[84] Karl Young, *The Drama of the Medieval Church* (Oxford: Clarendon Press, 1933), I, 369–410.

[85] Hamburger, *Rothschild Canticles*, figs. 17–18.

[86] Ibid., p. 80.

[87] Ibid., 83.

[88] Ibid., p. 83.

[89] Ibid., fig. 24.

[90] See the example of this subject in the *Heisterbach Bible* (Hamburger, *Rothschild Canticles*, fig. 131).

[91] Text in Young, *The Drama of the Medieval Church*, II, 361–64.

[92] Honorius Augustodunensis, *Sigillum Sanctae Mariae* (Munich, Bayerische Staatsbibliothek, Clm. 4550, fol. 1ᵛ); reproduced in Hamburger, *Rothschild Canticles*, fig. 148. See also the painting of the Mystic Marriage of the Sponsus and Sponsa in the Museum of Fine Arts, Boston; reproduced in Millard Meiss, *Painting in Florence and Siena after the Black Death* (Princeton: Princeton Univ. Press, 1951), fig. 99.

[93] See the printed Sarum breviary: *Breuiarum seu horarium domesticum* (Paris, 1531), Pt. 3, fol. cxv (STC 15830).

[94] See Brian E. Daley, "The 'Closed Garden' and the 'Sealed Fountain': Song of Songs 4.12 in the Medieval Iconography of Mary," in *Medieval Gardens*, introd. MacDougall, pp. 253–78.

[95] Pearsall and Salter, *Landscapes and Seasons*, p. 108; E. Bertaud, "Hortus: Hortulus, Jardin Spirituel," *Dictionnaire de Spiritualité*, VII, Pt. 1 (Paris: Beauchesne, 1969), 766–84.

[96] See *The Mirour of Mans Saluacioun*, ed. Henry, pp. 56–57, and Wilson and Wilson, *A Medieval Mirror*, p. 149; the source of the closed door symbol as a representation of Mary is *Ezechiel* 44.1–2.

[97] See Pearsall and Salter, *Landscapes and Seasons*, figs. 21, 32a, 32b, and also our discussion above.

[98] Ibid., p. 109.

[99] Niels M. Saxtorph, *Danmarks kalkmalerier* (Copenhagen: Politikens Forlag, 1986), p. 253. This depiction of the Virgin is influenced by the description of the Woman Clothed with the Sun in *Apocalypse* 12.

[100] See R. Berliner, "Arma Christi," *Münchner Jahrbuch der bildenden Kunst*, 36 (1955), 350–52, and Erwin Panofsky, "Imago Pietatis," in *Festschrift für Max Friedländer* (Leipzig: E. A. Seemann, 1927), pp. 261–304.

[101] See Sixten Ringbom, "Devotional Images and Imaginative Devotions," *Gazette des Beaux Arts*, 111 (1969), 159–70.

[102] The power of such images of Mary was suggestively portrayed by Daniel Rock, who noted her present state—"the light of glory in which she now lives in Heaven"—and men's consequent joy in her: "lamps and waxen tapers were kept burning . . . day and night before the B. V. Mary's image wherever it might be in the church" (*The Church of Our Fathers* [London: John Hodges, 1903], III, 224). Sometimes the tapers would be wreathed in flowers (ibid.). See also Eithne Wilkins, *The Rose-Garden Game* (New York: Herder and Herder, 1969), p. 124: "The garden is the original matrix in which the Saviour is conceived. . . . It is also the Paradise into which the Saviour draws the soul. The Virgin Mary, as the second Eve, transforms the original garden of Paradise, from which the human race was driven out, and she does so by containing it within herself."

[103] For an interesting example which places Mary in a garden in an Annunciation in the Hours of Mary of Guelders, see John Harthan, *Books of Hours* (London: Thames and Hudson, 1978), pp. 78, 80–81. As Harthan notes, the garden with its "rose-decked fence" was "a symbolic anticipation of Paradise," but the fashionably dressed figure of Mary was possibly modeled on the donor herself (p. 80).

[104] Wilson and Wilson, *A Medieval Mirror*, pp. 106–07; Stewart, *The Enclosed Garden*, figs. 6–8, 21, 32–33. See also Hamburger, *The Rothschild Canticles*, chaps. 4–5.

[105] See Wilson and Wilson, *A Medieval Mirror*, pp. 146–47, 152–53.

[106] *The Mirour of Mans Saluacioun*, ed. Henry, p. 53 (ll. 569–78); for the tower of David with its thousand shields, identified symbolically as a fortification against any spot of sin, see ibid., pp. 64–65.

[107] *Hore Beatissime Virginis Mariae* (Paris: Francisco Reynault, 1535), fol. lxviii (STC 15987). For a connection between the Mary Garden and the *Obsecro te*, see Roger S. Wieck, *Time Sanctified: The Book of Hours in Medieval Art and Life* (New York: George Braziller, 1988), chap. 8 and pp. 163–64.

[108] The sources for these items are liturgical and scriptural; for the latter see *Song of Songs* 2.1–2; 4.4, 12, 15; 6.9; *Wisdom* 7.26; *Ecclesiasticus* 24.17–19; *Genesis* 28.17; *Apocalypse* 3.12; and, for the rod of Jesse, *Isaias* 11.1. This example is not unique; see also, for example, Cod. Nonnbergensis 23.A.,16, fol. 104^v (microfilm at the Hill Monastic Manuscript Library), and the early sixteenth-century historiated initial published by Crisp, *Medieval Gardens*, I, fig. 182. But the iconography is older, and the earliest example seems to be a tympanum at Laon Cathedral; see Émile Mâle, *Religious Art in France: The Thirteenth Century*, trans. Marthiel Mathews, Bollingen Ser., 90, No. 2 (Princeton: Princeton Univ. Press, 1984), pp. 152–55, and Daley, "The 'Closed Garden' and the 'Sealed Fountain'," fig. 4. See also Yryö Hirn, *The Sacred Shrine* (London: Macmillan, 1912), pp. 435–70.

[109] Scoto de Vries and S. Morpurgo, *Il Breviario Grimani della Bibliotheca di S. Marco* (Leiden: A. W. Sijthoff, 1904–10), Pl. 1581 (fol. 831); Pearsall and Salter, *Landscapes and Seasons*, fig. 35b.

[110] Crisp, *Medieval Gardens*, I, figs. 131, 225.

[111] Greene, *Early English Carols*, Nos. 192–94, 199, 207; cf. Nos. 190–91.

[112] John Lydgate, *The Minor Poems*, ed. Henry Noble MacCracken, EETS, e.s. 107 (London: Oxford Univ. Press, 1911), Nos. 49, 54, 57, and esp. 63.

[113] John Sweetnam, *The Paradise of Delights, or the B. Virgins Garden of Loreto* (1620), sigs. **5ᵛ–6ʳ (STC 23531).

[114] These ranged from the "Hortus" or "Hortulus" which overlapped with the Primer and Book of Hours, to Albertus Magnus' *Paradise of the Soule* (St. Omer, 1617); both Edward Maihew (1613) and Luis de Granada (1609) published a *Paradise of Prayers*; there were Alfonso de Villegas' *Flos Sanctorum* (1609), Jerome Porter's *The Flowers of the Lives of Saincts of England, Scotland and Ireland* (Douay, 1632), and many more. It was a venerable tradition deriving from antiquity; Gellius, *Attic Nights* (written c. A.D. 2) cited as literary titles the following: woods, meads, the fruit basket, fruits of my reading, and the nosegay. For a brief survey of classical gardens, see A. Bartlett Giamatti, *The Earthly Paradise and the Renaissance Epic* (Princeton: Princeton Univ. Press, 1966), pp. 33–47.

[115] Richard Verstegan (pseud. for Richard Rowlands), *Odes in Imitation of the Seaven Penitential Psalmes, with Sundry other Poemes and ditties tending to deuotion and pietie*, English Recusant Literature 1558–1640, 53 (1601; rpt. Menston: Scolar Press, 1970), p. 48.

[116] Henry Hawkins, *Partheneia Sacra*, English Recusant Literature 1558–1640, 81 (1633; rpt. Menston: Scolar Press, 1971).

[117] Graham Hough, *A Preface to the Faerie Queene* (London: Duckworth, 1962), p. 107.

[118] Charles Joret, *La Rose dans l'Antiquité et au Moyen Âge* (Paris: E. Boullon, 1892); Wilkins, *The Rose-Garden Game*, pp. 105–25; Harvey, *Mediaeval Gardens*, *passim*. For the mystic rose in the *Paradiso*, see Canto XXXII.

[119] Rosemary Woolf, *The English Religious Lyric in the Middle Ages* (Oxford: Clarendon Press, 1968), p. 288n, citing Ambrose, *Hexaemeron* III.xi, and Basil, *De peccato, Sermones viginti quatuor de moribus* vii.

[120] Greene, *Early English Carols*, No. 173, st. 1; see also ibid., Nos. 174–76.

[121] British Library, MS. Sloane 2593, fol. 6ᵛ; Greene, *Early English Carols*, No. 175.

[122] *Religious Lyrics of the Fifteenth Century*, ed. Carleton Brown (Oxford: Clarendon Press, 1939), No. 44, ll. 5–6.

[123] See, for example, Albrecht Dürer's *Das Rosenkranzfest* (Wilkins, *The Rose-Garden Game*, Pl. VII); cf. the Rosary of the Virgin woodcut by Wolf Traut (c.1510) (Max Geisberg, *The German Single-Leap Woodcut: 1500–1550*, ed. Walter L. Strauss [New York: Hacker, 1974], IV, No. G.1415).

[124] See Frances Yates, "Queen Elizabeth as Astraea," *Journal of the Warburg and Courtauld Institutes*, 10 (1947), 20–82, Pl. 18c, and John N. King, *Tudor Royal Iconography* (Princeton: Princeton Univ. Press, 1989), pp. 223–66.

[125] Hawkins, *Partheneia Sacra*, p. 23.

[126] See Arthur Watson, *The Early Iconography of the Tree of Jesse* (London: Oxford Univ. Press, 1934); Christopher Woodforde, "A Group of Fourteenth-Century Windows, Showing the Tree of Jesse," *Journal of the British Society of Master Glass Painters*, 6 (1937), 184–90; H. T. Kirby, "The Jesse Tree Motif in English Stained Glass," *Journal of the British Society of Master Glass Painters*, 13 (1960–61), 313–20, 434–41.

[127] Sally-Beth MacLean, *Chester Art*, Early Drama, Art, and Music, Reference Ser., 3 (Kalamazoo: Medieval Institute Publications, 1982), pp. 24–25, fig. 6; in this case, the Tree of Jesse culminates at the top in the Coronation of the Virgin.

[128] See Eleanor Simmons Greenhill, "The Child in the Tree: A Study of the Cosmological Tree in Christian Tradition," *Traditio*, 10 (1954), 323–71.

[129] Gregory the Great, *Moralia* IX.80, as cited by Susan Snyder, "The Left Hand of God: Despair in Medieval and Renaissance Tradition," *Studies in the Renaissance*, 12 (1965), 58. See also Gilbert of Hoyland on the fountain in the *Song of Songs*: "it is not meant to cleanse but to irrigate; its whole purpose is not to scour filth but to increase fruitfulness" (*Sermons on the Song of Songs*, III, 446).

[130] Jan van Ruysbroek, *The Spiritual Espousals*, trans. Eric Colledge (London: Faber and Faber, 1952), p. 121.

[131] *The Complete Works of Saint Teresa of Jesus*, trans. E. Allison Peers (London: Sheed and Ward, 1946), I, 65–113.

108   J. T. Rhodes and Clifford Davidson

[132] Pearsall and Salter, *Landscapes and Seasons*, fig. 21.

[133] Walter S. Gibson, *Hieronymus Bosch* (New York: Praeger, 1973), fig. 63; Longnon and Cazelles, *Très Riches Heures*, Pl. 20; Backhouse, *Bedford Hours*, fig. 3.

[134] Bernard of Clairvaux, *Ad B. Mariam Sermo Panegyricus* (*Patrologia Latina*, CLXXXIV, 1011), as quoted in translation by Hirn, *The Sacred Shrine*, p. 448.

[135] Hawkins, *Partheneia Sacra*, p. 220.

[136] Evelyn Underhill, "*The Fountain of Life*: An Iconographical Study," *Burlington Magazine*, 17 (1910), 99–109, esp. p. 100.

[137] See Philip, *The Ghent Altarpiece*, figs. 19–20.

[138] Clifford Davidson, "Repentance and the Fountain: The Transformation of Symbols in English Emblem Books," in *The Art of the Emblem: Essays in Honor of Karl Josef Höltgen*, ed. Michael Bath, John Manning, and Alan R. Young (New York: AMS Press, 1993), pp. 6–37.

[139] Cesare Ripa, *Iconologia* (Rome, 1603), pp. 387–89. There is no fountain in the accompanying illustration; see Davidson, "Repentance and the Fountain," p. 7.

[140] Francis Bond, *Fonts and Font Covers* (London: Oxford Univ. Press, 1908), pp. 280, 287, 289, 294.

[141] A possible (fifteenth-century) survivor in England is at Milton Abbas; see Arthur Oswald, "Milton Abbey, Dorset—II," *Country Life*, 23 June 1966, p. 1654, fig. 9.

[142] James H. Marrow, *Passion Iconography in Northern European Art of the Late Middle Ages and Early Renaissance*, Ars Neelandica, 1 (Kortrijk: Van Ghemmert, 1979), pp. 84–86, Pl. V; cf. fig. 59.

[143] Jean Daniélou, *The Bible and the Liturgy* (1956; rpt. Notre Dame, Ind.: Univ. of Notre Dame Press, 1966), p. 193.

[144] William Maskell, *The Ancient Liturgy of the Church of England*, 3rd ed. (Oxford: Clarendon Press, 1882), pp. 166–67.

[145] "Heaven," l. 20; see George Herbert, *The Works*, ed. F. E. Hutchinson (Oxford: Clarendon Press, 1941), p. 188.

[146] *The Late Medieval Religious Plays of Bodleian MSS Digby 133 and E Museo 160*, ed. Donald C. Baker, John L. Murphy, and Louis B. Hall, EETS, 283 (Oxford: Oxford Univ. Press, 1982), pp. 24–95.

[147] See Clifford Davidson, "The Fate of the Damned," in *The Iconography of Hell*, ed. Clifford Davidson and Thomas H. Seiler, Early Drama, Art, and Music, Monograph Ser., 17 (Kalamazoo: Medieval Institute Publications, 1992), pp. 41–66.

[148] E. W. Ganderton and Jean Lafond, *Ludlow Stained and Painted Glass* (Ludlow: Friends of the Church of St. Lawrence, 1961), pp. 38–43, Pls. 21–22, 24.

[149] *The Fountayne or well of lyfe/ out of whiche doth springe most swete consolations/ right necessary for troubled consciences*, trans. "out of latyn into Englysshe" (London, 1532) (STC 11211); Davidson, "Repentance and the Fountain," fig. 5.

[150] See Hodnett, *English Woodcuts*, Nos. 677, 2043.

[151] Nikolaus Pevsner, *Devon*, 2nd ed., Buildings of England (Harmondsworth: Penguin, 1989), p. 737.

[152] Marrow, *Passion Iconography*, fig. 59; see also ibid., pp. 84–85, for the source of this iconography in *Isaias* 63.

[153] See especially F. C. Gardiner, *The Pilgrimage of Desire: A Study of Theme and Genre in Medieval Literature* (Leiden: Brill, 1971), *passim*.

[154] Alcuin, Epistle 104, *Patrologia Latina*, C, 318–19; as quoted in translation by Gardiner, *Pilgrimage of Desire*, p. 77.

[155] This terminology for heaven is from Southwell, *Poems*, p. 56.

Heaven's Fragrance

Clifford Davidson

In contrast to the stench of hell with its fecal odor, its decaying flesh, and its chemical brew of brimstone and other unpleasant smells,[1] heaven was always believed to be characterized by delightful and sweet fragrances.[2] Hence it was axiomatic that the angels would avoid "vices and sinnes as it were stinking thinges: and they loue vertues, as it were sweete smelles. And they seperate trueth from falshood, making distinction betweene cleane and vncleane, stinking and sweete smellyng."[3] In the *Ecclesiastical History* of the Venerable Bede, the account of the vision by the Monk of Melrose Abbey describes a paradise which is not yet heaven but which is separated by a wall from the odors of hell; this joyful place is a "plain, full of . . . a fragrance of growing flowers that the marvellous sweetness of the scent quickly dispelled the foul stench of the gloomy furnace [hell] which had hung around me." But heaven itself, which the person was not allowed to enter, sent forth such a "wonderful fragrance" that the pleasantness of the field of flowers seemed to be "very ordinary."[4]

Significantly, therefore, that which comes from heaven was asserted to share in the pleasantness of the odor of bliss, and also those who were in harmony with God were marked by the absence of unpleasant odors even in death. The followers of Jesus, the Second Person of the Trinity, were described in *2 Corinthians* 2.15 as people "in the good odour of Christ" (and thus opposed to those who share the "odour of death unto death" [ibid., 2.16]). In *Ephesians* 5.2 Christ is said to be the one who "hath delivered himself for us, an oblation and a sacrifice to God for an odour of sweetness." In one of his poems Paulinus of Nola had been able to associate sweet fragrance, probably of incense, with a living churchman, Aemilius, who was close to God's presence.[5] In this poem the procession to the altar and prayers are described as invoking a "fragrance . . . seeping down from the sky and gliding

down to my nostrils." "I recognize him," Paulinus writes of
Aemilius, "as one attended by God's fragrance, and as one whose
face gleams with heavenly beauty."[6] And Hildegard of Bingen, in
her *O dulcissime amator* (*Symphony of Virgins*), exclaims over the
"beautiful form" of Christ, who is identified with the "sweetest
fragrance [suavissime odor]/ of longed-for delights"—delights for
which the virgins yearn from their state of earthly banishment and
for which they sigh.[7] As indicated above, the angels too are associated with sweet fragrance and odors which have healing properties: "Truely they are sayde to haue Phyals with sweet smelling
things: for by dooing of them our wounds are brought to grace of
health."[8]

The fragrance of flowers is implied in the depictions of heaven
as a garden.[9] Flowers would hence be used to represent a condition
of heaven, as in the Pentecost ceremony in certain churches in
which wafers and flowers were dropped on the congregation from
the roof during the singing of the hymn *Veni Creator Spiritus*.[10]
Perfume is implied in other instances, as in the case of the water
that, along with white, red, and yellow wafers, was dropped at
Pentecost from the roof of the church at Calais.[11]

Incense, not favored in the early centuries of the Church except
for use in funerals,[12] was the substance that apparently in the late
Middle Ages was believed to be most typical of the fragrances of
heaven. Once the prejudice of the early Church against the use of
incense in pagan rites had been overcome, the command of God to
Moses in *Exodus* 31.11 to provide "the incense of spices" for the
temple and other biblical references served to rehabilitate its use,
which was to neutralize unpleasant odors and to ward off the devil.
Etheria, in her invaluable fourth-century account of her pilgrimage
to the Holy Land, reported that each week at the vigil of Sunday
"censers are brought . . . so that the whole basilica is filled with
odours" from the incense used prior to the reading of the gospel.[13]
A mosaic at San Marco in Venice depicts hanging censors,[14] and
this seems to be the practice that was affirmed in the third
"Apostolic Canon."[15] The *Leofric Missal* indicated that in the
Anglo-Saxon Church incense was burned during the festivals of
saints, "for they it is who are the lilies that gave out such a smell
of sweetness, and which they shed abroad over all parts of the
church at the beginning, just as incense wafts its fragrance now
throughout the material building."[16]

J. Wickham Legg notes that in the early fifth century St. Cyril was met on one occasion by men carrying lamps and women with censers.[17] By the sixth century portable censers with chains for censing were apparently in common use, as examples from the visual arts indicate.[18] The Seventh General Council of 787 would affirm the legality of offering incense before images of Christ, the saints, and the cross as well as at the gospel reading.[19] A pontifical of Prudentius, Bishop of Troyes, had provided a formula for blessing incense which asserted: "May the Lord bless this incense for the removal of every harmful stench, and kindle it for the perfume of its sweetness."[20]

St. Thomas Aquinas gave two reasons for the use of incense, the first of which was "to show reverence" for the Eucharist "by its agreeable scent [per bonum odorem] dispelling any bad smell about the place."[21] The second reason was

> to show the effect of grace, wherewith Christ was filled: *See the smell of my son is as the smell of a field at harvest.* From Christ it spreads to the faithful through his ministers; who *through us spreads the fragrance of the knowledge of him everywhere.* So when the altar, which signifies Christ, has been censed, then afterwards all are censed in turn.[22]

As a symbol of grace, coming from God to man, incense thus remained associated with heaven. But, as fragrant smoke that rises upward, its symbolic meaning also retained the meaning established in Psalm 140.2: "Let my prayer be directed as incense in thy sight; the lifting up of my hands, as evening sacrifice."

In the *Apocalypse* the opening of the "golden vials full of odours" revealed a fragrance that constituted "the prayers of the saints"—an act followed by the singing of a "new canticle" praising the Lamb (5.8–9). In its liturgical usage incense in the earthly Church was held to prefigure the presence of its fragrance in heaven, where its use was affirmed by the angel with the golden censer in *Apocalypse* 8.3–4:

> And another angel came, and stood before the altar, having a golden censer; and there was given to him much incense, that he should offer of the prayers of all saints upon the golden altar, which is before the throne of God. And the smoke of the incense of the prayers of the saints ascended up before God from the hand of the angel.

The angel with the censer is shown in a panel in the East Window of York Minster (fig. 15) which was painted by John Thornton of Coventry in 1405–08, and here the censer is depicted being cast down, as in *Apocalypse* 8.5.[23] The well-preserved angel holds the chain with his right hand, and with his left hand he empties the censer. The four chains and the censer are drawn with great clarity, though there is replacement glass immediately below. In the fourteenth-century illuminated Apocalypse in the Cloisters at New York, the angel holds the censer by the ring at the end of the chain and pours the flames down onto the earth,[24] while in Berlin, Staatliche Museen Kupferstichkabinett MS. 78.E.3, fol. 456^r, the angel is first shown censing and then casting the thurible with its chain to the ground.[25] Another Apocalypse manuscript provides a narrative beginning with a hand reaching down from a cloud to place heavenly incense in an incense boat with a spoon.[26] The incense boat is held by an angel who is censing with his right hand; he holds the chains near the ring at the end and swings the censer toward the altar, located to his right. On the right side of the altar the angel grasps the bottom of the smoking thurible, and with the right holds up the cover; then at the far right he empties out the contents of the smoking censer onto the ground.

Atchley calls attention to William Lyndewode's commentary on a constitution of Thomas Arundel: "For in censing, God is honoured just as he is honoured in the grandeur and beauty of a material church. For the grandeur of a material church signifies the image of the spiritual church which is the Kingdom of heaven. . . ."[27] In the liturgical practice described in Honorius of Autun's *Gemma Animae*, the bishop censed the altar while the choir sang the *Kyrie* "in representation of the angel in the Apocalypse."[28] But the *Gloria* was seen as the true "angel's song,"[29] and at Wells and Rouen it was accompanied by censing.[30]

It is quite interesting that in the late Middle Ages and thereafter censing, using a thurible, was frequently done in a particular pattern that affirmed its meaning in connection both to the sacrifice on the cross and the Mass and to the heavenly reward expected by the saints in heaven. The thurifer would swing the censer three times in the sign of the cross, then three times in a circle, symbolizing a (heavenly) crown.[31] The cross and the crown were, of course, among the most prominent symbols held by angels in representations in the visual arts to designate the effectiveness of the soteriological work instituted by Christ on earth and completed in heaven. In the early *Rabbula Gospels*, Christ at his Ascension is flanked by two angels holding out crowns, the sign of his victory over mortality and over the lapsarian condition.[32] In the fourteenth-century *Holkham Bible Picture Book*, the Ascension is again depicted with Christ as a full figure rising in the clouds, and in this case he is accompanied by two angel musicians and two censing angels.[33]

On a roof boss in the nave of York Minster, angels, having come from heaven to honor the Child, were censing him at the breast of his mother, the Virgin Mary.[34] The twelfth-century Hunterian Psalter at the University of Glasgow illustrates the Burial and Assumption of the Virgin with, at first, the shrouded body being lifted up by angels and other angels censing her; thereafter, the shrouded figure is taken upward toward heaven as four angels continue to cense her.[35] Incense is thus being brought from heaven by the angels who accompany her back to their abode, where they elsewhere are frequently shown censing the deity—e.g., on a supporter on a misericord at Ely Cathedral where the Second Person is blessing and on each side of him is an angel with a censer.[36] Other representations, for example, include illustrations of the Trinity on a thirteenth-century roof boss in the Lady Chapel in Chester Cathedral[37] and on various English alabaster carvings.[38] Typically the censing angels are swinging their censers high above the head of God the Father. The angels at the Father's left and right are holding the chain with the left hand and swinging the censer with the other as if in a snapping motion. This way of censing is associated with Northern Christianity; according to a later description noted by Atchley which is verified by examples in the visual arts, the chains were held in the one hand (the left is specified) while the other hand was used to toss the censer into the air—a movement that in medieval English practice was identified by the term 'castys.'[39] An example of this technique may be seen in a historiated initial in a *Life of St. Dunstan* (British Library, MS. Arundel 16, fol. 2^r) of c.1090,[40] but a more graphic illustration of it is depicted in a historiated initial in Bodleian Library MS. Auct. D.2.15, fol. 42^r, a Winchester Gospel Book of the twelfth century. The latter illumination shows Zacharias censing an altar; his right hand clasps the chains in the middle, and his left hand has just given a "cast" to the censer.[41] (In Southern Europe the custom was different; there the censer was often held in the right hand, grasping the chains close to its cover and swinging gently.[42]) But frequently the thurifer was shown holding the censer by the ring at the end of its chains and swinging it gently before him.[43] The censer with three chains and a fourth chain for its cover represents the standard in late medieval illustrations from Northern Europe. Such censers are being "cast" by the angels before the Lamb in the Ghent Altarpiece by Jan van Eyck, and here the four chains can be seen very clearly.

In England the angel sculptures at Westminster and in the angel choir at Lincoln Cathedral have been especially acclaimed.[44] Among the angels in the spandrels in the angel choir at Lincoln (erected 1256–80) is an especially fine figure with a censer (fig. 16); while the right hand of the angel and most of the chain are missing, the left hand with the end of the chain (the ring holding the chains together is intact) and the censer itself are undamaged.[45] Clearly the intent here was to show one of the functions of angels, who also sing, play instruments, render judgment (as in the Expulsion of Adam and Eve from the garden), and assist souls.[46] The design of the censing angel at Lincoln was probably influenced by a similarly placed angel swinging a censer in the north transept of Westminster Abbey.[47] Here, however, it is the left hand holding the chain that is broken away, while the chain (stylized and ropelike) and right hand remain intact. Originally sculptures like this would have been brightly colored with paint and gilt—another reminder of the sensory brightness of heaven itself. We may assume that the censers at both Lincoln and Westminster were gilt colored.

The presence not only of spices but also of incense at the discovery of the empty tomb by the three Marys—a moment of revelation when divine power has most forcefully asserted itself in this world—was affirmed in an early prayer for the blessing of incense: "O God, to whose sepulchre (as the Gospel tells) there came in the early morning women with spices, like holy souls carrying the virtues of holy works; and in whose sight there stood an angel, having a golden censer, (as has been revealed by a heavenly vision), to whom incense was given to add to the prayers of all the saints before the throne of the Lord. . . ."[48] However, in the earliest extant *Visitatio Sepulchri*, which appears in the *Regularis Concordia*, censers are provided not for the angel but for the holy women, who are impersonated by three brothers wearing copes and carrying thuribles with incense ("turibula cum incensu manibus gestantes") as they set forth to walk toward the tomb where a fourth brother is seated in representation of the angel.[49] This very scene, with the foremost of the Marys carrying a thurible before her, is shown in an illustration in the *Benedictional of St. Ethelwold* (British Library MS. Add. 49,598), a manuscript which is also associated with Winchester and dated 971–84; the other Marys carry spice jars, and all of them approach the angel, who is seated at the sepulcher (fig. 17).[50] The same scene is repeated in British Library MS. Egerton 809, fol. 27[v],[51] and is similarly treated in numerous other early English and German manuscripts. In a great many instances at least one of the Marys appears with a thurible.[52]

One of the most remarkable depictions is a paten of 1160–70 from Innsbruck that is now in the Kunsthistorisches Museum in Vienna;[53] the central scene shows an angel seated on an open coffer tomb (grave clothes are visible inside it) which is located within a larger tomb structure, of which the doors are open. The scroll held by the angel has the text "QVE · QVERITIS IN SEPVL.," which of course are the words spoken by the angel in the *Visitatio Sepulchri* ceremonies and plays. The foremost Mary gently tips her thurible toward the angel, and the others, as in the *Benedictional of St. Ethelwold*, hold spice jars.[54]

Examples which depict one of the Holy Women, usually but not always the foremost, approaching the tomb with a thurible may be found until the thirteenth century. The Shaftesbury Psalter (British Library MS. Landsdowne 383) of c.1130–40 shows the three Marys holding spice boxes, but the one in the rear also has a censer (fol. 13[r]).[55] In the Antiphonary of St. Peter (Codex Vinobenensis) of c.1160 from Salzburg, the Marys similarly all carry spice jars, but more typically it is the one in front who also swings a censer, in this case by grasping the middle of the chain; the angel, seated on the top of the tomb cover, has a red face.[56] In the carving on the plaque on the left arm of the Bury St. Edmunds Cross of c.1180–85 the foremost Mary again possesses a censer, in this instance on a long chain and with the appearance of swinging; the seated angel holds a scroll with the words "QVERITIS. NAZ IHM: RENVM. CRVCIFIX."[57] A wall painting at Brunswick Cathedral from the middle of the thirteenth century illustrates the scene at the tomb, at which the angel is seated, and here too the foremost Mary swings a censer.[58] But British Library MS. Arundel 157, fol. 11[r], and Royal I.D.x, fol. 6[r], English psalters dated in the early thirteenth century, are typical of later illustrations which show the Marys carrying only spice jars, though the interesting detail of the angel with a red face is retained from earlier depictions.[59]

In many continental versions of the *Visitatio sepulchri*—e.g., a typical example from Rheinau that exists in twelfth- and twelfth-thirteenth-century versions—the clergy, taking the women's roles, carried thuribles with incense in procession to the sepulchrum Domini, and, upon being invited to see "the place where the Lord was laid," proceeded to cense the location where the cross had been placed in the course of the *Depositio* ceremony on Good Friday.[60] This action was quite common, and in some instances the rubrics specify that the women should actually enter the tomb and then cense the place designated as a representation of the historical location where Jesus was buried.[61]

Incense was purchased in the sixteenth century for Holy Week at St. Andrew Hubbard, London; did its use in that season include either the *Depositio* or *Elevatio* ceremony on Good Friday or Easter morning?[62] But incense was definitely used for the censing of the sepulcher in the *Depositio* at Exeter and Salisbury and at the *Elevatio* at Norwich.[63] At Durham Cathedral before the Reformation, the Host and image of Christ placed in the Easter sepulcher on Good Friday were censed and reverenced with prayers, while on Easter morning the tomb was again censed by two monks on their knees with silver censers, whereupon "with great devotion and reverence, they tooke a marvelous beautifull Image of our Saviour, representing the resurrection, with a crosse in his hand, in the breast wherof was enclosed in bright cristall the holy Sacrament of the Altar. . . ."[64] After the elevation of this image of the Resurrection, it was brought to the high altar while the *Christus resurgens* was sung. During the singing of this item the censing continued as a way of showing reverence for the Savior who rose, ascended to heaven, and now sits at the right hand of the Father.[65] The iconographic significance of the censing is made more clear when we compare a fourteenth-century nave roof boss at York Minster (not extant, but replaced by a copy made from a drawing after a disastrous fire in the nineteenth century) which showed the Resurrected Christ holding the vexillum with his left hand and blessing with his right; he was seated on the tomb with a censing angel at his right side (the side especially identified with salvation and the entry into bliss) and stepping on sleeping soldiers (below, associated with the rejection of bliss).[66] A second angel at his left side held up the cover of the tomb to represent in yet another way Christ's victory over mortality (fig. 18).[67]

At terce on Pentecost in St. Paul's Cathedral, London, a censer with incense was used to represent the descent of the Holy Spirit. According to James Pilkington, "in the midst alley was their long censer reaching from the roof to the ground, as though the Holy Ghost came in their censing down in likeness of a dove."[68] William Lambarde's description of the ceremony informs us that the censer was lowered from an opening in the center of the roof vault, which was located 102 feet above the floor; the nave was 150 feet in length, so it was possible to seem to swing the censer almost to the West end and then nearly to the choir stairs, and thus to spread "a most pleasant Perfume of suche swete Thinges as burned thearin."[69] Presumably the censer was lowered during the singing of the hymn *Veni Creator Spiritus*; monastic churches commonly were filled with the smoke of incense at this point in the ritual.[70]

But the use of incense for the Pentecost ceremony and related rituals could additionally involve the presence of a live "actor" impersonating an angel. On the day following Pentecost (Monday of Whitsun Week) the mayor of London and the other members of the corporation, along with the rectors of the city churches, joined a procession at St. Peter's Church, Cornhill, between nine and ten o'clock in the morning. After arriving at St. Paul's Cathedral and being escorted to a location before the great rood screen, they heard the *Veni Creator Spiritus* by the vicars choral and organ. During the hymn one who was costumed as an angel descended with a thurible and censed them.[71]

So too an angel with incense had descended to cense Henry V at St. Paul's after his victory at Agincourt,[72] and a similar censing was reported when Henry VII came to the cathedral on 3 November 1487 after his victory at Stoke.[73] The latter occasion involved the use of "the greate senser of poulis by an Angell commyng oute of the roof during the whyche tyme the quire sange A solempne Anthyme. . . ."[74] The censer that was used for such ceremonies after 1429 was the great silver thurible weighing thirteen pounds and four ounces given by Mayor Henry Barton and intended for use at Pentecost.[75] At the Reformation this censer was inventoried along with the other church goods at St. Paul's prior to confiscation by the crown: "Item, a greate large Sensoure all silver with many windowes and battillments usedd to sense withall in the Penticoste weeke in the bodie of the Chirche of Pawles at the Procession tyme."[76] Such a ceremonial use of incense was not unique to St. Paul's, for at Norwich the sacrists' rolls suggest that at Pentecost a man impersonating an angel was made to descend to cense the rood.[77] The opening at the center of the roof of the nave at Norwich from which the descent was made is still visible.[78]

While on the one hand incense was said to symbolize God's glory generally,[79] it also was understood to be a characteristic of the odors that would be found in heaven. For a church building to be filled with incense and other fragrances, therefore, was to make it a true foreshadowing of heaven just as its luminescent windows prefigured the glorious light that would unendingly illuminate the place of bliss. Such was the earthly setting for the prayers of the saints and of all other Christian men and women, whose invocations would rise up to the feet of the deity like incense. The church structure was in fact a point where the temporal and eternal intersect,[80] and the intersection is made explicit in part through the sacrifice of incense. So too the Easter sepulcher in the Resurrection ceremony or play is both the most important stage property associated with medieval drama and also a triumphant sign of the abrogation of earthly limitations—and hence it is a location which, like the altar where the elements of the Mass are consecrated, is worthy of being censed. It is a censing that will be continued eternally in the heavenly city where the saints and all those who have overcome death and received salvation will praise God and enjoy him forever.

NOTES

[1] The Monk of Melrose—quoted by the Venerable Bede (*Ecclesiastical History* V.12)—described hell as having "an indescribable stench [fetor incomparabilis] which rose up" with the "vaporous flames" and "filled all these abodes of darkness" (*Bede's Ecclesiastical History of the English People*, ed. and trans. Bertram Colgrave and R. A. B. Mynors [Oxford: Clarendon Press, 1969], p. 491). See also Thomas H. Seiler, "Filth and Stench as Aspects of the Iconography of Hell," in *The Iconography of Hell*, ed. Clifford Davidson and Thomas H. Seiler, Early Drama, Art, and Music,

Monograph Ser., 17 (Kalamazoo: Medieval Institute Publications, 1992), pp. 132–40.

[2] For a listing of "frequently recurring motifs" which were used to describe heaven, see Aron Gurevich, *Medieval Popular Culture: Problems of Belief and Perception*, trans. János M. Bak and Paul A. Hollingsworth (Cambridge: Cambridge Univ. Press, 1988), p. 123.

[3] *Batman vppon Bartholome, his Booke De Proprietatibus Rerum* (London, 1582), fol. 5^r.

[4] Bede, *Ecclesiastical History*, pp. 492–95 (V.xii).

[5] Paulinus of Nola, *The Poems*, trans. P. G. Walsh (New York: Newman Press, 1975), pp. 251–52 (No. 25). The poem is quoted by E. G. Cuthbert F. Atchley, *A History of the Use of Incense in Divine Worship* (London: Longmans, Green, 1909), p. 179. Atchley's encyclopedic work is properly regarded as the standard reference book on the subject of the use of incense in Christian tradition; it has been invaluable in the preparation of the present article.

[6] Paulinus, *Poems*, pp. 251–52.

[7] Hildegard of Bingen, *Symphonia*, ed. and trans. Barbara Newman (Ithaca: Cornell Univ. Press, 1988), pp. 220–23.

[8] *Batman vppon Bartholome*, fol. 4^v.

[9] See above, pp. 71, 85, 88–90, 93, 95.

[10] Atchley, *History*, pp. 300–01. Flowers and wafers were also dropped from above in the Ascension Day ceremony at Moosburg, Germany; see above, p. 5. For the location of *Veni Creator* in the liturgy, see *Breuiarium seu horarium domesticum . . . ad vsum insignis ecclesie Sarum* (Paris: C. Chevallon, 1531), Pt. 1, fol. cliii, and *Breviarium ad usum insignis ecclesie Eboracensis*, ed. Stephen Lawley, Surtees Soc., 71, 75 (Durham, 1880–83), I, 503.

[11] Thomas Coryat, *Coryat's Crudities* (Glasgow: James MacLehose and Sons, 1905), I, 153. Coryat, a hostile Protestant observer, noted: "about the Middle of their Masse there was an extreme crackling noise from a certain hollow place in the vault of the middle of the Church. . . . After the noyse there was powred downe a great deal of water, immediately after the water ensued a great multitude of Wafer-cakes, both white, redde and yellow: which ceremony was done to put them in minde of the cloven tongues, that appeared that day of Pentecost to the Apostles in Hierusalem."

[12] The use of incense would of course be denounced during the Protestant Reformation. *The Book of Common Prayer* of 1549 and 1552 omits all mention of it.

[13] L. Duchesne, *Christian Worship: Its Origin and Evolution*, 5th ed. trans. M. L. McClure (1920; rpt. London: S.P.C.K., 1931), p. 544.

[14] Otto Demus, *The Mosaic Decoration of San Marco, Venice*, ed. Herbert L. Kessler (Chicago: Univ. of Chicago Press, 1988), Pl. 33; see also the wall painting of the Mass of St. Clement in the Church of San Clemente at Rome (Otto Demus, *Romanesque Mural Painting* [London: Thames and Hudson, 1970], Pl. 48).

[15] Atchley, *History*, p. 201.

[16] *The Leofric Missal, as Used in the Cathedral of Exeter during the Episcopate of Its First Bishop, A.D. 1050–1072*, ed. F. E. Warren, Henry Bradshaw Society (Oxford: Clarendon Press, 1883), p. 130, as quoted in translation by Daniel Rock, *The Church of Our Fathers* (London: John Hodges, 1903), I, 164. Hanging censers suspended by three chains above the altar appear in the *Utrecht Psalter* (fols. 131–32, 147–48, 151–53, 156, 161, 167).

[17] J. Wickham Legg, *Church Ornaments and Their Civil Antecedents* (Cambridge: Cambridge Univ. Press, 1917), p. 20. For the comment that candles and incense were used "much in the same manner as incense and lamps were in use in the Emperor's court," see ibid., p. 20, citing the *Ordo Romanus Primus*.

[18] See the sixth-century carving on the tomb of Marino Morosini at San Marco, Venice (Atchley, *History*, p. 319), and the mosaic at the Church of S. Vitale, Ravenna, which shows one of the clerks accompanying the Emperor and Bishop Maxianus holding a censer, which is without a lid and supported by three short chains (Giuseppi Bovini, *I Monumenti Antichi di Ravenna* [Milan: "Silvana" Editoriale d'Arte, 1955], Pl. 43; Atchley, *History*, p. 180, Pl. following p. 180).

[19] Atchley, *History*, p. 153.

[20] Edmond Martène, *De Antiquis Ecclesiae Ritibus*, 2nd ed. (Antwerp, 1736–38), I, 525; as quoted in translation by Atchley, *History*, p. 203.

[21] Thomas Aquinas, *Summa Theologiae*, Blackfriars ed. (New York: McGraw-Hill, n.d.), LIX, 169 (3a.83.5.2)

[22] Ibid.

[23] Representation of the Seventh Seal, Row 6 from the top, panel 7.

[24] *The Cloisters Apocalypse* (New York: Metropolitan Museum of Art, 1971), I, fol. 12^r.

[25] *The Apocalypse in the Middle Ages*, ed. Richard K. Emmerson and Bernard McGinn (Ithaca: Cornell Univ. Press, 1992), fig. 16.

[26] Montague Rhodes James, *The Apocalypse in Latin MS. 10 in the Collection of Dyson Perrins* (Oxford: Oxford Univ. Press, 1927), Pl. 10b. In yet another Apocalypse manuscript the hand which places incense in the boat is that of an angel; see M. R. James, *The Apocalypse in Latin and French (Bodleian MS. Douce 180)* (Oxford: Roxburghe Club, 1922), p. 22.

[27] William Lyndewode, *Provinciale, seu Constitutiones Angliae* (Oxford, 1679), p. 298n (V.5, *s.v. thurificationis*), as quoted in translation by Atchley, *History*, p. 130.

[28] *Gemma Animae* I.vii, as cited in Atchley, *History*, p. 218; for the Latin text, see *Patrologia Latina*, CLXXII, 546.

[29] William Maskell, *The Ancient Liturgy of the Church of England*, 3rd ed. (Oxford: Clarendon Press, 1882), pp. 36–37.

[30] Atchley, *History*, p. 190.

[31] Ibid., p. 256 and Pl. facing p. 257; this illustration represents early twentieth-century practice.

[32] See Kurt Weitzmann, *Late Antique and Early Christian Book Illumination* (New York: George Braziller, 1977), Pl. 36.

[33] W. O. Hassall, *The Holkham Bible Picture Book* (London: Dropmore Press, 1954), fol. 38^r.

[34] John Browne, *The History of the Metropolitan Church of St. Peter, York* (London, 1847), I, 141; II, Pl. CI. The nave bosses were lost in a fire in the nineteenth century, and the replacements, made on the basis of Browne's drawings, are satisfactory copies except in the case of this boss in which a baby bottle was substituted for the breast of the Virgin—an instance of misplaced Victorian prudery.

[35] T. S. R. Boase, *The York Psalter* (London: Faber and Faber, 1962), Pl. 6.

[36] G. L. Remnant, *A Catalogue of Misericords in Great Britain* (Oxford: Clarendon Press, 1969), p. 19.

[37] Sally-Beth MacLean, *Chester Art*, Early Drama, Art, and Music, Reference Ser., 3 (Kalamazoo: Medieval Institute Publications, 1982), pp. 49, fig. 27; angels also are swinging censers on a boss representing the Virgin and Child (ibid., pp. 29–30, fig. 10)

[38] Francis Cheetham, *English Medieval Alabasters* (Oxford: Christie's-Phaidon, 1984), Nos. 228, 230, 232, 234–35, fig. 1, Pl. VI; in some cases the censers are missing.

[39] George James Aungier, *History and Antiquities of Syon Monastery* (London: J. B. Nichols, 1840), p. 337.

[40] C. M. Kaufmann, *Romanesque Manuscripts, 1066–1190*, Survey of Manuscripts Illuminated in the British Isles, 3 (London: Harvey Miller, 1971), No. 7, fig. 12.

[41] Otto Pächt and J. J. G. Alexander, *Illuminated Manuscripts in the Bodleian Library, Oxford*, III: *British, Irish, and Icelandic Schools* (Oxford: Clarendon Press, 1973), No. 131, Pl. XIII (131b).

[42] Atchley, *History*, pp. 321–22.

[43] See, for example, the censing angels on each side and above Christ in a twelfth-century copy of St. Augustine's *City of God* in the Bodleian Library (MS. Laud. misc. 469, fol. 7ᵛ); see Pächt and Alexander, *Illuminated Manuscripts in the Bodleian Library*, III, No. 112, Pl. XII (112a).

[44] M. D. Anderson, *The Medieval Carver* (Cambridge: Cambridge Univ. Press, 1935), p. 82.

[45] Arthur Gardner, *English Medieval Sculpture* (1951; rpt. New York: Hacker, 1973), p. 123, fig. 228.

[46] Ibid., pp. 116–25.

[47] Ibid., fig. 208.

[48] *Leofric Missal*, p. 131, as quoted in translation by Atchley, *History*, p. 398; see also the *Benedictional of Archbishop Robert*, Henry Bradshaw Soc., 24 (London, 1903), p. 94.

[49] *Regularis Concordia: The Monastic Agreement of the Monks and Nuns of the English Nation*, ed. and trans. Dom Thomas Symons (New York: Oxford Univ. Press, 1953), pp. 49–50; see also Pamela Sheingorn, *The Easter Sepulchre in Eng-*

land, Early Drama, Art, and Music, Reference Ser., 5 (Kalamazoo: Medieval Institute Publications, 1987), pp. 20–21.

[50] George Frederic Warner and Henry Austin Wilson, *The Benedictional of St. Aethelwold* (Oxford: Roxburghe Club, 1910), fol. 51[v]; see also Elzbieta Temple, *Anglo-Saxon Manuscripts 900–1066,* Survey of Manuscripts Illuminated in the British Isles, 2 (London: Harvey Miller, 1976), No. 23. The *Benedictional and Pontifical of Archbishop Robert* (Rouen, Bibliothèque Municipale Y.7), closely related to the *Benedictional of St. Ethelwold,* contains a copy of the scene at the tomb (fol. 21[v]; see Temple, *Anglo-Saxon Manuscripts,* No. 24).

[51] Atchley, *History,* Pl. facing p. 398.

[52] Among these manuscripts are the *Mainz Sacramentary* of c.1000, illuminated in St. Albans (Mainz Cathedral Treasury, MS. Kautsch 4, fol. 84[v]), the late Ottonian MS. Egerton 809, fol. 27[v], and the Sacramentary of Henry II; for the latter, see Georg Swarzenski, *Die Regensburger Buchmalerei des X. und XI. Jahrhunderts* (Leipzig: Karl W. Hiersemann, 1901), pp. 63ff, Pl. II, fig. 21. While the tomb in this illumination is reminiscent of the design to be seen in a famous early fifth-century ivory in the British Museum (O. M. Dalton, *Catalogue of Ivory Carvings of the Christian Era* [London: British Museum, 1909], No. 7, Pl. IVc), the ivory does not, of course, include censing by one of the Holy Women—and indeed does not even show the angel. For another important example, see Otto Pächt, C. R. Dodwell, and Francis Wormald, *The St. Albans Psalter* (London: Warburg Institute, 1960), Pl. 31a.

[53] Gertrud Schiller, *Ikonographie der christlichen Kunst,* III (Gütersloh: Gerd Mohn, 1971), fig. 275.

[54] See also the illumination accompanying the *Quem queritis* with musical notation in Piacenza, Bibl. Capit., MS. 65, fol. 235, as reproduced by Bamber Gascoigne, *World Theatre: An Illustrated History* (London: Edbury Press, 1968), fig. 53; in this example the foremost of the three Marys swings a censer as they approach the tomb in which the angel is situated.

[55] Kaufmann, *Romanesque Manuscripts,* No. 48.

[56] Georg Swarzenski, *Die Salzburger Malerei* (Leipzig: Karl W. Hiersemann, 1908), Pl. C, fig. 339.

[57] Thomas F. Hoving, "The Bury St. Edmunds Cross," *Metropolitan Museum of Art Bulletin,* 22 (1964), 321, fig. 3.

[58] Otto Demus, *Romanesque Mural Painting* (London: Thames and Hudson, 1970), Pl. 273.

[59] On this motif see Andreas Petzold, "'His face like lightning': Colour as Signifier in Representations of the Holy Women at the Tomb," *Arte Medievale*, 2nd ser. 6, No. 2 (1992), 149–55.

[60] Walther Lipphardt, *Lateinische Osterfeiern und Osterspiele* (Berlin: Walter de Gruyter, 1975–90), II, Nos. 315, 315a.

[61] See, for example, ibid., II, Nos. 532 (Berlin), 536d (Breslau). An interesting group of items with such rubrics is to be found in Scandinavia; see Audrey Ekdahl Davidson, *Holy Week and Easter Ceremonies and Dramas in Medieval Sweden*, Early Drama, Art, and Music, Monograph Ser., 13 (Kalamazoo: Medieval Institute Publications, 1990), pp. 39, 51, 72, 99–100; Nils Holger Petersen, "Another *Visitatio Sepulchri* from Scandinavia," *Early Drama, Art, and Music Review*, 14 (1991), 18. Curiously, there is no evidence for a tomb large enough to be entered in Scandinavia, but evidently these rubrics were all copied from sources where such an Easter sepulcher was used. Rites using a "walk-in" Easter sepulcher of this kind have been studied by Dunbar Ogden ("The *Visitatio Sepulchri*: Public Enactment and Hidden Rite," *Early Drama, Art, and Music Review*, 16 [1994], 95–102).

[62] John C. Crosthwaite, "Ancient Churchwardens' Accounts of a City Parish," *British Magazine*, 32 (1847), 277; 35 (1849), 178, 180, 185. A brief description of the English rites of the *Depositio* and *Elevatio* with special reference to the use of incense is to be found in Atchley, *History*, pp. 296–300, but for a more recent study which is more comprehensive see Sheingorn, *The Easter Sepulchre in England*, passim.

[63] Sheingorn, *The Easter Sepulchre in England*, pp. 115, 249, 348.

[64] *A Description or Briefe Declaration of All the Ancient Monuments, Rites, and Customes belonginge or beinge within the Monastical Church of Durham before the Suppression*, Surtees Soc., 15 (London, 1842), p. 10. At Freising, the image taken from the Easter sepulcher was both censed and sprinkled with holy water (see Lipphardt, *Lateinische Osterfeiern*, No. 568).

[65] *A Description or Breife Declaration*, p. 11.

[66] Browne, *The History of the Metropolitan Church of St. Peter*, I, 142–43; II, Pl. CXI. That the soldiers are demonic is evident from another example from York Minster, painted glass by Robert the Glazier (1339) that places a devil's mask on the shield of one of them; see Clifford Davidson and David E. O'Connor, *York Art*, Early Drama, Art, and Music, Reference Ser., 1 (Kalamazoo: Medieval Institute Publications, 1978), pp. 91–92, and Thomas French and David O'Connor, *York Minster: A Catalogue of Medieval Stained Glass*, Fascicule 1: *The West Windows of the Nave*, Corpus Vitrearum Medii Aevi, 3 (Oxford: Oxford Univ. Press, 1987), Pl. 11a.

[67] Around the outside of the roof boss the holy women appear on their way to the empty tomb, but these figures are less clear than would be desired on Browne's drawing.

[68] James Pilkington, *The Works*, ed. James Scholefield, Parker Soc., 35 (Cambridge: Cambridge Univ. Press, 1842), p. 540.

[69] William Lambarde, *Dictionarium Angliae Topographicum et Historicum* (London, 1730), pp. 459–60; see also above, p. 7. For the suppression of the censing ceremony at St. Paul's in 1548, see *Chronicle of the Grey Friars of London*, ed. John Gough Nichols, Camden Soc. (1877; rpt. New York: AMS Press, 1968), II, 2.

[70] See Atchley, *History*, p. 303.

[71] *Munimenta Gildhallae Londoniensis*, ed. Henry Thomas Riley, Rerum Britannicarum Medii Aevi Scriptores, 12, Pt. 1 (1859; rpt. Nendeln: Kraus, 1968), I, 29; W. Sparrow Simpson, *S. Paul's Cathedral and Old City Life* (London: Eliot Stock, 1894), pp. 61–64. Censings were repeated on the following Tuesday and Wednesday. When the rite was suppressed by the Protestant reformers, it was replaced by sermons on each of the three days following Pentecost; see ibid., p. 83. In the case of this ceremony, it may be assumed that the incense would have been intended as a purifying agent. Like the sound of a bell, incense was believed to drive away demons; a blessing quoted by Atchley (*History*, p. 395) concluded as follows: "bless this censer, we beseech thee, by thy majesty, and grant that the incense which is offered in it unto thee, may put demons to flight, repel spectres, and cause unclean thoughts to depart; and that our prayers to thee may ever be acceptable in its odour." For the Latin text, see *Patrologia Latina*, CXXXVIII, 1031.

[72] *Memorials of Henry V*, Rerum Britannicarum Medii Aevi Scriptores, 11 (1851), p. 129; cited by Atchley, *History*, p. 304n.

[73] British Library, MS. Cotton Julius B.xii, fol. 34^r–34^v.

[74] Ibid.

[75] Simpson, *S. Paul's Cathedral and Old City Life*, p. 62.

[76] John Orlebar Payne, *St. Paul's Cathedral in the Time of Edw. VI* (London: Burns and Oates, n.d.), p. 5; there were five smaller silver censers (ibid.).

[77] M. E. C. Walcott, *Traditions and Customs of Cathedrals*, 2nd ed. (London: Longmans, Green, 1872), p. 196.

[78] See *Norfolk Archaeology*, 8 (1874–79), 330.

[79] Atchley, *History*, p. 206.

[80] See the chapter "The Symbolism of the Center" in Mircea Eliade, *Cosmos and History: The Myth of the Eternal Return*, trans. Willard R. Trask (1954; rpt. New York: Harper and Row, 1959), pp. 12–17.

The Light of Heaven:
Flame as Special Effect

Philip Butterworth

In my article "Hellfire: Flame as Special Effect," I considered the use of mirrors and lenses as means of increasing the power of light employed in the staging of hell.[1] The lighting devices chosen to enhance theatrical productions tended to operate on a relatively domestic scale; water-filled globes, or condensers, and the principles upon which they operated "could have used stronger light sources in the form of torches, lanterns, or sunlight. . . ."[2] In the present essay, I propose to discuss the nature of some of these larger devices as they relate to the power of heaven.

Although the representation of heaven in medieval theater may have taken on different forms according to the mode and purpose of presentation, perhaps its most potent manifestation may be seen in the use of light. The brilliance of heavenly light is not only conveyed by angels but also by physical representation of the sun and stars and elemental forces such as thunderbolts and lightning.

It might be useful to make a distinction between lighting employed for its scenic contribution to heaven and that which represents the intervention of God at some miraculous moment or demonstration of power. Light employed for its scenic value may also operate as a means of illuminating the theatrical or religious event—e.g., the Florence *Annunciation* and *Ascension*. This use of light may additionally function in the act of worship. My interest, however, must remain focused on light as a special effect and thus must be less concerned with light for illumination or worship.

Flame as Light. Although the biblical narrative suggests a number of requirements and opportunities for the provision of light in various plays, such needs are seldom articulated in "explicit" stage directions. However, some references to the production of light do exist in these kinds of stage directions, although the information

128

tends to indicate the effect to be produced and not the means of achieving it. For instance, in the *Passio Domini* in the Cornish *Ordinalia* at the point of Christ's death, an ambiguous stage direction instructs: "Here the sun is darkened."[3] This requirement indicates neither the nature of the sun nor the style or method by which the effect is realized. It is not even clear that a change of light is involved, for the sun may have been a physical representation other than a light source. Some stage directions do provide more information with regard to the effect sought even if the technique is not indicated. In *The Life of St. Meriasek* at the point where Silvester baptizes Constantine, the following stage direction occurs: "*Cum in aquam descendisset baptismatis mirabilis enituit splendor lucis Sic inde mundus exiuit et christum se vidisse asseruit*"[4] ("*When he went down into the water of baptism there shone forth a marvellous splendour of light. So thence he came forth clean, and declared that he had seen Christ*"). What is meant by "*mirabilis enituit splendor lucis*" or "*a marvellous splendour of light*"? Other stage directions make similar requirements. At Bourges, for instance, when the angels are required to set free from prison St. Peter and St. Paul there should appear "a great light."[5] A similar direction at Bourges requires that "St. Michael must present the soul to Jesus Christ. Having done this, they come down from Paradise accompanied by all the angelic hierarchy, and as soon as Jesus Christ reaches the monument there must be a great light at which the apostles are amazed."[6]

What is meant by the description "a great light"? At Mons in 1501 during the *Resurrection* the following direction is recorded: "And the two angels remove the stone, and Jesus rises and puts his right leg out of the tomb first, and there should issue with him a great brightness and smoke of incense and light."[7]

Again what is meant by "a great brightness"? A late reference in an early seventeenth-century play, *The Second Maiden's Tragedy*, contains a similar but more involved direction: "*On a sodayne in a kinde of Noyse like a Wynde, the dores clattering, the Toombstone flies open, and a great light appeares in the midst of the Toombe.*"[8]

Once more, the phrase "a great light" is encountered. Clearly, requirements such as "a great light," "marvellous splendour of light," and "great brightness" as expressed by these stage directions must be relative terms and refer to intensity and/or illumination.

Light levels for outdoor performance might be said to exist on a scale operating between darkness and bright sunlight. An equivalent indoor scale might work from darkness to artificial levels of light produced by candle, lantern, torch, or cresset. The kind of light required by these stage directions appears to be greater than that which might be expected from conventional flame sources. Although evidence exists to demonstrate the use of candles, torches, and cressets in volume for play production during the visits of Elizabeth to Cambridge and Oxford in 1564 and 1566,[9] the purpose of such lighting was to illuminate the play as an event, whereas the light required by the foregoing stage directions seems to be concerned with particular theatrical statements. Ways of achieving specific lighting effects which may be described as "great light" or "great brightness" must be concerned with the ability to reflect, direct, intensify, or focus light.

In my article on hellfire, I referred to a lighting device described by Hugh Platte as "a large Cilinder like vnto a halfe Lanterne, all of Latten kept bright and glistring, the same being inwardly garnished with diuerse steele Looking-glasses, so artificially placed as that one of them might reflect vnto an other."[10] Two earlier descriptions of this sort of device which make use of the same principle are recorded by John Baptista Porta in his *Magia Naturalis* of 1565. The first account of "How to make an Amphitheatrical Glass" requires that a "circle" is made "on a Table" of "what largeness you desire. . . ." An octagonal shape is created within the circle and on 7 of the 8 lines of the octagon:

> let Looking-glasses be raised perpendicularly; for the face that shall be against the Looking-glass, placed in the middle, will fly back to the beholder of it, and so rebounding to another, and from that to another, and by many reflections you shall see almost infinite faces, and the more the Glasses are, the more will be the faces: If you set a Candle against it, you shall see innumerable Candles.[11]

Porta, in his second version of an "Amphitheatrical Glass," declares that he "will now make one that is far more wonderful and beautiful. For in that the beholder shall not see his own face, but a most wonderful, and pleasant, and orderly form of pillars, and the basis of them, and variety of Architecture." Although Porta is not too prescriptive concerning the size of this device, he does indicate his preference:

I hold the best to be where the diameter is two foot and a half: divide
the circumference into equal parts; as for example into fourteen; the
points of the divisions shall be the places, where the pillars must be
erected. Let the place where the spectator must look, contain two parts;
and take one pillar away, so there will be thirteen pillars: . . . then raise
Looking-glasses upon the lines of space between, not exactly, but
inclined: . . . Hence by the reciprocal reflection of the Glasses, you shall
see so many pillars, basis, and varieties, keeping the right order of
Architecture, that nothing can be more pleasant, or more wonderful to
behold. . . . If you set a Candle in the middle, it will seem so to multiply
by the Images rebounding, that you shall not see so many Stars in the
skies, that you can never wonder enough at the Order, Symmetry, and
the Prospect.[12]

Clearly, these arrangements of angled mirrors are capable of
creating greater intensity from a single candle. Not only is the
brightness of flame a relative phenomenon, but also the effect produced by its position in terms of the viewer in a given space is also
relative. Sunlight directed onto a small hand-held mirror may be
projected further towards the viewer in such a way as to create a
brilliance which will dazzle the eye, for the small mirror is capable
of creating intense light that may seem disproportionate to its size.
The devices described by Porta and Platte which reflect and re-
reflect light produced by a candle may not communicate the same
effect as a single hand-held mirror lit by the sun, but this sort of
lantern as a source of light is capable of being perceived as
brilliant.

An important distinction needs to be made between the intensity of the light source and its effect. The "great light" required by
the Bourges directions and the "*marvellous splendour of light*"
determined by the stage direction in *St. Meriasek* may well indicate
use of reflectors in the form of mirrors or metal basins since the
light is presumably intended to fall upon St. Peter, St. Paul, and
Constantine respectively. At Bourges, the apostles would have been
able to "perform" their "amazed" response to the source of the
reflected light and at the same time be caught in its effect.

The light required by the stage directions in the respective
tombs of the Mons *Resurrection* and the later *Second Maiden's
Tragedy* indicates an intensity which may be produced by one or
more devices consisting of angled mirrors. The confinement of
such light within the tomb would create strong focus for the
viewer. The effect may be further enhanced if the tombs were lined

with reflective material. However, the Mons requirement of "a great brightness and smoke of incense and light" may indicate use of fireworks. Ingredients such as camphor ($C_{10}H_{16}O$) and/or orpiment (arsenic trisulphide As_2S_3) are recorded in early accounts of firework mixtures, and both are capable of burning to produce intense white light.[13]

Although mirrors may have been the principal means of achieving intensity, other qualities of light such as radiant or shimmering kinds are likely to have been accomplished using some form of condenser. Perhaps the most complete form of this device was that developed by Furtenbach in the seventeenth century and known as the "Glory Box."[14] The apparatus was used at dramatic moments such as the appearance or intervention of God. Furtenbach suggests: "With very little expense a powerful light can be placed behind a round double glass filled with water and put at the very center of the 'glory'."[15] The "glory" is a specially designed box some three feet square and two feet deep which is lined with reflecting materials, some of which represent the sun's rays. The glass vessel is a crystalline globe five inches in diameter. Furtenbach writes:

> This globe must be carefully made by the glassmaker from two pieces of crystalline glass set two fingers' distance apart. It is filled with water to which a little bit of red coloring is added. It must be made with a neck or hole the width of a finger to put the water in by, and also with a peg (*Zapfen*). By the peg and the neck it is made fast to the box. Or if no better can be had, a glass flask with a curved side can be used.[16]

The effect produced by the water-filled glass is said to produce light "like an eye that sends out sunbeams towards the spectators to cause great wonder by its shimmering . . . a shimmering and shining splendor that the man who looks at it too closely would lose his sight."[17] The basic detail concerning the "crystalline globe" as described by Furtenbach is almost identical to the instruction made by Platte some seventy years earlier.[18] There are, however, some significant differences between the requirements of Platte and Furtenbach. In the former, a candle flame produces the light source which is placed in the center of the "double glass." The light required here seems to demand a more powerful source than candle flame. It is possible that a number of closely arranged candles might have produced sufficient power, although lanterns or torches are more likely to have been used. A light source powerful enough to qualify for Furtenbach's description of "a powerful light" seems to have been too big to fit into the middle of his five-inch "crystalline glass." Given that the effect of the "glory" is a two-dimensional one, it does not matter that the light source is placed behind the glass rather than in the middle. In the event that the "crystalline glass" could not be obtained, Furtenback suggests that "a glass flask with a curved side can be used."[19]

Larger condensers appear to be suggested by the description given by John Rovenzon:

> For such of the workes as require light to worke by in the night, being distant from the places where the Furnaces are, there is a new-deuised luminary of glasse, or glasses filled with water, & a candle placed to giue light through it, which giueth a very great light a great distance off, with small charge; and may be conuerted to excellent vse, being placed in high places, in crosse-wayes, and streets of Citties and Townes, to the sauing of lanthorne, and candle-light, and the auoyding of inconueniences happening by darknesse.[20]

Although the light source in this instance is still the candle, it does seem that the "glasses filled with water" need to be larger than those suggested by Platte or Furtenbach if the intended application is to take place in the street. Rovenzon's reference to "the saving of lanthorne, and candle-light" seems to refer to the notion that one candle or lantern could be placed in the center of a number of symmetrically arranged globes "placed in high places." This is not a fanciful suggestion if later lacemaker's practice is considered (see fig. 19). The lacemaker's lamp was sometimes arranged in a group of four lamps known as a "candle block" or "flash."[21] The wooden stems or bases of the individual lamps were secured to the top of a wooden stool. A candle was placed in the middle of the four globes, and the work of four lacemakers sitting around the "candle block" could be illuminated. In some instances it was possible to tilt the wooden stem holding the globe in order to direct the light onto the lacemaker's work. The illumination produced by Rovenzon's device would have been greater if the light source had been a lantern or torch.

Such an elaboration took place at the nuptials of Cosimo I and Eleanora of Toledo in Florence in 1539. Vasari records the following:

Appresso ordino con molto ingegno una lanterna di legname a uso
d'arco dietro a tutti i casamenti, con un sole alto un braccio, fatto con
una palla di cristallo piena d'acqua stillata, dietro la quale erano due
torchi accesi, che la facevano in modo risplendre, che ella rendeva
luminoso il cielo della scena e la prospettiva in guisa, che pareva
veramente il sole vivo e naturale; e questo sole, dico, avendo intorno un
ornamento di razzi d'oro che coprivano la cortina, era di mano in mano
per via d'un arganetto tirato con si fatt'ordine, che a principio della
comedia pareva che si levasse il sole, e che salito infino al mezzo
dell'arco scendesse in guisa, che al fine della comedia entrasse sotto e
tramontasse.[22]

(Nearby he set up with great ingenuity a lantern of timber by means of
an arc [or arch] behind all the apartments, with a sun above, a braccio
across, made with a crystal sphere filled with distilled water, behind
which two torches were lighted which somehow made it glow so that it
rendered the sky luminous of the scene and the stage picture in such a
way that it appeared to be truly the living, natural sun; and this sun, I
say, having round about a decoration of golden rays which covered the
curtain was drawn little by little by means of a winch so that at the
beginning of the performance it appeared that the sun rose, and that
having finally climbed to the middle of the arc, it descended in the same
way, that at the end of the play it entered underneath the set.)

The description seems to suggest that the lantern consists of a
wooden frame or cradle that holds two torches and the crystal
sphere in a fixed relationship. The cradle is set just behind the arc
or arch and no doubt placed on a track of a circumference which
is effectively the same as the arc or arch. A winch maneuvers the
cradle from the base of the arc or arch, over the top and back down
the other side. One winch, if suitably geared, could have moved the
whole cradle. If the winch was not geared, then two winches may
have been necessary—one to pull the cradle up to the top of the
arch, and another to control the descent. The size of the crystal
sphere is recorded as a "braccio" across, which is a measurement
of just under two feet. This globe represents a considerable
difference of scale to the ones considered earlier. The flickering
flames of the two torches seem to have provided greater strength
as the light source, and the effect is likely to have been one of
shimmering radiance rather than still, focused light as produced by
the relatively constant candle flame of the lacemaker's lamp. The
effect of this sphere representing the sun is enhanced by "avendo
intorno un ornamento di razzi d'oro che coprivano la cortina. . . ."

Presumably the curtain was in some way attached to the frame of the globe in order that the globe and the "razzi di'oro" could move together. Perhaps the "razzi d'oro" were capable of reflecting light in the same way as those in Furtenbach's "Glory box." The idea of decorative rays or beams to support and complete the light effect produced by a condenser is suggested by the list of properties of the Lincoln Cordwainers and their *pageant of Bethelem*:

> Item a great hed gildyd sett w^t vii Beamez & vii glassez for ye sam And on long beame for ye mouthe of ye said hed
> Item iij^{re} greatt stars for ye sam w^t iij^{re} glassez And a cord for ye sam steris[23]

It seems likely that the purpose of the "vii glassez" is concerned with contributing to the effect of the "vii Beamez" which are clearly an integral part of the "great hed." The function of the "vii glassez" seems to be concerned with the production of light which is intended to coincide with the "vii Beamez" or produce sufficient illumination to be reflected by the "vii Beamez." The assumption to be made is that the "great hed" is effectively a two-dimensional representation consisting of "vii Beamez" painted or fashioned with reflective material to take the light produced by the "vii glassez." The "vii glassez" were presumably filled with liquid and lit from behind. Each of the "vii glassez" would have been positioned opposite appropriate holes at the narrow ends of the "vii Beamez" towards the center of the "great hed." Candles or lanterns or torches may have produced the light source. Like the "great hed" the "iij^{re} greatt stars" seem to have been large two-dimensional painted or gilded stars, possibly with radiating points or beams and openings at their centers to accommodate the "iij^{re} glassez." If the *pageant of Bethelem* centered around a nativity scene, then the light of the "iij^{re} greatt stars" would perhaps have needed to appear or disappear or even change position. The "cord for ye sam steris" seems to have been the means of aligning the "iij^{re} glassez" with holes at the center of the "iij^{re} greatt stars." Whether the cord pulled the "iij^{re} greatt stars" or the "iij^{re} glassez" into their respective positions is not clear. Presumably the "iij^{re} greatt stars" might have been more manipulable the "iij^{re} glassez" filled with liquid.

The principal means of achieving focus and direction of light with condensers depends upon the height and distance of the flame relative to the "bellie" of the globe. Vertical down light is suggested by Serlio in a receipt in which a piece of burning camphor, placed in a vessel containing water, is lit by a candle from below.[24] The burning camphor as the light source was presumably intensified through the base of the glass vessel. Another example of the use of vertical down light is given in *The Dialogues of Leoni di Somi* as part of a description concerning a pastoral feast:

> still greater splendour was provided by several great globes filled with water, cleverly set in the middle of each archway. Above these, lamps had been placed in such number that each arch seemed lit up by a blazing sun. Indeed, it seemed brighter than high noon.[25]

Again, the use of "great globes" implies vessels of a dimension greater than those used in lacemaker's lamps and may have been as large as the one used by Aristotle San Gallo.

It is clear that the descriptions of light required by the foregoing stage directions appear similar to the effects described by eye-witnesses and other writers on the production of light. The need for "a marvellous splendor of light," "a great light," and "a great brightness" as expressed by stage directions is not essentially different from the descriptions of light produced by various vessels. Furtenbach suggests that the "powerful light" of his "Glory box" would create "great wonder by its shimmering . . . a shimmering and shining splendour that the man who looks at it too closely would lose his sight."[26] Rovezon in his account of the condenser describes the light produced as "a very great light." The point concerning these descriptions is that they are apparently as vague as the requirements of the stage directions. This should not be too surprising given the absence of an appropriate technical vocabulary and/or the technical means of measuring light. Even though a late-twentieth-century person may have experienced greater extremities of artificial levels of light than a medieval counterpart, he or she would still need relative terms to describe lighting in a production as "great lighting" or "ingenious lighting effects." Although the terms are similar, the meaning is clearly different. Lighting in the theater of today tends to make use of specially designed lanterns with a power consumption typically between 500 and 3000 watts. The viewer who observes such power is aware of the effect caused by this capacity when he or she describes "great lighting."

A figure of 50 lux was recently recorded in a test to measure the intensity of light which falls onto a prescribed surface from a

20 cm. (8 inch) condenser.[27] It is suggested that this level of light may be compared to that which has been adopted by museums "as a maximum for the illumination of sensitive exhibits, such as watercolours and tapestries."[28] No doubt this level of light when dispersed in a gallery or museum may seem relatively gloomy. However, such an amount of light when concentrated on a small area—e.g., a lacemaker's pillow—and in a relatively darker context may appear more intense.

Flame as Message. A number of stage directions indicate flame effects as signals from heaven. Typical of such instructions is that in the Chester Draper's play of *Cain and Abel*: "Then a flame of fyer shall descende upon thee sacrafice of Abell."[29] In *The Life of St. Meriasek* four outlaws are the target of a stage direction which states: "*Hic ignis venit super illos*" ("Here fire comes upon them").[30] In the Chester Drapers' stage direction the flame effect clearly comes from above. If Abel's sacrifice is located on a pageant wagon, then the signal from God presumably appears from the top of the wagon. An appropriate technique to produce such directed flame is to blow combustible powder through a tube and over a flame. Powdered rosin or collophone would have been a suitable powder, as would powdered sulphur mixed with aqua ardens.[31] The purpose of the fire which "comes upon" the outlaws in *The Life of St. Meriasek* is that of a warning from God and may refer to a similarly directed flame of fire.

Instructions found in stage directions for flames of fire are sometimes the literal or practical descriptions of the effect required. The same effect however, may be referred to by the more theatrically conscious instruction for "lightning." The list of effects required by the *Mystery of the Acts of the Apostles* at Bourges in 1536 contains the following description:

> The Jews try to get hold of the Virgin Mary's body to take it from the apostles, and immediately their hands wither and they are blinded by the fire the angels throw (*gectent*) at them. Belzeray [*a Jewish prince*] puts his hands on the litter on which the Virgin Mary is being carried, and his hands remain attached to the said litter and much fire in the form of lightning (*fouldre*) is thrown at them, and the Jews must fall to the ground, blinded.[32]

The effect indicated here revolves around the notion that the angels "throw" something which is or causes simulated lightning. If the angels throw actual fire, then some material of substance must be fired first. For example, pieces of tow or oakum dipped in tallow and fired may fulfil the task, providing that the angels are able to protect their hands with suitable covering. Various recipes exist for concoctions capable of being pasted upon the hands in order to provide appropriate protection.[33] Alternatively, the lightning effect may be created by the powder and tube method or simply by casting a powder such as rosin over fire.

In *The Conversion of St. Paul* shortly after the arrival of Saul on horseback, the following stage direction indicates: "*Here comyth a feruent, wyth gret tempest, and Saule faulyth down of hys horse; þat done, Godhed spekyth in heuyn.*"[34] How is the direction for a "*feruent, wyth gret tempest*" to be interpreted? Although part of the action referred to by this stage direction is that contained in *Acts* 9.3–4, the instruction "*wyth gret tempest*" is confined to the play and is thus an interpretation of the biblical narrative. The source of the stage direction has consequently influenced writers as to the meaning of the word "feruent." F. J. Furnivall in marginal notes to his edition of the play writes that Saul is "struck by lightning, and falls off his horse."[35] Mary del Villar regards "feruent" as a "blaze of light,"[36] and Darryll Grantley interprets the word as "a flash."[37] Baker, Murphy, and Hall suggest that "there would have been simple devices of gunpowder for the divine light. . . ."[38] Thus the "lux de caelo" of *Acts* 9.3 is variously interpreted. So what is the effect and how is it created? The stage direction is not clear whether the "*feruent*" produces the sound of the "*gret tempest*" or if the latter is produced by other means and timed to accompany the former.[39] The implication is that the "*feruent*" and the "*gret tempest*" are different, yet contributory aspects to the overall dramatic effect. Although the term 'tempest' is primarily associated with wind, accompanying sound is also typical.[40] The word 'feruent' may well refer to the provision of bright light as determined by *Acts* 9.3, but derivatives of the word also refer to heat.[41] If the "*feruent, wyth great tempest*" is the cause of Saul falling from his horse, then the moment must be one of intended dramatic impact. The speed with which the effect is completed seems to be important. As indicated earlier, a relatively instant flash of light is capable of being produced by powdered rosin coming into contact with fire or flame. The powder and tube technique may satisfy the requirement of implied movement and speed by the words "*Here comyth a feruent*," but other techniques applicable to stage directions which suggest "thunderbolts" may also be relevant. Although the thunderbolt may be regarded as a streaking flash of light, it does not appear to be the same effect as that of lightning created by powdered rosin sprinkled onto fire or "rosen punned fine."[42] Nor does the thunderbolt produce the sound of thunder; this needs to be created by other means.

Typically thunderbolts are used as a signal or statement from God or Heaven to an earthly recipient. The eye-witness account offered by Abramo, the Russian bishop of Souzdal, of the Florence *Annunciation* in 1439 indicates one method of creating the effect: "In the meantime a fire comes from God and with a noise of uninterrupted thunder passes down the three ropes towards the middle of the scaffold, where the Prophets were, rising up again in flames and rebounding down once more, so that the whole church was filled with sparks."[43] It is unlikely that the rope itself is the conductor of the fire even though it is seen to pass "down the three ropes."[44] Rather like the "*feruent*," "*wyth gret tempest*," it is also unlikely that the fire which "passes down the three ropes" is the source of the thunder. The "noise of uninterrupted thunder" that accompanies the fire seems to be produced in some other way. The technique employed appears to be the one referred to as "fireworks on lines"; "rockets on lines"; "squibs on lines"; "runners on lines"; or "swevels."[45] A number of seventeenth-century plays record the use of fireworks on lines in both "implicit" and "explicit" stage directions.[46] John Bate describes how to make "swevels":

> SWevels are nothing else but Rockets, having instead of a rod (to ballast them) a little cane bound fast unto them, where through the rope passeth. Note that you must be carefull to have your line strong, even & smooth, and it must be rubd over with sope that it may not burn. If you would have your Rockets to returne againe, then binde two Rockets together, with the breech of one towards the mouth of the other, and let the stouple that primeth the one, enter the breech of the other. . . .[47]

The technique offered by Bate's description is not unique among early firework writers,[48] although the main aspects are well illustrated here. The "Rockets" referred to in this account are not ones balanced by sticks, as we understand the term today; they simply exist as a tube containing a basic gunpowder mixture that is ignited by connecting stouple. Such rockets were also capable of being made of different lengths in order to match the distance covered.[49] Bate's method, outlined here, offers a partial means of achieving the effects described by the bishop of Souzdal for the Florence *Annunciation*. If the term "feruent" as used in the stage direction in *The Conversion of St. Paul* may be regarded as synonymous with the term "thunderbolt," then Bate's description of the operation of "SWevels" also provides a partial method of realizing the instruction in the stage direction; the technique presupposes the use of a suitable wire or rope.

During the performance of the Modane play of *Antichrist* in 1580 it is recorded that "they shall project fireworks in the air and along the cord (*par la corde*) whenever necessary for the said mystery. . . ."[50] As part of a comprehensive series of effects for thunder and lightning Serlio suggests that "you must draw a piece of wyre ouer the Scene, which must hang downewards, whereon you must put a squib couered ouer with pure gold or shining lattin which you will: and while the Bullet is rouling, you must shoote of some piece of Ordinance, and with the same giuing fire to the squibs, it will worke the effect which is desired."[51] The "squib" of Serlio's account performs the same function as the "Rocket" in Bate's description. Indeed, the two terms were often interchangeable in early accounts, particularly where translation took place. Reference to the "Bullet is rouling" in Serlio's account indicates one of the known methods of producing thunder indoors. The technique of rolling cannon balls (or equivalent) down a wooden trough is known to have existed in the sixteenth century, and evidence concerning later practice is well established.[52] The coordinated shooting of "some piece of Ordinance" is yet another example of how more than one effect is often required to create an accumulative effect.

In appearance the thunderbolt is essentially a fizzing or flaming streak of fire delivered at rapid speed. The use of rockets or squibs to create thunderbolts is not the only means available, for a similar yet simplified technique is indicated by the following nineteenth-century account:

> When a thunderbolt is to strike an object, a wire is run from the flies to the object which is to be struck. A rider runs on the wire. The rider consists of a section of iron pipe. Around it is secured asbestos by means of wire. The asbestos is soaked with alcohol, and is lighted just

at the instant when it is to be projected upon the object. It is usually held by a string, which is cut. It rushes flaming through the air, and produces the effect of a ball of fire striking the object.[53]

The simplicity of this technique invites speculation as to its practicability in the sixteenth century. A piece of cane, previously soaked in vinegar (frequently thought to retard combustion) may have worked instead of a piece of iron pipe, and tow fastened to the cane and soaked in aqua vitae may have provided the combustible material of the thunderbolt. If the device is made of cane it would clearly be lighter in weight than the one consisting of iron pipe, but gravity would still enable this technique to work.

Heavenly responses to earthly actions are invariably powerful and unequivocal. The purpose of such intervention is to admonish, punish, or signify the miraculous. Other than words spoken by God or angels most communications from heaven to earthly recipients are conducted through special effects consisting of sound and/or light. God is not usually seen to administer the effect; it is communicated on his behalf. The effects may appear to exist independently or be delivered by angels. Characters in plays are usually left to determine the significance of such intervention, which is frequently one of surprise.

NOTES

[1] Philip Butterworth, "Hellfire: Flame as Special Effect," in *The Iconography of Hell*, ed. Clifford Davidson and Thomas H. Seiler, Early Drama, Art, and Music, Monograph Ser., 17 (Kalamazoo: Medieval Institute Publications, 1992), pp. 67–101.

[2] Ibid., p. 78.

[3] *The Ancient Cornish Drama*, ed. Edwin Norris (1859; rpt. New York: Benjamin Blom, 1968), I, 458–59.

[4] *The Life of Saint Meriasek*, ed. and trans. Whitley Stokes (London: Trübner, 1872), pp. 104–05.

[5] *The Staging of Religious Drama in Europe in the Later Middle Ages: Texts and Documents in English Translation*, ed. Peter Meredith and John E. Tailby, Early Drama, Art, and Music, Monograph Ser., 4 (Kalamazoo: Medieval Institute Publications, 1983), p. 101.

[6] Ibid., p. 102.

[7] Ibid., p. 114.

[8] *The Second Maiden's Tragedy*, ed. W. W. Greg, Malone Society Reprints (Oxford, 1910 [for 1909]), p. 61.

[9] John J. Nichols, *The Progresses and Public Processions of Queen Elizabeth* (London, 1823), I, 167; *Cambridge*, ed. Alan H. Nelson, Records of Early English Drama (Toronto: Univ. of Toronto Press, 1989), I, 234, and II, 1136; W. Y. Durand, *"Palæmon and Arcyte, Progne, Marcus Geminus*, and the Theatre in which they were acted, as described by John Bereblock (1566)," *PMLA*, 20 (1905), 504–05.

[10] Hugh Platte, *The Jewell House of Art and Nature* (London, 1594), p. 32.

[11] John Baptista Porta, *Natural Magick* (1658; facsimile rpt. [ed. Derek J. Price] New York: Basic Books, 1957), p. 359; this publication is the English translation of *Magia Naturalis* (Naples, 1558).

[12] Porta, *Natural Magick*, pp. 359–60.

[13] *OED*, *s.v.* 'camphor' (sb.1); John Babington, *Pyrotechnia Or, A Discovrse of Artificiall Fire-Works* (London, 1635), p. 11; Robert Jones, *A New Treatise on Artificial Fireworks* (London, 1765), pp. 6–8; A. H. Church, *The Chemistry of Paints and Painting* (London: Seeley, 1890), p. 90.

[14] *The Renaissance Stage: Documents of Serlio, Sabbattini and Furtenbach*, ed. Barnard Hewitt (1958; rpt. Coral Gables: Univ. of Miami Press, 1969), pp. 224–27; Gösta M. Bergman, *Lighting in the Theatre* (Stockholm: Almqvist & Wiksell International, 1977), p. 85.

[15] *The Renaissance Stage*, ed. Hewitt, p. 224.

[16] Ibid., p. 226.

[17] Ibid., pp. 224–25.

[18] Platte, *The Jewell House*, pp. 31–32.

[19] For discussion, see my "Hellfire," p. 75.

[20] John Rovenzon, *A Treatise of Metallica* (London, 1613), sigs. C2^v–C3^r; A. Sauzay, *Marvels of Glass-Making in All Ages* (London: Sampson Low, Son, and Marston, 1870), p. 214.

[21] Leroy Thwing, *Flickering Flames: A History of Domestic Lighting through the Ages* (1958; rpt. Rutland, Vermont: Charles E. Tuttle, 1970), opp. p. 105; David J. Eveleigh, *Candle Lighting* (Aylesbury: Shire, 1985), p. 3.

[22] *Le Vite de' più eccellenti pittori, scultori ed architettori scritte da Giorgio Vasari*, ed. Gaetano Milanesi (Florence: Sansoni, 1878–85), VI, 442; A. M. Nagler, *Theatre Festivals of the Medici 1539–1637* (New Haven: Yale Univ. Press, 1964), p. 10; Bergman, *Lighting in the Theatre*, p. 56.

[23] *Records of Plays and Players in Lincolnshire, 1300–1585*, ed. Stanley Kahrl, Malone Society Collections, 8 (Oxford, 1974), p. [96]; Butterworth, "Hellfire," p. 96n.

[24] Sebastiano Serlio, *The Book of Architecture*, introd. A. E. Santaniello (1611; facs. rpt. New York: Benjamin Blom, 1970), Book II, fol. 26^v.

[25] Allardyce Nicoll, *The Development of the Theatre*, 5th ed. (London: George G. Harrap, 1970), p. 277.

[26] *The Renaissance Stage*, ed. Hewitt, p. 224–25.

[27] H. J. Yallop, "The Lacemaker's Globe," *Report and Transactions of the Devonshire Association*, 123 (1991), 189–93.

[28] Ibid., p. 192; see also Yves le Grand, *Light, Colour and Vision* (London: Chapman and Hall, 1957), pp. 82–83.

[29] *The Chester Mystery Cycle*, ed. R. M. Lumiansky and David Mills, EETS, s.s. 3, 9 (London, 1974–86), I, 36.

[30] *The Life of Saint Meriasek*, ed. and trans. Stokes, pp. 120–21.

[31] Philip Butterworth, "Fire and Flame as Special Effects in the Medieval and Tudor Theatre," unpubl. Ph.D. diss. (Univ. of Leeds, 1993), pp. 267n, 268n.

[32] *The Staging of Religious Drama*, ed. Meredith and Tailby, p. 101; G. G. Coulton, *Life in the Middle Ages* (Cambridge: Cambridge Univ. Press, 1929), II, 138–40.

[33] *The Book of Secrets of Albertus Magnus*, ed. Michael R. Best and Frank H. Brightman (Oxford: Clarendon Press, 1973), pp. 89, 109–10; Porta, *Natural Magick*, p. 299; Platte, *The Jewell House*, p. 31; J. C. Cannell, *The Secrets of Houdini* (1931; rpt. New York: Hutchinson, 1973), p. 118.

[34] *The Late Medieval Religious Plays of Bodleian MSS Digby 133 and E Museo 160*, ed. Donald C. Baker, John L. Murphy, and Louis B. Hall, Jr., EETS,

144   Philip Butterworth

283 (London, 1982), p. 7.

[35] *The Digby Plays*, ed. F. J. Furnivall, EETS, e.s. 70 (1896; rpt. London, 1967), p. 34.

[36] Mary Del Villar, "The Staging of the Conversion of Saint Paul," *Theatre Notebook*, 25 (1970–71), 67.

[37] Darryll Grantley, "Producing Miracles," in *Aspects of Early English Drama*, ed. Paula Neuss (Cambridge: Boydell and Brewer, 1983), p. 87.

[38] *The Late Medieval Religious Plays*, ed. Baker *et al.*, p. xxx.

[39] See ibid., p. 18, for stage direction at l. 501.

[40] *OED*, *s.v.* 'tempest' (sb.1).

[41] Ibid., *s.v.* 'fervent' (a.).

[42] *The Buggbears* IV.i.27, in *Early Plays from the Italian*, ed. R. Warwick Bond (Oxford: Oxford Univ. Press, 1911), p. 123; *OED*, *s.v.* 'pound' (v.1).

[43] *The Staging of Religious Drama*, ed. Meredith and Tailby, p. 245; Bergman, *Lighting in the Theatre*, p. 36; William Donald Young, "Devices and Feintes of the Medieval Religious Theatre in England and France," unpubl. Ph.D. diss. (Stanford Univ., 1959), pp. 75–76.

[44] See Young, "Devices and Feintes," p. 76.

[45] John Bate, *The Mysteryes of Natvre and Art* (London, 1634), pp. 76–77; John Babington, *Pyrotechnia*, pp. 16–17; Robert Norton, *The Gvnner Shewing the Whole Practise of Artillerie* (London, 1628), p. 152.

[46] Nichols, *The Progresses and Public Processions of Queen Elizabeth*, III, 118; Jean Wilson, *Entertainments for Elizabeth I* (Woodbridge: Boydell, 1980), p. 114. In *Northward Ho* by Thomas Dekker and John Webster, the practice is alluded to as follows:

> Bell.   But what say you to such young Gentlemen as these are.
> Baud.   Foh, they as soone as they come to their lands get vp to *London*, and like squibs that run vpon lynes, they keepe a Spitting of fire, and cracking till they ha spent all, and when my squib is out, what sayes his punke, foh, he stinckes. (IV.iii.88–92)

See *The Dramatic Works of Thomas Dekker*, ed. Fredson Bowers (Cambridge:

Cambridge Univ. Press, 1953–61), II, 459. In John Marston's *The Fawn*, the following description occurs in response to a question about the nature of the birthday celebrations for Prince[ss] Dulcimel:

> Page.   There be squibs, sir; which squibs, running upon lines, like some of our gaudy gallants, sir, keep a smother, sir, with flishing and flashing, and, in the end, sir, they do, sir—
> Nym.   What, sir?
> Page.   Stink, sir. (I.ii)

See *The Works of John Marston*, ed. A. H. Bullen (London: 1887), II, 121. An explicit stage direction in Dekker's *If this be not a Good Play, the Devil is in it* (II.i.193) requires *"Fire-workes on lines"* (*The Dramatic Works*, ed. Bowers, III, 150).

[47] Bate, *The Mysteryes of Natvre and Art*, pp. 76–77.

[48] See n. 45, above.

[49] Babington, *Pyrotechnia*, p. 17.

[50] *The Staging of Religious Drama*, ed. Meredith and Tailby, p. 105.

[51] Serlio, *The Book of Architecture*, Book II, fol. 26ᵛ.

[52] Nicolo Sabbatini, *Pratica di fabricar scene e machine ne' teatri* (1638; facs. rpt. Rome: 1955), p. 126; *The Renaissance Stage*, ed. Hewitt, p. 172; Lily B. Campbell, *Scenes and Machines on the English Stage during the Renaissance* (Cambridge: 1923), p. 157; Richard Southern, "The stage groove and the thunder run," *Architectural Review*, 95 (1944), 135–36, and *Changeable Scenery* (London: Faber and Faber, 1952), p. 230; Frances Ann Shirley, *Shakespeare's Use of Off-Stage Sounds* (Lincoln: Univ. of Nebraska Press, 1963), p. 7.

[53] Albert A. Hopkins, *Magic: Stage Illusions, Special Effects and Trick Photography* (1898; rpt. New York: Dover, 1976), pp. 303–04; Nicoll, *The Development of the Theatre*, p. 61; N. D. Shergold, *A History of the Spanish Stage from Medieval Times until the End of the Seventeenth Century* (Oxford: Clarendon Press, 1967), p. 281.

"A Similitude of Paradise":
The city as Image of the City

Robert D. Russell

The history of Christian representations of cities is almost as long as the history of Christian art. It is true that there are no urban images in the catacombs, but from the time that Christian art emerged from its early obscurity there has been no hesitation about depicting cities. One thinks, for example, of the early fifth-century mosaic representations at S. Maria Maggiore in Rome which illustrate Bethlehem and Jerusalem on either side of the triumphal arch and the representation of Jericho in the Old Testament scenes along the nave walls. Since the purpose of these early pictures of cities was more symbolic than topographical, the standard image settled on was compact and self-contained but still possessed of all the necessary parts of a city, most particularly the walls with their towers and gates. All of these early depictions of cities followed virtually the same essential pattern, and hence the artist frequently included the name of the particular city which the image was intended to represent in order to designate the place where the action of the scene took place (fig. 20).

In addition to these early mosaic representations of cities in S. Maria Maggiore, there are frequent depictions of them in early Christian manuscripts as well. Whether miniature or mosaic, however, the essential form of the city does not vary much at all from one representation to the other. Surviving copies of an illustrated late antique manuscript, the *Corpus Agrimensorum Romanorum*, provide evidence that the standard Christian representation of a city was essentially a continuation of a late Roman convention.[1] The hexagonal shape given to these images of cities, with the towers marking the corners, is first encountered in the *Corpus Agrimensorum Romanorum*.

Soon, however, it became possible to represent in a particularly recognizable way at least one city of especial importance to

Christians: Jerusalem. This was a result of the building program carried out there in the early fourth century by the emperor Constantine. The most important—and the most easily recognized— Constantinian church was that of the Anastasis with its basilican martyrium, a courtyard containing the hill of Golgotha, and beyond that the rotunda of the Resurrection itself. It has recently been argued that the apse mosaic of the church of S. Pudenziana in Rome (402–17) depicts these very Constantinian buildings as part of its background (fig. 21).[2]

Apparently not until the Carolingian period, however, did the conventions of urban representation begin to be extended to representations of the heavenly Jerusalem. At least this is the period to which the earliest surviving representations can be dated. Charlemagne was himself enthusiastic about Augustine's *Civitas Dei*, and some scholars have argued that the Frankish king was attempting to create his own new Jerusalem at Aachen rather than merely a new Rome north of the Alps. It does seem that the original mosaic of the domical vault of Charlemagne's palatine chapel was based on the fourth chapter of the *Apocalypse* of St. John: Christ enthroned, surrounded by the twenty-four elders.[3]

It is also in the Carolingian period that illustrated copies of the *Apocalypse* began to appear. There are at least four surviving manuscripts with extensive cycles of illuminations traceable to the ninth century. These are the earliest examples of images of the heavenly as well as the earthly Jerusalem.[4] Not surprisingly we find the heavenly Jerusalem represented essentially as any number of earthly cities had been. The basic urban ideogram had not changed from the earlier period: a set of towered, crenellated walls containing some more or less distinguishable structures.

Despite their general conventionality, there are still some specific relationships between these early images of the heavenly Jerusalem and the description found in the *Apocalypse* of St. John which describes the City as having "a wall great and high, having twelve gates, and in the gates twelve angels, and names written thereon, which are the names of the twelve tribes of the children of Israel" (21.12). The subsequent verses of the chapter specify that the twelve gates are distributed three to a side in the city walls and that the walls themselves are oriented cardinally (21.13). The square form suggested by this description is thereafter explicitly stated when it is said that the city "lieth in a foursquare" with each wall stretching 12,000 furlongs (*stadia*) or about 1500 miles. Further, this squaring of the form is actually cubing it, and the city is described as being equal in length, width, and height (*Apocalypse* 21.16).

Without much difficulty we may imagine that this particular urban form would cause trouble for anyone who attempted a diligent and complete representation of it. Medieval artists who took St. John's description as their starting point invariably selected certain of its aspects rather than dealing with the impossibility of rendering visually what the words described. The square form and the twelve gates were straightforward enough and often would be rendered literally. More frequently, however, the artists would pick and choose and assemble a vision of the Heavenly City made up of what they took to be its most important visual elements. Not surprisingly, these important features tended to be the things that were important elements of the representations of earthly cities: walls and towers. The foursquare form was something that could be sacrificed if necessary, and the twelve towers were obviously regarded as a more important link to the recognition of the city than its shape, if we may judge from the representations in the tenth-century Cambrai manuscript and the ninth-century *Valenciennes Apocalypse* (fig. 22).

The image in the *Valenciennes Apocalypse* and another representation of the city in the *Bamberg Apocalypse* from c.1000 (fig. 23) actually are illustrating a slightly later moment in St. John's description of the City. According to *Apocalypse* 22.1–2, the center of the city was the throne of God and the Lamb, from which flowed the river of the water of life. On either side of this "river of the water of life, clear as crystal, proceeding from the throne of God and of the Lamb" was located "the tree of life." All of these elements are literally depicted in one of the relatively rare representations of the heavenly City not found in a manuscript. These are the frescoes found in the two vaults of the entrance bays of the early twelfth-century Benedictine church of S. Pietro al Monte at Civate, in the mountains of the Brianza, north of Milan (fig. 24).[5] Not only is this a remarkably complete depiction of the heavenly Jerusalem, but its location within the church itself is also important for what it reveals about how these images were understood by those who saw them.

Since the time of the Fathers, the interpretation of the Heavenly

Jerusalem of *Apocalypse* 21 has been a complex one. Following the well-known fourfold medieval hermeneutic consisting of a literal, an allegorical, an anagogical, and a tropological meaning, the City was understood on different levels in different ways. The literal understanding of Jerusalem was as the biblical Jewish capital city: the location of the temple and the place where many of the events recorded in the Gospels were acted out. The second or allegorical sense of the City comes into play here at Civate, and I will return to it in a moment. The anagogical understanding was of earthly Jerusalem, the "lower-case" city, as it were, standing for the "upper-case" City or heavenly Jerusalem. The temporal city in Palestine points us to the eternal City. As Abbot Suger of Saint-Denis was to say in the 1140's: "Mens hebes ad verum per materialia surgit" ("The dull mind rises to truth through that which is material").[6] Tropologically, Jerusalem was the human soul.

As indicated above, however, it was the second, or allegorical, level of understanding that achieved significance in the Benedictine church at Civate. In this sense the heavenly City was the Church: *Ecclesia.* This association, which may be traced back to Augustine, had become standard in all the medieval commentaries on the *Apocalypse.*[7] Haymo, a ninth-century bishop of Halberstadt, can be taken as representative when he says in his commentary on the *Apocalypse* that "haec civitas sancta Ecclesia est. . . ."[8] We thus see why this particular image is squeezed into the tiny vaults of the entrance bays of the church itself: as the worshippers came into the church they would be reminded vividly that they were entering Paradise. Architectural decoration has become eschatological fact.

Rather than multiplying examples of variations on the theme of the heavenly Jerusalem (something that would not be difficult to do), I would like to examine two or three less obvious visual uses of this close identification of the earthly city and the heavenly Jerusalem. The visual evidence adduced is generally late medieval, from the fourteenth and fifteenth centuries, but the ideas themselves that these pictures embody can easily be traced back to the earlier Middle Ages. A vivid application of this relationship is in fact seen in the visual association of a real, recognizable city with Jerusalem. Since relatively few medieval Europeans had actually visited Jerusalem—and since there is remarkably little evidence that people were at all interested in what the contemporary city actually looked like anyway—Jerusalem remained recognizable in essentially the same way it had been back in the early centuries of Christian art: as an element in a known story or scene.

The Crucifixion was a well-known scene that was also precisely located: it took place outside of Jerusalem (*John* 19.17). A Crucifixion (fig. 25) painted by Botticelli near the end of his career, around 1500, presents the scene in a relatively common way, though with the addition of a recognizable view of Florence in the background. While it is sometimes argued that in the Renaissance heaven was brought down to earth, it may well be the case both here and generally that what was actually taking place was the sacralization of the secular.[9] That is, what is occurring here is the conscious equation of Florence and Jerusalem. The Italians were the first ones to do this sort of thing, not because of their precocious naturalism in the visual arts but rather, I think, because they had the oldest and most highly developed system of urban political theory in medieval Europe. Urban political theology might be an even better way of putting it.[10] However faulty this system may have been in practice, the theory could easily lead to such an identification of a specific earthly city with a more "holy" place.

Another example, Florentine again but in this instance from the fourteenth rather than the fifteenth century, is found in one of the miniatures of the Biadaiolo illuminator, dated around 1340 (fig. 26). Florence is again the scene, recognizable largely because of the baptistry—Dante's *bel San Giovanni*—prominently located in the middle of the picture on the right. In the foreground are some starving Sienese being succored by Florentine citizens. The miniature was partly intended as political propaganda, but it also recalls the allegorical method of commentators like Haymo, who, in speaking of the heavenly Jerusalem, interpreted the four sides of the foursquare City as the three theological virtues: faith, hope and charity, to which *operationem*—"doing"—was added.[11]

So virtue and virtuous action are specifically associated with the city. Again, Italian art provides the most unequivocal and well-known examples of cities sanctified by the virtuous actions of their citizens. For example, in one of the scenes of the life of St. Francis from the fresco cycle in the upper church of S. Francesco at Assisi, the simple man recognizes the saint and spreads his cloak for him (fig. 27). The event is taking place not just in a generalized urban setting but recognizably in the central square of medieval Assisi itself with the communal palace on the left and the still surviving ex-temple of Minerva in the center. While the scene is presented in a matter-of-fact manner, the story and the characters effectively sanctify the locus of the action.[12]

What is undoubtedly the most famous appearance of a city in a medieval work of art is found at Siena in the Sala della Pace (Hall of Peace) of the civic palace, the Palazzo Pubblico. In 1338–39 the Sienese painter Ambrogio Lorenzetti was commissioned by the Nine, the oligarchic governing board of the city, to fresco the walls of the room with an extended allegory of Good and Bad Government. I will not attempt to explore this immensely complicated and rich cycle of frescoes beyond pointing out one figure that plays a fundamental role in the scenes on the wall that show the effects of good government in the city and the countryside (figs. 28–29).[13] This figure is the personification of *Securitas* (Security) that, hovering over the city wall, carries a gibbet with a corpse (fig. 30). At first glance such a representation seems to be gruesomely out of place in a scene that otherwise is filled with order and calm and beauty both within and outside the city. But the caption provided for the figure also provides the real explanation of her presence: "Senza paura ognuom franco camini/ elavorando semini ciascuno/ mentre che tal comuno/ manterra questa donna in signoria/ che alevata arei ogni balia" ("Without fear each man may walk, and working each may sow, while this lady will keep such a city under her rule, for she has removed all power from the guilty"). She is to be understood not as a warning but rather as one of the chief signs of the effects of good government, which is what the pictures on this wall are are intended to depict. Security is a result of justice, which is the chief civic virtue and which distinguishes a city virtuous in itself from one that is virtuous as a result of its saints—e.g., the image of Assisi discussed above. "Jerusalem is built as a city that is at peace with itself," says the Psalmist (*Ps.* 122.3). "Per iustitiam autem conservatur pax civitatis" ("for the peace of a city is preserved through justice"), says St. Thomas Aquinas.[14] Returning us from cities in general specifically to the city of God, Augustine says that "right [by which he means *moral right*] is that which flows from the fountain of justice."[15] Tertullian also connects the "regnum . . . iustorum" with the "civitas nova Hierusalem."[16]

This brings us finally to the effects of such thinking on actual cities in the Middle Ages—or at least to its effects on one city, Brescia, in northern Italy. Like all of the other important cities in

Lombardy which managed to gain true independence from external domination during the course of the twelfth century, Brescia was intensely preoccupied with working out the ramifications of self-government. From this city comes what seems to be the earliest appearance in any of these north Italian communes of a building used specifically for communal judicial activities.[17] Probably the existence at Brescia of this early structure was at least partly responsible for the fact that by Lombard standards this city was relatively late in building itself a full-blown communal palace. The present complex was not begun until the early 1220's, nearly a generation after the first North Italian town halls appeared (fig. 31). When it was finally built, however, the Brescian palace was not located *in medio civitatis* (in the middle of the city), which was the preferred site for these palaces in virtually every other Lombard city. Rather, it was built to the north of the double cathedral where it was situated facing onto one of the town's main squares—very near the site, mentioned above, of the earlier civic loggia associated with civic judicial activities. This position located the new palace more towards the western edge of the city than near its center (fig. A). My intention here is not to undertake an examination of this particular Lombard communal palace, which I will be doing elsewhere, but rather to associate this complex of buildings with other events from the first half of the thirteenth century in Brescia that I suspect are intimately connected with what I have been discussing so far. Such an assertion necessitates a brief overview of a half-century of Brescian urban development, beginning soon after the Peace of Constance in 1183—the event that marked the beginning of legitimate communal government not only in Brescia but also generally in Lombardy.

In 1186–87 Brescia undertook to build a new set of city walls, largely on the same foundations that the Romans had used for the first walls but also incorporating settlements which had sprung up to the west of the original city. The late twelfth century was a time of increasing prosperity for Brescia, and within a generation even the new walls had been outgrown; hence communal Brescia had yet another chance to remake itself and to think about what it wanted to be. The surviving evidence suggests that city planning here was operating at a more organized level (that is, it was slightly less *ad hoc*) than was usually the case in North Italian cities of the thirteenth century. The new communal palace, begun in 1223, was in-

A. Brescia, indicating: (1) the location of the Roman city, (2) the communal palace, (3) the late twelfth-century, (4) the new city, 1227 and thereafter.

tended to replace the older civic structures such as the wooden loggia from the 1180's, mentioned above. As a Lombard town hall, the new building served two purposes: it was intended to house the communal council, and it was to serve as the seat of civic justice.[18] For various reasons, the communal palace at Brescia, or the *Broletto*, as it came to be called, was a particularly elaborate and complex undertaking, eventually consisting of three connected palaces, and its construction carried on into the early fourteenth century (fig. B).[19]

However, in 1237, in the midst of the building of this communal complex, the city of Brescia embarked on another ambitious and very well documented program of civic improvement and expansion.[20] Essentially this urban expansion involved the construc-

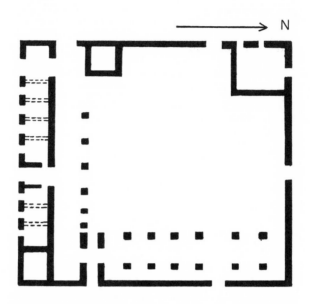

B. Groundplan of the communal palace (Broletto), Brescia (c.1223–32).

tion of new walls to the west and south of the early medieval city. Such an undertaking is hardly surprising for an Italian city in the thirteenth century; many cities were growing in population and making the requisite enlargements to their surrounding walls. Significant in the case of Brescia, however, are the extent to which it is clear that the enlargements were thought out beforehand and the particular form that was intended for the city once the expansion was complete.

In addition to the walls themselves, a system of streets and roads was projected, both inside and outside the gates. These streets are remarkable in medieval urbanism both for their size and for their orthogonal regularity. The main thoroughfares leading from the old city gates to the new ones were planned to be eighteen braccia (about 8.5 meters) wide, and this was also the width of the connecting streets within the walls. Running immediately inside the new wall was a spacious boulevard forty-five braccia (almost 21.5 meters) wide, which expanded even more—to fifty braccia (23.75 meters)—whenever it approached one of the new gates.[21] As far as possible these new streets were to be regular in their layout, running straight from the old gates to the new walls and intersected at right angles by the secondary streets.[22]

Such a program of course flies in the face of general notions about the essentially chaotic nature of medieval urban development. We do not usually imagine thirteenth-century cities growing like this, and questions about details and intentions come immediately to mind. While the documentation concerning the projected enlargements is ample, it does not at a first reading provide us with any hint of what was in the minds of the Brescians as they worked out the details of this elaborate expansion to the city. Why for example, expand in the direction that was chosen, to the southwest? Why this much, and not more, or less? Were these new walls intended to annex already inhabited *sobborghi*, or, as in the case of Florence towards the end of the thirteenth century, were they simply going to enclose much empty space that could be filled up over the years?

Fortunately it is possible to go a considerable distance towards finding the answers to these questions with the information that is available. If we consider this urban expansion of the 1230's and beyond as being intimately tied up with other community endeavors, particularly the construction of the communal palace complex, then individual pieces of information begin to coalesce and form themselves into reasonable possibilities. For example, in the fourteenth century, when the most important chronicler of Brescia, Jacopo Malvezzi, composed his history, he was able to say about the communal palace not only that "it was built on a square plan" but that it was "placed just about in the middle of the city": "Et . . . incoeperunt Brixienses construere Palatium Populi . . . quasi in medio civitatis. . . . Est autem editionis ejus figura quadrata, habens ad alterum angulum versus Occidentem et ad Austrum, Turrim altam. . . ."[23] As is evident from a glance at a plan of the city, the building was not centrally located when it was first built in the 1220's, for then it was very close to the western edge of the city (fig. A). However, by the time that the thirteenth-century urban boom was over—that is, by the time that Malvezzi knew the city—this had become a very accurate statement of its location. He never knew a time when the palace had not been at the center of the town.

The suspicion arises, then, that this ultimate central location of the communal palace might not have been simply an accidental by-product of other, unrelated civic actions. Given the concern, which has been noted above, that other Lombard communes exhibited about the placement of their own civic palaces in the middle of their cities, the final location of the Brescian *Broletto* does not seem to have been an unforeseen result of the city's expansion. The answers to some of the questions posed above, therefore, might well be deduced from Malvezzi's statement about the location of the town hall *quasi in medio civitatis*. The direction chosen for the enlargement of the city walls and the actual dimensions of the enlargement appear to have been related to a desire for a more central location for the communal palace. Even if the palace itself could not be moved so that it was in the middle of the town, it was possible to rearrange the town itself, so to speak, so that the eventual result was the same: the palace—the *sedes* (or in Augustine's phrase, the *fons*) *iustitiae*—had always existed *in medio civitatis*.[24] The shape itself of the newly walled city echoed that of the communal complex: both were squares, or reasonably close to squares, and the square is the shape of the new Jerusalem of the *Apocalypse*. Furthermore, in the surviving documents relating to these thirteenth-century expansions, the new gates are carefully ennumerated: there are twelve of them.[25]

Beginning in 1245, the commune undertook a program of construction of civic fountains, including, it seems, one that was placed in the courtyard of the communal palace.[26] In 1254, the city's streets were paved, including the new grid behind the expanded walls.[27] The description of the heavenly Jerusalem from the twenty-first chapter of the *Apocalypse* continues into the twenty-second chapter, which opens with the river of life flowing through Paradise. This heavenly river was often in the Middle Ages equated with the allegorical *fons vitae*, the fountain of life. And such allegorical fountains were easily associated with actual ones. Further interweaving reality and allegory, in the thirteenth century there was a river that flowed through Brescia immediately to the west of the communal palace complex which, though it has long since been paved over, is still evident in nineteenth-century maps of the city (fig. A).[28] The biblical precedent for paving streets is, of course, found in this very description of the heavenly Jerusalem in the *Apocalypse* (21.21). While the streets of Brescia may not have been golden, they were at least paved as a part of the general expansion and refurbishment of the city undertaken in the middle of the thirteenth century.

If the case I am attempting to make for an equation of Brescia and the paradisiacal Jerusalem of the *Apocalypse* were based only on this kind of circumstantial evidence, it would then be a weak one indeed. Even given the evidence presented in the first part of this paper that the medieval mind imagined the heavenly City literally as it was described in the twenty-first chapter of the *Apocalypse*—and that there are many cases where earthly cities were associated, visually or metaphorically, with Jerusalem and Paradise—the association of Brescia with the heavenly City could not be regarded as proven.[29] There is, however, some very powerful additional evidence that the Brescians were themselves thinking along these very lines of an earthly manifestation of Paradise. In 1251 a new chapter was added to the civic statutes prohibiting the tearing down of houses "so that the city will not be disfigured by ruins." It should not be forgotten that this was an addition to the statutes made while the city was immersed not only in the construction of its new civic palace but also in the expansion of its walls and the creation of a new system of streets and city gates. In the statutes of 1313 this prohibition was renewed, though now with the added explanation: "since it is said that cities have been made in the likeness of Paradise" (". . . ne civitas deformeretur ruinis . . . cum dicatur quod civitates facte sunt ad similitudinem Paradisi").[30] Given such a view of urban construction and reconstruction which so willingly conflates literalism with allegory and metaphor, it seems distinctly possible that in this case, and perhaps more frequently than we have thought so far elsewhere, medieval cities themselves were envisioned as partial but nonetheless true reflections of heaven—i.e., as the New Jerusalem come down to earth.

NOTES

[1] The *Corpus Agrimensorum Romanorum* describes the various aspects of Roman city planning and foundation. While the oldest extant manuscript is no older than the fifth century, it is assumed that the present *Corpus* is based on early Roman sources. Likewise, even though the surviving illustrations of cities in the manuscripts are generally assigned to the sixth century, they are thought to derive from earlier models. For a modern edition, see Carl Olof Thulin, ed., *Corpus Agrimensorum Romanorum* (Leipzig: B. G. Teubner, 1913); see also C. Thulin,

Die Handschriften des Corpus Agrimensorum Romanorum (Berlin: Verlag der Königlichen Akademie der Wissenschaften, 1911), and E. Baldwin Smith, *Architectural Symbolism of Imperial Rome and the Middle Ages* (New York: Hacker, 1978), p. 66.

[2] On the Anastasis complex, and Constantinian building in general, see Richard Krautheimer, *Early Christian and Byzantine Architecture*, 4th ed. (New Haven: Yale Univ. Press, 1986). For the proposal that the background architecture represents the fourth-century Constantinian architecture in Jerusalem see Bianca Kühnel, *From the Earthly to the Heavenly Jerusalem* (Rome, Freiburg, and Vienna: Herder, 1987), pp. 63–72.

[3] The original mosaic has been replaced, but surviving evidence attests to its subject; see H. Schnitzler, "Das Kuppelmosaik des Aachener Pfalzkapelle," *Aachner Kunstblätter*, 29 (1964), 17–44.

[4] The *Trier Apocalypse* (Trier Stadtbibliothek, c.31), considered to be the earliest of this group, is dated in the first quarter of the ninth century; see Peter Klein, *Trierer Apokalypse, Kommentarband* (Graz: Akademische Druck- und Verlagsanstalt, 1973). The Cambrai manuscript (Bibliothèque Municipale, MS. 386) appears to be a tenth-century copy of the Trier codex. A second group of Carolingian *Apocalypse* manuscripts is represented by the early ninth-century Valenciennes manuscript (Bibliothèque Municipale, MS. 99) and a tenth-century copy of it, now in Paris (Bibliothèque Nationale, Nouv. acq. lat. 1132); see Franz von Juraschek, *Die Apokalypse von Valenciennes* (Linz, 1954), and Henri Omont, "Un nouveau manuscrit illustré de l'apocalypse au XIe siècle; notice du ms. lat. nouv. acccq. 1132 de la Bibliothèque nationale," *Bibliothèque de l'École des Chartres*, 83 (1922), 1–24. See also Henri Omont, "Manuscrits illustrés de l'Apocalypse aux IXe et Xe siècles," *Bulletin de las Societé francaise de réproduction des manuscrits à peintures*, 6 (1922), 62–95.

[5] See A. Giussani, *L'abbazia di S. Pietro al Monte sopra Civate* (Como: Tipografia Cavalleri e Fossati, 1912); Pietro Toesca, *Monumenti dell'antica abbazia di S. Pietro al Monte di Civate* (Florence: Bencini and Sansoni, 1946); and Gian Piero Bognetti and Carlo Mancora, *L'abbazia benedettina di Civate* (Milan: Amici della Casa del Cieco, 1957).

[6] This inscription was placed by Suger on the bronze doors (now lost) of the west front of his new church (Erwin Panofsky, ed., *Abbot Suger on the Abbey Church of St.-Denis and Its Art Treasures*, 2nd ed. [Princeton: Princeton Univ. Press, 1979], p. 48).

[7] Kühnel, *From the Earthly to the Heaven Jerusalem*, pp. 77–78; see also J. Ratsinger, *Volk und Haus Gottes in Augustins Lehre von der Kirche* (Munich, 1954), and Yves M.-J. Congar, "'Civitas Dei' et 'Ecclesia' chez saint Augustine," *Revue des études augustiniennes*, 3 (1957), 1–14.

[8] Haymonis Halberstatensis Episcopi, *Enarratio in Apocalypsin*, in *Patrologia Latina*, CXVII, 1192.

[9] An example of an essentially similar depiction, though in a different biblical scene, is found in a Florentine antiphonary of the early sixteenth century where an initial has a scene of God appearing to king David, who is on his knees outside of the walls of Florence (Florence, Duomo, cod. H n.17, c.140; reproduced in Mirella Levi d'Ancona, *Miniatura e miniatori a Firenze dal XIV al XVI secolo* [Florence: L. S. Olschki, 1962], I, Pl. 1).

[10] See, for example, Maria Consiglia de Matteis, ed., *"La teologia politica comunale" di Remigio di Girolami* (Bologna: Pàtron, 1977).

[11] *Patrologia Latina*, CXVII, 1201. It is intriguing that Haymo twice, in relating the Church to the heavenly City, makes specific reference to the sanctifying nature of baptism: "Sancta dicitur, quia quotidie per baptismum sanctificatur . . ." (ibid., CXVII, 1192, 1198). While I am not claiming that the Biadaiolo illuminator was using the Carolingian bishop's commentary on the *Apocalypse* as the source for this miniature, it is nevertheless clearly not accidental that the baptistry appears in such a noticeable way.

[12] This is also a good example of the most common method used by Italian medieval artists when they wanted to locate an action in a specific and actual place. They would simply reproduce one or two recognizable buildings in an otherwise generic urban view. Besides being a remarkably effective way of localizing action, it also provides a revealing glimpse of what structures were considered to be the important ones in Italian cities in the late Middle Ages.

[13] These justly famous frescoes have received extensive attention by scholars, and hence only the most important can be listed here. The beginning point is Aldo Cairola and Enzo Carli, *Il palazzo pubblico di Siena* (Rome: Editalia, 1963). See also George Rowley, *Ambrogio Lorenzetti* (Princeton: Princeton Univ. Press, 1958), and Nicolai Rubenstein, "Political Ideas in Sienese Art: The Frescoes by Ambrogio Lorenzetti and Taddeo di Bartolo in the Palazzo Pubblico," *Journal of the Warburg and Courtauld Institutes*, 21 (1958), 179–207. More recent treatments include Uta Feldges-Henning, "The Pictorial Programme of the Sala della Pace: A New Interpretation," *Journal of the Warburg and Courtauld Institutes*, 35 (1972), 145–62; Quentin Skinner, "Ambrogio Lorenzetti: The Artist as Political Philosopher," *Proceedings of the British Academy*, 72 (1986), 1–56; Randolph Starn, "The Republican Regime of the 'Room of Peace' in Siena, 1338–40," *Representations*, 18 (1987), 1–32; and Chiara Frugoni, *A Distant City* (Princeton: Princeton Univ. Press, 1991), esp. pp. 118–93.

[14] *In octo libris politicorum Aristotelis* (Venice, 1500), sec. 271; as quoted in Rubenstein, "Political Ideas in Sienese Art," pp. 187–88.

[15] *The Political Writings of St. Augustine*, ed. Henry Paolucci (Chicago, 1987), p. 39.

[16] See Kühnel, *From the Earthly to the Heavenly Jerusalem*, p. 76.

[17] The loggia of the commune (*laubia comunis brixie*) was first noted in a document dated 1183 (Federico Odorici, *Storie bresciane dei primi tempi sino all' età nostra* [Brescia: Pietro di Lor. Gilberti, 1853–65], VI, 49 [No. 157]), but it has long since disappeared without a trace. It was undoubtedly located very near to the site of the present communal palace or town hall.

[18] Until the Peace of Constance (1183), which marked the settlement of the differences between the Lombard communes and the emperor Frederick Barbarossa—a settlement in which Barbarossa conceded that he no longer had any control over these cities—the juridical structures of North Italy were similar to those in cities all through the Empire. That is, the bishop was also the chief judicial authority of the town, and all civic cases were essentially heard in ecclesiastical courts. The Peace of Constance was mostly an official acknowledgement simply of the status quo, but in its treatment of civil law it made substantial changes—changes which had important ramifications for subsequent communal development. After the ratification of the Peace, the responsibility for civic justice was removed from the hands of the bishops and placed with secular communal authorities. This was one of the most important changes in communal organization and one that seems to have resulted in the development of communal palaces in the decades after the signing of the Peace. See Carlo Guido Mor, "Il tratatto di Costanza e la vita comunale italiana," *Popolo e stato in Italia nell' età di Federico Barbarossa* (Turin: Deputazione Subalpina di Storia Patria, 1970), p. 367.

[19] While an extended discussion of the *Broletto* of Brescia would be inappropriate in the present paper, a thumbnail sketch of the building history may be useful. As has already been mentioned, the initial palace, comprising the southern block of the complex, was begun in 1223. At approximately the date when this palace was finished—i.e., in 1226 or soon after—work began on the second (eastern) wing, which was completed and in use by 1232. It is unclear what exactly stood on the site of the present west wing, but the palace that exists there now seems to have been built at the end of the thirteenth century. During the communal period, the northern boundary of the *Broletto* was simply a wall, and the present palaces that make up the north part of the palace complex date from the fifteenth through the early seventeenth century.

[20] The principal source of information concerning these thirteenth-century public works is the *Liber Potheris comunis civitatis Brixiae*, Monumenta Historiae Patriae, 19 (Turin: E Regio Typographeo, 1890), especially cols. 426ff.

[21] Outside of the walls was an open area that was fifty braccia wide, a moat of the same width, and finally another encircling road that was eighteen braccia

wide.

[22] The single exception to this general principle was a dominant diagonal road entering the city from the southwest and forming a break in the orthogonal regularity of the new part of the city which is easily recognizable in plans. This exceptional street appears to have been an important pre-existing artery, connecting Brescia to the rich plains of the Po valley.

[23] Jacobo Malvecio [Malvezzi], *Chronicon Brixianum ab origine urbis ad annum usque MCCCXXXII*, Rerum Italicarum Scriptores, 14 (Muratori, n.d.), p. 901.

[24] *Political Writings of St. Augustine*, ed. Paolucci, p. 39.

[25] *Liber Potheris*, cols. 931–44. These documents are dated 1284. While the Brescians did not go so far as to place three gates in each of the sides of the newly enlarged city, this may be reasonably explained as related to already existing gates and roads. Since the city was not being built *ex novo*, frequent compromises for the sake of expediency were necessary.

[26] Fountains are mentioned regularly in the civic statutes, and it is abundantly clear that the city took its responsibilities as the provider of water seriously; in the *Statuta clausorum statutorum* of 1293, several chapters are dedicated to this subject (Brescia, Archivio di Stato, MS. Bibliotheca Queriniana 1044 1/2, fols. 186^r–187^v and *passim*).

[27] Gabriele Rosa, "Il Broletto di Brescia," in *Brixia 1882* (Brescia: Tipografia Pagnoncelli, 1882), p. 2.

[28] It may well be this river that was referred to in the civic statutes of 1277 as the "flumen sancti luce" (Brescia, Archivio di Stato, MS. Bibliotheca Queriniana 1044 1/2, fol. 76^r).

[29] The association of cities and Paradise was not restricted solely to the Italian peninsula in the Middle Ages; the early-fourteenth-century *Tractatus de Laudibus Parisius*, by Jean of Jandun, puns on the words *Parisius* and *paradisus* (*Paris et ses historiens aux XIVe et XVe siècles*, ed. Adrien Jean Victor le Roux de Lincy [Paris: Imprimerie Impériale, 1867], pp. 32–79). I am indebted to Michael Davis for this northern example.

[30] Brescia, Archivio di Stato, MS. Bibliotheca Queriniana, Arch. Civ. 1043 1/2, fol. 63^v.

The Musical Repertory

Richard Rastall

When a saule es purified be luf of God, illumynd be wysdom, stabild be
þe myght of God, þan es þe eghe of þe saule opynd to behalde gastly
þings, & uertus, & angels, & haly saules, & heuenly thyngs. Þan es þe
saule abil, because of clennes, to fele þe touchyng, þe spekyng of goode
aungels.—Walter Hilton, *Of Angels' Song*, ll. 71–76

The treatise *Of Angels' Song* by Walter Hilton (d. 1396)[1] is the
only medieval work known fully to discuss the nature of angelic
singing. The touching and speaking of angels is not bodily but
spiritual, and the soul may be in such condition, says Hilton, that
"if oure lord uouchesafe, þe saule may here & fele heuenly sowne,
made be þe presence of aungels in louyng of God" (ll. 79–81).
Hilton characterizes angelic song, then, as the sound that angels
make "in loving of God"—that is, the sound of the angelic praise
of the Creator. The preconditions necessary for anyone to hear
angelic song are such that few mortals have ever had the experience; in fact, it is Hilton's thesis that the soul must be in so great
a state of grace that those who think they hear angels singing
should assume that the Devil is trying to deceive them.[2] The soul
of one who hears angels singing is very close to God because of its
perfect love ("charite": see ll. 11–13); such a soul is perfectly
reformed, returned to its initial state (ll. 13–15)—that is, to the
state prior to the Fall of Man. For this state to occur, the mind
must be fixed on God and spiritual things, the reason must be freed
from all worldly things and illuminated by grace to behold God
and spiritual matters, and "þe wyl & þe affeccion" must be purged
of worldly love and inflamed with love of the Holy Spirit (ll.
15–22). The soul cannot be continually in this condition in earthly
life, but only in heavenly bliss; but the nearer a soul comes to this
condition, the more nearly perfect it is (ll. 22–25). Nor does every
soul that is in perfect charity hear angelic song, but only one that
"es so pouried in þe fyre of luf, þat al erthly sauour es brent oute
of it . . ." (ll. 97–100). Given these conditions, though, the soul

162

may "synge a new sang, & sothly may he here a blisful heuenly soun & aungels sang."[3]

What the song is, no mortal can tell. It is beyond mortal imagining and understanding; and so, although it can be experienced in the soul, it cannot be described by any mortal, nor discussed in any terms that a mortal could use or understand.[4]

This intellectual view was of little relevance to those who wished to represent angelic song iconographically or dramatically for the education or comfort of the populace at large.[5] For this purpose, something more specific was needed, something comprehensible to ordinary men and women. That had in fact been the more common need from the beginning of the Judeo-Christian tradition with its emphasis on communication between God and humans. The scriptures therefore provided the basic evidence of this communication and made possible a whole medieval tradition of the nature of the music that characterized heaven. In tracing this tradition we can list the texts sung by angels in Latin and vernacular drama, in various literary works such as the *Legenda Aurea* and in medieval iconography, and we can also compile some evidence about the use of musical instruments in such works.[6] This essay will discuss the textual repertory, the case for singing liturgical texts, and the nature of the polyphonic repertory used for angelic music.[7]

The proper activity of all angels, and of the souls of the saints, is the praise of God, the *laudes dei*. The original and influential description of the *laudes dei* is Isaias' vision of heaven in which the seraphim are depicted as praising God:

Et clamabant alter ad alterum, et dicebant: Sanctus, sanctus, sanctus Dominus exercituum; plena est omnis terra gloria eius. (*Isaias* 6.3)

(And [the seraphim] cried one to another, and said, Holy, holy, holy is the Lord God of hosts, all the earth is full of his glory.)

Their praise is ceaseless because they constantly strive to praise God adequately; and they call to one another in order to share their knowledge of God.[8] Isaias' vision has a New Testament parallel: in *Apocalypse* 4.8–11 St. John describes the inhabitants of heaven and reports the words of praise that they utter:

Et quatuor animalia, singula eorum habebant alas senas, et in circuitu et

intus plena sunt oculis; et requiem non habent die et nocte, dicentia:
Sanctus, sanctus, sanctus Dominus Deus omnipotens, qui erat, et qui est, et qui venturus est.
Et cum darent illa animalia gloriam, et honorem, et benedictionem sedenti super thronum, viventi in saecula saeculorum, procident viginti quatuor seniores ante sedentem in throno, et adorabunt viventem in saecula saeculorum, et mittent coronas suas ante thronum, dicentes:
Dignus es, Domine et Deus noster, accipere gloriam, et honorem, et virtutem, quia tu creasti omnia, et propter voluntatem tuam erant et creata sunt.

(And the four living creatures had each of them six wings; and round about and within they are full of eyes. And they rested not day and night, saying Holy, holy, holy, Lord God Almighty, who was, and who is, and who is to come.
And when those living creatures gave glory, and honour, and benediction to him that sitteth on the throne, who liveth for ever and ever;
The four and twenty ancients fell down before him that sitteth on the throne, and adored him that liveth for ever and ever, and cast their crowns before the throne, saying,
Thou art worthy, O Lord our God, to receive glory, and honour, and power; for thou hast created all things, and for thy will they were, and have been created.)

The hymn of praise spoken by the four beasts (or "living creatures," as the Douay-Rheims translation identifies them) is obviously closely related to that of Isaias' vision; that of the twenty-four elders ("ancients") is quite different, although it presents ideas found in the *Psalms* and elsewhere.[9]

The seraphim who cry to God in Isaias' vision are the angels closest to God. Of the nine orders of angels, arranged in three groups of three orders each,[10] the first species (Seraphim, Cherubim, and Thrones) were believed to be the closest to God's throne; the second species (Dominions, Powers, and Virtues) less close; and only those furthest away, the lowest orders (the third species, consisting of Principalities, Archangels, and Angels), had anything at all to do with Mankind. This is not to say that these last three orders are close to men, however. Angels are terrible beings; indeed "an angel is so terrible that even for an event as important as the Annunciation it was only an archangel—the lowest order but one—which bore God's message. Even so, his first words were 'Fear not': which are the first words of almost any biblical angel."[11] The angel of the Annunciation was the archangel Gabriel

(*Luke* 1.26).[12] In other cases God's unnamed messengers are simply designated "angel"; while these may usually be assumed to be of the lowest rank of all, the term is a generic one and was sometimes used for a being of higher rank.[13]

These biblical texts of the *laudes dei* were used in the composition of the liturgy. The hymn of Isaias' vision appears near the opening of the prose hymn *Te deum laudamus*:

Tibi omnes angeli, tibi celi et universe potestates: Tibi cherubyn et seraphyn incessabili voce proclamant: Sanctus, Sanctus, Sanctus, Dominus deus sabaoth. Pleni sunt celi et terra maiestatis glorie tue.[14]

(To thee all angels cry aloud: the heavens, and all the Powers therein. To thee, Cherubin and Seraphin: continually do cry, Holy, holy, holy, Lord God of Sabaoth; heaven and earth are full of the majesty: of thy glory.)

It appears again in the Preface of the Mass:

Et ideo cum angelis et archangelis cum thronis et dominacionibus cumque omni milicia celestis exercitus ymnum glorie tue canimus sine fine dicentes.
Sanctus. Sanctus. Sanctus. Dominus deus sabaoth. Pleni sunt celi et terra gloria tua. . . .[15]

(And therefore with Angels and Archangels, with Thrones and Dominations and with all the host of the heavenly army we sing the hymn of thy glory, evermore saying:
Holy, Holy, Holy Lord God of Hosts. Heaven and earth are full of thy glory. . . .)

The Mass Preface shows that the hymn sung by mortals is in emulation of the praise of the angels: "Therefore with . . . all the host of the heavenly army we sing the hymn . . . Holy, holy, holy. . . ." It is, as it were, authenticated by its heavenly origin. In fact, any angelic text that could have a liturgical use might become part of the earthly liturgy on an appropriate occasion. Gabriel's greeting to the Blessed Virgin—"Ave, gratia plena; Dominus tecum; benedicta tu in mulieribus" (*Luke* 1.28)—became a Mass offertory, while different versions with "Maria" added were used in a variety of liturgical forms for both Mass and daily Office on

Marian feasts. A less widely-used example is the words of the two men clothed in white—obviously angels—to the apostles after the Ascension (*Acts* 1.11): "Viri Galilaei, quid statis aspicientes in caelum? Hic Jesus, qui adsumptus est a vobis in caelum, sic veniet quemadmodum vidistis eum euntem in caelum" ("Ye men of Galilee, why stand ye gazing up into heaven? This Jesus who is taken up from you into heaven, shall so come, as ye have seen him going into heaven"). This text, up to "sic veniet," became the first antiphon for the Feast of the Ascension, and with slightly different wording appears in several other places in the liturgy of the day.

Nor did the liturgy take only angelic texts, either in biblical form or as the starting point for modified or largely newly composed items. Suitable hymns of praise delivered by mortals were treated as parallel to the angelic *laudes dei*, like the people's greeting to Christ at his entry into Jerusalem on Palm Sunday:

> Osanna Filio David. Benedictus qui venturus est in nomine Domini: osanna in altissimis. (*Matthew* 21.9)

> Osanna. Benedictus qui venit in nomine Domini; benedictum quod venit regnum patris nostri David. Osanna in excelsis. (*Mark* 11.9–10)

> Benedictus qui venit rex in nomine Domini: pax in caelo et gloria in excelsis. (*Luke* 19.38)

> Benedictus qui venit in nomine domini. Hosanna in excelsis. (Preface of the Mass)

The words of the individual mortals who did God's will were sometimes incorporated into the liturgy—the *Magnificat* is perhaps the best-known example of this—and the words of Christ himself could also be used. Other significant biblical texts too were used in the liturgy at appropriate places. The *Psalms* in particular offered a number of prophetic writings about the Messiah, and the *Song of Songs*, regarded as an allegory of Christ and his bride the Church, provided texts suitable for Marian and other occasions.

One of the most important biblical texts used in the liturgy is the angelic *Gloria in excelsis deo* at the annunciation to the shepherds. After the angel had told the shepherds of the Christ Child in Bethlehem (*Luke* 2.10–12), "a multitude of the heavenly army" praised God with the words "Gloria in altissimis Deo, et in terra pax hominibus bonae voluntatis" (2.14). In fact, the liturgy uses the older Latin version, with "excelsis" for the Vulgate's "altissimis," and in that form the text appears twice in the liturgy for Christmas Day: as the verse of the first responsory, *Hodie nobis caelorum rex*, at Matins, and as the *Benedictus* antiphon at Lauds. The responsory verse treats the text with no additions; the *Benedictus* antiphon, which has a different chant, adds two Alleluias. The responsory verse was normally treated in a somewhat dramatic fashion: in several English uses it was sung by a group of boys bearing lighted candles and singing from some elevated position in the church.[16] The text as taken from the Bible occurs only in these two places in the liturgy, but it was important enough to act as the starting point for a longer and more generalized hymn of praise, the *Gloria* of the Mass ordinary.

The *Gloria in excelsis deo* illustrates an important fact about biblical texts in medieval iconography and drama—namely, that in most cases the artist or author used a liturgical text rather than a strictly biblical one. Representations of the annunciation to the shepherds only rarely use the Vulgate version, with "altissimis," and normally use the liturgical version with which, after all, most people were more familiar in the late Middle Ages. Though the subject is probably a complex one, it is generally true that liturgical texts are more often used than the Vulgate version of the biblical texts that gave rise to them.[17] One reason for this is that the liturgical position itself provided a text with a specific significance if it did not originally have one; for example, the psalm-text "Attolite portas, principes" (Psalm 23.10; *AV* 24.10) is only a generalized reference to the Messiah, but it was thought especially appropriate for Christ's entry into hell in various Harrowing of Hell plays because of its use in the Consecration of a Church, where there is a ritualized forced entry and an exorcism of evil spirits by the officiating prelate.[18]

That the angels sang the same liturgy as the Church on earth was, I think, generally accepted in the late Middle Ages. Several stories in the *Legenda Aurea* seem to depend on this, for example. In the section on the Assumption of the Virgin Mary, the *Legenda Aurea* tells how, at the Virgin's funeral procession, Peter began the apostles' singing of *Exiit Israel de Egypto, Alleluia*, and that "Affuerunt et angeli cum apostolis concinentes et terram totam sonitu mirae suavitatis replentes" ("angels . . . were present with the apostles, singing with them and filling the whole earth with the dulcity of their music").[19] This is put to dramatic practice in the N-town Assumption play, where the angels sing the Alleluias.[20]

In the section on St. Thomas of Canterbury, the angelic singing of earthly liturgy is used in an even more positive way. The *Legenda Aurea* relates how, after Thomas' martyrdom in 1170, "Dum igitur clerici requiem aeternam inciperent et pro eo missam agerent defunctorum, subito, ut ajunt, angelorum chori adstantes voces cantantium interrumpunt, martiris missam incipiunt, laetabitur justus in domino, concinuntet caeteri clerici prosequuntur" ("At the moment when his clergy was about to chant for him the *Requiem aeternam*, the Mass for the Dead, it is said that a choir of angels came and interrupted the singers, and began to chant the Mass of the Martyrs, *Laetabitur justus in Domino . . .*").[21] In correcting the Canterbury clergy by singing the introit to the Mass of a Martyr instead of that of the Mass for the Dead, the angels indicated that the former Mass was appropriate.

In most cases the Bible says that the texts were said, not that they were sung; yet in medieval drama, in writings such as the *Legenda Aurea*, and in some religious paintings of the late Middle Ages such texts are often presented as being sung. There are three main reasons why the biblical speech should so commonly have become singing in late medieval presentation.

First, the use of liturgical texts, normally sung and often with their own—sometimes very well-known—chants, would automatically bring to mind the musical setting associated with the text. This is probably why texts are so often sung in the *Legenda Aurea*, where quotations are normally from the liturgy rather than direct from the Bible. Second, the psalmist's frequent exhortations to the faithful to *sing* God's praises were highly influential in promoting the idea of sung praise as especially effective. David was known as a musician, not least because of the psalms beginning "Cantate Domino canticum novum" (Psalms 97 [*AV* 98], 149; cf. 95 [*AV* 96]), but there are many other psalms that express the same idea, while some also exhort the faithful to play instruments and to dance in God's praise. This whole attitude of the *Psalms* to music is summed up in the very last psalm (150):

Alleluia.
Laudate Dominum in sanctis eius;

laudate eum in firmamento virtutis eius.
Laudate eum in virtutibus eius;
   laudate eum secundum multitudinem magnitudinis eius.
Laudate eum in sono tubae;
   laudate eum in psalterio et cithara.
Laudate eum in tympano et choro;
   laudate eum in cordis et organo.
Laudate eum in cymbalis bene sonantibus;
   laudate eum in cymbalis iubilationis.
Omnis spiritus laudet Dominum.
Alleluia.

This psalm was known not only in its Latin version but also in a number of English paraphrases. It is significant that Robert Mannyng should use part of it to illustrate his story of Robert Grosseteste's approbation of music in *Handlyng Synne* (1303):

yn harpe, yn thabour, and symphan gle,
wurschepe God, yn troumpes, and sautre,
yn cordys, an organes, and bellys ryngyng,
yn al þese, wurschepe ӡe heuene kyng.[22]

The ideas presented here were also repeated by Isaias (12.5, 42.10). The *Psalms* were not the earliest scriptures to take this view, however, even if they were the best known in the Middle Ages. Moses and the children of Israel had sung a hymn of praise to God after the destruction of the Egyptian might in the Red Sea (*Exodus* 15.1): "Cantemus Domino; gloriose enim magnificatus est, equum et ascensorem deiecit in mare" ("Let us sing to the Lord: for he is gloriously magnified, the horse and the rider he has thrown into the sea").[23] The concept of musical performance in God's praise was, we may assume, widespread in the Middle Ages.

The third reason for this is the commonly-understood place of music in the universe. The ancient world had seen the physical universe as founded on simple mathematical proportions which themselves created musical sounds.[24] Such a theory did not explain angelic music, however, since the angels are not part of the material universe.[25] For this reason Boethius had described a fourth category, *musica divina*, further discussed by his great medieval admirer Jacobus Leodiensis in Chapters XI and XII of the *Speculum Musice* of c.1330.[26] Jacobus distinguished within *musica divina* between *musica divina* proper, the music of God himself which is inaudible, and *musica caelestis*, which is the music of angels and saints.[27] The idea of *musica caelestis* depends on the fusion of two concepts: the structure of the spiritual universe, equivalent to the spheres of the material universe, and the *laudes dei*, or praises of God.[28]

For the above reasons, heaven was seen as a musical place. The tradition of the *laudes dei* as angelic singing appears at least as far back as the hymns of Prudentius (348–413) and Sedulius (fifth century); the latter's *A solis ortus cardine* (st. 7, ll. 1–2) asserts: "Gaudet chorus caelestium/ et angeli canunt Deum" ("The chorus of the heavens rejoices/ and the angels sing God's praise").[29] These hymns also made the direct connection between angelic music and the earthly praise of God. By the time of the great trope writing period the singing and playing of instruments as a normal part of the *laudes dei*, both in heaven and on earth, was an important element in liturgical accretion of all kinds. This is illustrated in the following *Sanctus* trope from a twelfth-century Sicilian troper (now Madrid, National Library MS. 19,421):

Clangat hodie vox nostra melorum symphonia . . .

. . .

Personet nunc tinnula, armonie organa musicorum chorea
Tonorum, quam dulcia, alternatim concrepant voce, modulamina.
Diapason altissona, per vocum discrimina, tetracordis figurarum alta conscendens culmina:
Sustollant nostra carmina ad Celi fastigia, ymnis angelicis coherenda
Patri melodia. (ll. 1–6)[30]

(Let our voices ring out today with the concord of melodies. . . . Now let the bell ring out, [let] the organs [*or* instruments] of harmony, the choral songs of the music makers sound forth in alternation with the voice: how sweet are the modulations of the notes! The deepest diapason, climbing the high peaks of the tetrachord, figure by figure, through the varied notes of our voices: let it raise our songs to the roofs of Heaven, to unite the melody with angelic hymns to the Father.)

In all, it was probably inevitable that the tradition should play a large part in dramatic representations, in writings such as the *Legenda Aurea*, and in pictorial representations of heaven.

In these last we can sometimes identify the texts that the angels sing. The great majority of texts are clearly liturgical and were presumably sung to the chants normally associated with them.[31] JoAnna Dutka has listed fifty-five Latin texts sung in the English play cycles. Most of them are identifiably liturgical, and they come from a wide variety of liturgical types:[32] the nineteen liturgical items in the Chester cycle, for instance, include antiphons, antiphonal Mass-chants, a responsory, a responsory verse, canticles, hymns, and the Apostles' Creed.[33] Chants for the daily Offices far outnumber those from the Mass, and relatively simple chants—antiphons and congregational pieces—predominate over soloistic music.[34] The situation varies slightly in different types of play, and perhaps from one country to another, but this result is broadly true for all large-scale civic dramas that use amateur singers as well as professionals.[35]

Iconographic representations of angels vary greatly in the amount of verbal and musical detail that they show. Angelic messengers are usually accompanied by their verbal text (if at all) on a scroll, without music. Where the message is to be understood as sung, the music is sometimes shown but often represented in a rather impressionistic way—sufficient to show that it *is* music, but not clearly enough for identification.[36] There are examples in which the music is shown accurately, and in most of these cases the obvious plainsong tune is depicted. Where the choral presentation is a "set piece" the angelic host often shows the normal distinction between instrumentalists playing by ear and singers reading from a book or an unbound piece of parchment.

The most interesting cases from a musical point of view are items of notated polyphony (part-music) found in pictures and playbooks. Here the usual relationship between the words and their plainsong setting no longer obtains. For performance in a play the priority is for the text to be recognizable, the polyphonic style being special in any case. Since a dramatic performance is not a liturgical one, there is no necessity for specially composed polyphony to be chant-based. There are, however, too few examples in English drama for a general picture to emerge. As we shall see, the only liturgical text in the polyphonic settings of York XLV (the Weavers' *Assumption of the Virgin*) is not set as a liturgical piece, while the angelic *Gloria* in Chester VII (the Paynters' *Pagina Septima de Pastoribus*) may or may not be chant-based. A pre-existent setting of a liturgical text is more likely to be based on the chant, however, because its original liturgical function would normally demand that.[37] In an iconographic presentation of polyphony, the text is again the priority, but in addition, if the point is to be made that the part-music is something special, the music itself should be recognizable. This is not to say that the chant must be used and be seen to be used; rather, pictures showing polyphonic settings presumably rely on a locally-known setting of special significance. There are a few late medieval paintings in which this is the case, and some are discussed here briefly; the list is not comprehensive, but simply allows certain points to be made with respect to specific examples.

First, it will be convenient to discuss the paintings in which the *Ave regina . . . Mater regis* of Walter Frye appears. Frye may have worked at Ely Cathedral in the 1440's and early 1450's, and is probably the man of that name who was apparently working in London in the later 1450's.[38] There is no evidence that he ever traveled or lived abroad, and this is particularly interesting in view of the largely Continental provenance of sources of his music. Brian Trowell has pointed out that Frye's three best-surviving pieces occur thirty-six times in twenty-three sources, only one of which is English.[39] Of these three, the *Ave regina . . . Mater regis* also survives in three paintings, none of them English. Two are by the Master of the Embroidered Foliage, however, so that an association with the city of Bruges seems certain.[40] This association is partly confirmed by the Bruges connection of the Master of the St. Lucy Legend, whose painting of the Assumption of Our Lady includes a related musical setting (discussed below), and also by the use of Frye's work by the Bruges-based Jacob Obrecht as a basis for his *Ave regina celorum* Mass.[41]

Frye's work is a setting of the rhymed antiphon *Ave regina celorum, Mater regis angelorum*, not to be confused with the better-known *Ave regina celorum, ave domina*:

> Ave regina celorum
> Mater regis angelorum
> O Maria flos virginum
> Velud rosa vel lilium
> Funde preces ad dominum
> Pro salute fidelium.[42]

This text may be a contrafactum. Manfred Bukofzer noted that the chant is used also for an antiphon in honor of St. Edmund, *Ave rex gentis Anglorum*;[43] and although both texts go back to the thirteenth century and arguments can be advanced for the priority of either, it is on balance more likely that the Edmundian text is the original and that the Marian text was a more generally usable adaptation.[44] Sylvia Kenney has suggested that the substitution took place before the piece left England and that the *Ave regina . . . Mater regis* text is in fact an English one. However all this may be, the plainsong does not share its first-mode chant with any other text. One might expect polyphonic settings of it to use the chant in the normal way,[45] but Kenney has shown that fifteenth-century settings, at least, normally did not use the chant.[46] Frye's setting is indeed in the wrong mode to do so (being virtually in F major). It is possible that Frye's *Ave regina* is itself a contrafactum of a secular piece despite the absence of any vernacular-texted version. The piece is closely related formally to the ballade, and several other of Frye's secular pieces have been given Latin texts so that the absence of the chant makes one suspicious of the piece's status as originally a sacred work. Kenney has demonstrated too how the six-line sacred text may have been adapted to replace an original text of eight lines, as a ballade would have.[47] However, John Caldwell has pointed out that Frye's structure is a normal responsorial form, with lines 5–6 as the verse and lines 3–4 returning as the repeat (ll. 7–8). It is therefore unnecessary to resort to contrafactum as an explanation of the form of the *Ave regina*.[48]

Frye's *Ave regina*, then, is an unusual piece in many ways. Not the least of these is its appearance in three paintings, two of which I shall discuss here. The first is a painting of the Virgin and Child with angels, by the Master of the Embroidered Foliage, now in the R. G. Grog Collection in Paris;[49] it seems to have been painted in Bruges in the 1480's. Kenney has conveniently reproduced the painting as the frontispiece to *Walter Frye and the Contenance Angloise*, with a detail showing the music as Plate 5.[50] The layout of the painting is shown in fig. C. The Virgin is seated in the center of the picture with the Child in her lap and two flying angels holding her crown above her head. On her right (to the left of the picture) are three angel singers (1, 2, 3) reading from a book held by the nearest (1). On her left are three angel instrumentalists (4, 5, 6) playing lute, fiddle, and recorder. Each of these groups has its own leader (1, 4), nearer to us in the picture and distinguished from his more plainly-dressed fellows by the richly ornamented cope that he wears. These copes are fastened at the front with a morse (medallion clasp): that of the singer is square, while the lutenist's is round or elliptical. The leader of the singers holds the book. In each group the innermost angel (2, 5) looks at his leader, although that singing angel is in fact beating time with his right hand.

C. Virgin and Child. R. G. Grog Collection, Paris.

The music in the book is written in void notation with black semiminims (quarter notes) and a few semibreve (whole-note) ligatures.[51] It is legible enough to be identified when compared with a known piece, but it could not have been transcribed accurately if it had not survived elsewhere. On the left-hand page is the Cantus part of Frye's piece, up to the beginning of bar 19; on the right, the Tenor up to the end of bar 17.[49] That is, the painting shows rather less than half of the piece, which is forty-four bars long in Kenney's edition. Although the pitches of the notes are unclear, as are many of the individual symbols, most of the note-shapes and ligatures are recognizable, the vertical movement of the notes seems generally accurate, and there appear to be no corrections or second thoughts. Music can also be seen on the previous verso; this too would be identifiable as a known piece but cannot be transcribed as it stands. Unfortunately, the music is only a small fragment and no text is visible, so the piece may remain unidentified.[53]

The painting raises some interesting questions of performance. In medieval iconography, two such groups of musicians should normally be regarded as separate consorts, representing two performances separated in space and/or time; they do not constitute evidence of mixed vocal and instrumental performance. In the present instance, however, it will be sensible to reconsider this situation. To begin with, the page-turn is at different places in the music, which would cause problems for the singers. This is known in actual music-books, and performance is not impossible if the leaf is turned in such a way that the Cantus singer can see the previous opening while the Tenor singer is already reading from the new one; but it is not an ideal situation.[54] On the other hand, there are three singers for two parts: which singers are singing which part? It does not help that none of them is actually reading from the book; perhaps they have memorized the music, even if only near the page-turns.[55] Alternatively, perhaps all three singers are engaged on only one voice-part, despite the presence of two. In this case, the three instrumentalists are perhaps playing the other voices of a three- or four-part version of the piece.[56] I shall return to this question.

The second painting, also a Virgin and Child by the Master of the Embroidered Foliage, is now in the Chiesa di Santa Maria degli Angeli in Polizzi Generosa, Sicily.[57] Kenney has shown details of the painting, but not the whole picture.[58] The layout of the painting is shown in fig. D. Here there are only two singers and two instrumentalists (playing lute and ?recorder), again on the left and right of the picture, respectively. As before, the leader of the singers and the nearer instrumentalist (the lutenist) wear richly decorated copes. These incorporate foliage very like that in the background of the first painting, and again each is fastened with a jeweled morse (the singer's is rhombic, and the lutenist's elliptical). Here the angel holds not a book but a strip of parchment, apparently about 22 inches long and some 4–5 inches deep, on which is written music and text associated with a single staff. This strip, with the music written along the length of the parchment, is itself unusual. I am not aware of any such strip surviving, nor of any literary or documentary mention of one.[59] However, there are several depictions of such sources, so that we must assume that the format existed in the late Middle Ages, perhaps as the most ephemeral of performance copies.[60] Moreover, there may have been a relationship (or perhaps a confusion in the minds of some artists) between the single-line scroll of text previously mentioned and the musical strip. In some depictions the text-scrolls are held by the angels almost as if they were using them to speak from, while the scroll held by the four angels constituting the angelic host in an illustration by Simon Marmion may presumably contain both text and music of the Christmas *Gloria*.[61]

D. Virgin and Child. S. Maria degli Angeli, Polizzi Generosa.

The music of the painting in Santa Maria degli Angeli is the Tenor part of Frye's piece, again in void notation with black semi-minims (quarter notes) and some semibreve (whole-note) ligatures. There are apparently no corrections or second thoughts. The first three notes cannot be read, but then the music continues identifi-ably (with a brief lacuna where the angel's finger intervenes) to the beginning of bar 15.[62] At that point the parchment folds over so that the onlooker cannot see any further, apart from an inch or two at the very end of the strip, which shows the end of the staff continuing right to the edge of the strip but without any notation on it. The visible notated music takes up about three-quarters of the available space, so the music could perhaps reach the half-way cadence at bar 21 before that final, unused part of the strip. What can be seen of the other side of the parchment is blank, and there is no other piece of parchment in the picture. It is therefore unclear how the performance of the piece will be completed, since the notated music for bars 22 onward appears not to be available.

It may be, however, that bars 1–21 of the piece were regarded as a suitable and self-sufficient unit for the purpose. Because of the ABCB structure of the piece, with both text and music of lines 3–4 (bars 13–21) repeated at the end as lines 7–8 (bars 36–44), an ending at bar 21 presents no problem of musical or textual incompleteness.[63] Moreover, the "verse" section of the text that starts the second half of the piece (ll. 5–6 in the text as given above) is less directly suitable for a Virgin and Child scene, which is one of simple angelic adoration in which prayers for the salvation of humankind have no particular relevance. In effect, this is a more selective use of Frye's *Ave regina* than in the Paris picture, with only the first half of the piece being performed.

The performance circumstances shown again suggest a mixed vocal and instrumental texture. The singers have only the Tenor part, and presumably the instrumentalists provide one or two other voices. Compared to the Paris painting, this is a smaller-scale performance in various ways—two singers and two instrumentalists instead of three in each category, and only part of the Frye piece—so that a two-voiced setting might well be expected. However, we need not assume this, as the lute could play the Contratenor part if the recorder played the Cantus.

At this point we should note that pictures of the Virgin flanked by a group of singers on one side and instrumentalists on the other are not confined to altar-panels, nor to the school of Bruges.[64] The iconography at issue here is a standard one associating the Virgin with "all kinds of music"—that is, vocal, string, and wind music. We have, then, a situation in which an iconographical convention is allied to a real piece of music together with a group of singers and a group of instrumentalists. The deliberate accuracy of the notated music and, to a large extent, of the instruments suggests that the observed performance practice too may be realistic. Against this, iconographic accuracy of the observed details is not normally matched by the accuracy in depiction of the performance practice, where iconographic convention overrides realism. On balance it seems doubtful if the *performance* of Frye's *Ave regina* is necessarily depicted accurately and realistically, however accurate the notation and other details in the paintings.[65] This is an area in which we still know far too little, however, and it will be worthwhile to collect information on possible performance practice from these paintings in case it can be confirmed by means of other types of evidence.

The many sources of Frye's *Ave regina* suggest a number of conclusions. That the piece was well known, even popular, in Bruges during the 1480's can hardly be in question.[66] Its text was certainly considered highly suitable for an angelic concert in honor of Our Lady, and in this respect the relatively loose liturgical affiliations of the text may have encouraged both its extra-liturgical uses and a non-liturgical composition without plainsong cantus firmus. Beyond this, however, the depiction of it in three paintings suggests not only a strong connection between the religious life of Bruges and that of the paintings' intended destination but, also more specifically, the use of Frye's piece in particular to symbolize that connection. I feel doubtful, however, about the extent to which the depictions illustrate the actual conditions of performance of the piece in Bruges in the 1480's.

It is interesting nevertheless to note that a related *Ave regina* setting appears in another Bruges painting of c.1485.[67] This, one of the most remarkable paintings of the late fifteenth century, is the Assumption of Our Lady attributed to the Master of the St. Lucy Legend and now in the Samuel H. Kress Collection in the National Gallery of Art, Washington, D.C. It has been discussed at length by Emanuel Winternitz and more briefly by others; and it has been reproduced in works by Winternitz, Kenney, and Strohm and elsewhere.[68] Fig. E shows the main outlines of the painting. The Blessed Virgin is depicted during her Assumption, surrounded by many angels and with her feet resting on the crescent moon. Eight angels, four on each side (1, 2), support her during her ascent, their hands gently laid on her hair and robes. Four of these angels wear the decorated copes and jewelled morses seen in the other paintings. Immediately behind these eight, near the edges of the picture, are four other angels: those on the right (3) play lute and shawm; of those on the left (4), the lower angel plays a portative organ, while the other supports the topmost of the "lifting" angels on that side. A final group of four angels around the Virgin is disposed in pairs behind and above her shoulders (5, 6). These are the singers of an anonymous setting of *Ave regina celorum . . . Mater regis*, and I shall return to them presently.

E. Assumption of the Virgin. National Gallery, Washington, D.C.

Immediately beyond and above these angels the eye reaches a circular entrance in the clouds, through which can be seen heaven itself, with the throne of God placed at the top center of the picture. Framing the entrance, and on the viewer's side of it, are four more minstrel angels: fiddle and treble shawm on the right (7), tenor shawm and harp on the left (8). Within the entrance, the eye is drawn to the throne of God, with the Father and Son seated symmetrically and the Holy Spirit in the form of a dove hovering between them. The hangings around this scene are supported by three flying angels, one on each side and one placed centrally behind the Holy Spirit. On either side of the throne are groups of musicians, forming an arc from the sides to the space between the entrance to heaven and the throne. Those on the right are instrumentalists playing harp, dulcimer, lute, and three pipes of some kind, perhaps shawms (9). Those on the left, eleven in all, form two groups of singers (10, 11); to these too I shall return. It should be assumed, I think, that the actual numbers of angels in these groups, separately and in total, are of some symbolic significance.[69]

Some groups of musicians in this painting are hard to define: do the various groups of instrumentalists join up with groups on the other side, or with those above or below? Fortunately this is not a difficult issue in the case of the nearer singers, who are isolated from the instrumentalists above and below them but identified as a single singing group by the music that they sing. On each side of the picture the nearest singing angel holds a single parchment leaf from which he and the angel standing immediately behind him read. These membranes contain the music of a two-part setting of *Ave regina celorum . . . Mater regis* so that we have a clear performance situation in which two voice-parts are each performed by two singers. The nearest angel on the left-hand side wears a decorated cope fastened with a circular morse depicting God in glory.[70]

Each parchment membrane would in real life measure some 8 inches or more across by 10 or 12 inches high. Three staves can be seen on each, together with the associated music and text, and it seems likely that another two staves could be accommodated on the bottom of each membrane, which is folded away from the viewer. It is impossible to be certain, but it does not seem that any music is written on the dorse of either membrane. What is visible, then, may be about sixty percent of the piece. On the right, the text of the Tenor part is probably incomplete, for the Cantus part, on the left (held by the coped angel), shows that after a long melismatic setting of "Ave" the text quickly reaches "angelorum" by the end of the second stave. The less florid style of the second line's setting, if continued, would certainly allow the next four text-lines to be set in the music of the next three staves, which would bring the piece to an end at the bottom of the membrane. I think we may take it, therefore, that the membrane held by each of these angels contains the whole of a voice-part of this *Ave regina* setting. It should be noted that in this situation lines 5–6 of the text *are* immediately relevant: once assumed and crowned, Mary became Man's greatest intercessor with the Son.

The music is in white mensural notation, with black semi-minims (quarter notes) and a few semibreve (whole-note) ligatures. The Tenor part is so labelled, under the large coloured initial "A" at the beginning of the first staff; the Cantus part also has the large initial "A" but (as was usual) no voice-name. The music is clearly written and most of it can be transcribed with little difficulty. As in the case of the depictions of Walter Frye's *Ave regina*, there are places where the painter has certainly made a copying error, and others where the music is too indistinct in relation to the staff for a certain transcription to be made. There is also at least one place (the fourth ligature in the Tenor part) where the painter seems to have corrected an error. Enough of the music can be transcribed, however, for us to gain a clear idea of the kind of piece that it is. Like Frye's setting, it is in triple time, in the key of F major (or mode VI, not the mode of the chant), and makes no use of the chant for this text. Its two-part imitative texture is perfectly satisfactory as it stands but does not preclude the possibility of a third voice. Like Frye's, this setting may have been reduced for iconographic purposes. It is an attractive piece, and in Example 1 I give a transcription of as much as can be seen.[71]

This piece seems so closely related to Frye's that one is tempted to suggest it as an emulation of the more famous work, especially in view of its non-liturgical nature and the identity of mode.[72] Comparison with sections of Frye's work in Example 2 will show that both pieces begin with an initial statement ending on a pause (on "Ave" in Frye's setting and on "regina" in the Washington one) and that this cadence in the anonymous setting is perhaps related to the approach to the principal cadence in Frye's. However, both this figure and the extension of it into the longer cadence appear in the song "Go hert, hurt with adversitie," as Example 3 shows, so it would be unwise to read too much into these superficial similarities. Moreover, there is evidence for some sort of tradition of non-liturgical settings of the *Ave regina* text, for a setting similar to the Washington one, but apparently earlier, can be found in Bologna, Biblioteca Universitaria, MS. 2216, fol. 31[v].[73] This too is a two-voiced setting in F major and triple time, but, more surprisingly, the opening motif is very closely related to that of our anonymous setting (see Example 4).

Example 1: Washington *Ave regina*

There remains the question of the other groups of singers (10, 11) in the Assumption panel. Having discussed the two notated parts of the *Ave regina*, Kenney turned to the music visible in the book used by group 10 and suggested that it is "a pure fabrication of the artist."[74] In a sense she was right, for the piece is not quite clear enough to be recognizable, although one can see that the notation consists of void notes and ligatures on a staff with clefs. It is unclear whether the clefs are all the same or different on the two pages of the open book. There is, then, an element of impressionism about it that makes one suspicious of trying to identify the music; and although the opening of the music on the left-hand page looks a little like the start of the Contratenor part of the Frye *Ave regina*, detailed comparison shows that the artist cannot have had that piece in mind. Nor does the line seem to fit with the two-part

Example 2: Frye, *Ave regina*

(a) bars 1-4

(b) bars 19-21 = 42-4

Example 3: *Go hert, hurt with adversitie*, bars 7–10

Example 4: Bologna *Ave regina*, bars 1–3, voice I

Ave regina

Ave regina just discussed. This is no surprise, of course: not only are these angels singing from a different type of source from the others—a bound book instead of a single membrane—but they are within the boundaries of heaven rather than outside them.

This music is nevertheless of great interest, for the artist has gone to some lengths to show us that it is void mensural notation with semibreve (whole-note) ligatures (no semiminims/quarter notes can be seen). The singers are of considerable musical ability, then, and indeed all six of them are wearing the embroidered copes that seem to indicate seniority, while the nearest has on his breast the heavy round morse seen elsewhere. This group also has its book on a lectern. The five angels behind them, singing from their own book held by the outermost two, are all dressed in plain white and are clearly of lesser importance. Are these two groups singing the same piece, or are they involved in different performances?

In all other groups in this painting, coped angels mix with those in more plain attire.[75] As in the other paintings, this probably indicates leading angels in each group. The division of the two groups 10 and 11, therefore, with all of the first group in copes and all of the second group plainly dressed, is a strong visual indication that they do not work together—in other words, that they are not singing two voice-parts of a polyphonic piece. There follow from this two conclusions. First, the less senior angels presumably sing plainsong, though they are facing us and we cannot see what is written in their book. Second, the coped angels are singing measured monody, of a kind rare in actual sources and not (as far as I know) discussed by either medieval theorists or modern scholars.[76]

These three paintings form a group, or are part of a group, of depictions of the worship of the Blessed Virgin that seem to follow a firmly-established tradition in a number of areas (notated music, angelic vestments and decoration, etc.), not the least interesting being the repertory of polyphony and its mode of performance.[77] It will be instructive, then, to bear this tradition in mind when considering the staging of a Marian play such as the Assumption plays of the York and N-town cycles, in which the use of music, the costuming and effects, and the complexity of the staging itself suggest the kind of opulent presentation seen in the paintings. The N-town Assumption, originally a separate saint play, uses both vocal and instrumental resources, although it is impossible to say what instruments were intended. The York Assumption, notable for the most extensive collection of complete notated pieces in the English drama of the time, also suggests a conspicuous consumption in its staging that is exceptional even by the standards of late fifteenth-century Marian art.

I have discussed elsewhere both the music of York XLV (the Weavers' *Assumption of the Virgin*) and the voices that sang it, and I need offer only some brief contextual comments here.[78] In this play, as apparently in the *Assumption* of the Master of the St. Lucy Legend, numerological considerations are important in giving practical expression to ideas of divine harmony and proportion. It is not just that the play divides into three exactly equal scenes of eight stanzas each, which is the kind of structure seen in other York pageants; the apparently anomalous positioning of the second music-cue after stanza 9 is explicable only in numerological terms.[79] The play has a large cast and was expensive in terms of props and costumes as well as of the actual staging with its mechanical device for lifting the Virgin.[80] It is hard not to believe that the twelve speaking angels of the surviving text were all boy singers: the roles bear the characteristics of a scene that could be played by inexperienced actors and rehearsed separately from the rest of the cast. It may be coincidence that the choirboys of York Minster were increased from seven to twelve in 1425, but the boys of the Minster are certainly the most likely source for the angels singing in Play XLV.[81] And although it would not be necessary for all twelve to sing the notated music, we should probably expect that at least the majority would do so.[82]

As for the music itself, it might be thought that *Ave regina celorum* would be sung during the Assumption play, but in fact it has been sung at the end of Play XLIV, the Drapers' *Death of the Virgin*, as the angels go to Mary in preparation for her assumption. In the Assumption play itself three texts are sung:

1. Surge, proxima mea, columba mea, tabernaculum glorie, vasculum vite, templum celeste. (cf. *Song of Songs* 2.10, 13–14)

(Arise, you who are closest to me, my dove, tabernacle of glory, vessel of life, celestial temple.)

2. Veni de Libano, sponsa, veni, coronaberis. (*Song of Songs* 4.8)

(Come away from Lebanon, my bride, come: you shall be crowned.)

3. Veni, electa mea, et ponam in te tronum meum:
quia concupivit rex speciem tuam. (York use, Mattins responsory for the
Assumption, partly from Psalm 44.12)

(Come, my chosen one, and I shall place you upon my throne:
for the king has desired your beauty.)

These three texts all appear in the *Legenda Aurea*, where they are found in the order 3, 2, 1.[83] Numbers 1 and 2 were probably transmitted to the play via the *Legenda Aurea*, although it may be that this work was not the only source for them. In these the Bridegroom addresses the Bride according to the standard interpretation of that most erotic of love-poetry, the *Song of Songs*. *Veni electa mea* is liturgical, being the fourth respond at Matins on the feast of the Assumption in the York use, but it is not set liturgically in the play.[84] The music is apparently not chant-based, and there is no indication that the responsory-verse *Audi filia* is associated with it. Although the text does not derive from the *Song of Songs*, its imagery matches that of the other two texts.

The texts are set for two equal boys' voices, once in the body of the play text and again, in rather more elaborate settings, at the end of the play. The second version of *Veni de Libano* breaks very briefly into four-part chords, so that the two voice-parts demand at least two singers each, which compares with the pictorial representations already discussed (but not with my feeling that all twelve of the speaking angels should sing). This music is the work of one composer. Although the music was copied into the surviving source during the period of the copying of the manuscript itself (1463–77), the musical style suggests a date for the composition rather earlier, perhaps in the 1440's. To some extent the notational style—full black notation with red coloration–supports this earlier dating.[85]

The history of angelic singing in the West is a long one. The few biblical texts of angelic utterance were modified for liturgical use, and liturgical items, in their turn, were then attributed to angels in the representation of particular events. The worship of God by angels and men gave rise to a wealth of ideas connected with singing and the playing of instruments in liturgical accretions, especially in the ninth to the eleventh centuries, and this eventually bore fruit in various forms in the late Middle Ages—in the visual arts, in literature, and in drama. The vernacular drama of the fifteenth and early sixteenth centuries in particular exhibits a fascinating synthesis of the visual and musical elements of this tradition, resulting in a rich presentation of heaven to the eyes, ears, and intellect of the beholder. Such a presentation allowed ordinary sinful mortals some glimpse of those "gastly þings, & uertus, & angels, & haly saules, & heuenly þyngs" that, as Walter Hilton noted, were so rarely experienced in real life by even the most holy of men and women.

NOTES

[1] See *Two Minor Works of Walter Hilton*, ed. Fumio Kuriyagawa and Toshiyuki Takamiya (Tokyo, 1980). The line-numbers in citations in my paper refer to this edition.

[2] See Richard Rastall, "The Sounds of Hell," in *The Iconography of Hell*, ed. Clifford Davidson and Thomas H. Seiler, Early Drama, Art, and Music Monograph Ser., 17 (Kalamazoo: Medieval Institute Publications, 1992), pp. 102–04.

[3] *Two Minor Works of Walter Hilton*, ed. Kuriyagawa and Takamiya, ll. 102–03.

[4] Richard Rolle of Hampole also regarded angelic song as indescribable in any human terms; see, for instance, Hope Emily Allen, ed., *English Writings of Richard Rolle* (1931; rpt. Gloucester: Alan Sutton, 1988), p. xxviii.

[5] It was a vital principle controlling the use of angelic singing in religious drama, but that is another matter. This subject is discussed in my book *The Heaven Singing: Music in Early English Religious Drama* (Woodbridge: Boydell and Brewer, forthcoming), chap. 5.

[6] This would not provide a clear theoretical or philosophical framework that would explain the repertory's use, which is outside the scope of the present essay.

[7] I treat only English evidence here: widening the discussion to include Continental evidence would certainly add information, but it would not substantially affect this essay.

[8] P[atrick] L. Little, "The Place of Music in the Medieval World-System," Ph.D. diss. (Univ. of Otago, 1975), p. 142.

[9] I have here simplified the relationship between *Isaias* 6.3 and the New Testament and liturgical texts. This relationship is explored in Eric Werner, "The Genesis of the Liturgical Sanctus," in *Essays Presented to Egon Wellesz*, ed. Jack Westrup (Oxford: Clarendon Press, 1966), pp. 19–32.

[10] Little, "The Place of Music," p. 15. This is, of course, not the only order proposed in the Middle Ages, but it is a common one; see the remarks by Clifford Davidson, above, pp. 13–14, and additionally C. S. Lewis, *The Discarded Image* (Cambridge: Cambridge Univ. Press, 1964), pp. 71–72. In the course of a discussion of various orderings, Kathi Meyer-Baer, *Music of the Spheres and the Dance of Death* (1970; rpt. New York, Da Capo Press, 1984), p. 24, deals with the "beautiful angels," the highest order of the original ten, which fell with Lucifer; see also ibid., p. 81.

[11] Little, "The Place of Music," pp. 15–16.

[12] The archangel Michael, stated by St. John to be the leader of the heavenly forces against the fallen angels (*Apocalypse* 12.7, and see also *Jude*, verse 9), may be the prince of that name who visited Daniel (*Daniel* 10.13, 21) but is not unequivocally said to visit any mortal.

[13] Gabriel is named as an archangel by Luke, but he is also designated "the angel" elsewhere, so not every "angel" is necessarily of the lowest rank. The man named Gabriel who speaks to Daniel in *Daniel* 8.15–27 and 9.21–27 may be understood to be the archangel of that name.

[14] Wolfgang Hopyl, *Antiphonale Sarisburiense* (Paris, 1520), I, 20^v–21^r (ll. 3–6).

[15] *The Sarum Missal*, ed. J. Wickham Legg (1916; rpt. Oxford: Clarendon Press, 1969), p. 220; the translation which follows is from *The English Missal* (1958).

[16] See Frank Ll. Harrison, *Music in Medieval Britain* (London: Routledge and Kegan Paul, 1958), pp. 99, 107.

[17] It is possible that the older scriptural version was being used—that is, the pre-Vulgate version from which liturgical texts had been taken—but this is very unlikely.

[18] This matter was discussed by Daniel Sheerin in an unpublished paper, "'Signum uictoriae in Inferno': An Allusion to the Harrowing of Hell in Late Medieval Dedication Rituals," presented at the Twenty-First International Congress on Medieval Studies in May 1986.

[19] Jacobus de Voragine, *Legenda Aurea*, ed. Th. Graesse (Vratislava: Koebner, 1890), p. 508; the translation is from Jacobus de Voragine, *The Golden Legend*, trans. Granger Ryan and Helmut Ripperger (1941; rpt. New York: Arno Press, 1969), p. 453.

[20] See *The N-Town Play*, ed. Stephen Spector, EETS, s.s. 11-12 (Oxford: Oxford Univ. Press, 1991), I, 402 (*s.d.* following 41.370). As Spector notes (II, 533), the N-town Assumption play is closely related to the *Legenda Aurea*

account.

[21] *Legenda Aurea*, ed. Graesse, p. 68; trans. Ryan and Ripperger, p. 70. The translators date this episode to 1174; this is due to a misunderstanding on their part. Immediately before the section quoted here the *Legenda Aurea* states that Thomas was canonized as a martyr in 1174 (*recte* 1173); see Graesse's edition, p. 68.

[22] Robert [Mannyng] of Brunne, *Handlyng Synne*, EETS, o.s. 119, 123 (London: Kegan Paul, Trench, Trübner, 1901–03), I, 158–59 (ll. 4769–72).

[23] See also *Exodus* 15.21.

[24] For a discussion of this matter, see Rastall, "The Sounds of Hell," p. 115 and esp. n. 36 on p. 129. The ancient view of the universe was transmitted to the Middle Ages by Boethius (c.480–c.525) and others, notably Cassiodorus (c.485–c.580) and Isidore of Seville (c.560–636).

[25] Angels have no bodily form, for all that they appear to men in human likeness, and the Middle Ages understood their depiction with wings and haloes to be "symbolic rather than genuinely descriptive" (Little, "The Place of Music," p. 16; see also Lewis, *The Discarded Image*, p. 71). God and his angels therefore do not inhabit the material universe, and are outside time and place. They do, however, permeate the whole physical universe, for otherwise humans could have no relationship with God, and angels could not visit them. The spiritual universe, then, is outside the known dimensions of the physical one, but it was convenient to conceptualize it along similar lines.

[26] It must be stressed (as Little does in "The Place of Music," p. 45) that *musica divina* is not merely an addition on a par with the other three but a qualitatively distinct category, concerned with the spiritual rather than the material universe.

[27] See David S. Chamberlain, "Philosophy of Music in the *Consolatio* of Boethius," *Speculum*, 45 (1970), 80–97, esp. 95–96 and n. 90; and Kay Slocum, "*Musica Coelestis*: A Fourteenth Century Image of Cosmic Music," *Studia musica*, 14 (1991), 3–12

[28] Little discusses this matter fully ("The Place of Music," pp. 125–62).

[29] *Liber Hymnarius* (Solesmes: Abbaye Saint-Pierre de Solesmes, 1983), p. 24.

[30] Text and translation from Donald Ireland, "The Tropes to the Sanctus and Agnus Dei in Three Norman-Sicilian Manuscripts of the 12th–13th Centuries," unpublished M.Ph. diss. (Univ. of Leeds, 1985), II, 120–25. Tropes are hard to date, both individually and as a genre, but the most concentrated period of trope-

writing seems to have resulted in the repertory of tropes found in manuscripts of the tenth and eleventh centuries. Later accretions include texts composed for Latin sung dramas, with their own settings in chant style.

[31] The painted glass in the Beauchamp chapel in Warwick (c.1447–49) includes the texts and chant for the introit *Gaudeamus omnes in domino* and the antiphon *Ave regina celorum, ave domina*; and a two-voiced polyphonic setting of (exceptionally) the Mass *Gloria*; see Clifford Davidson and Jennifer Alexander, *The Early Art of Coventry, Stratford-upon-Avon, Warwick, and Lesser Sites in Warwickshire*, Early Drama, Art, and Music, Reference Ser., 4 (Kalamazoo: Medieval Institute Publications, 1985), p. 178, and Charles F. Hardy, "The Music in the Painted Glass of the Windows in the Beauchamp Chapel at Warwick," *Archaeologia*, 61 (1909), 583–614.

[32] JoAnna Dutka, *Music in the English Mystery Plays*, Early Drama, Art, and Music, Reference Ser., 2 (Kalamazoo: Medieval Institute Publications, 1980), pp. 18–51.

[33] Not all of them can be identified with certainty, however, when two or more liturgical pieces have the same text incipit.

[34] See my list in R. M. Lumiansky and David Mills, *The Chester Mystery Cycle: Essays and Documents* (Chapel Hill: Univ. of North Carolina Press, 1983), pp. 142–54.

[35] For the broad differences between civic dramas and institutional plays, see my comments in *Contexts for Early English Drama*, ed. Marianne G. Briscoe and John C. Coldewey (Bloomington: Indiana Univ. Press, 1989), pp. 197–99.

[36] More rarely, notes are accurately written in a "nonsense" tune that cannot possibly represent a real piece: see, for instance, the painted glass representation (c.1420–50) of an angel singer in the church of St. Milburga, Wixford (Davidson and Alexander, *The Early Art of . . . Warwickshire*, p. 178, fig. 61).

[37] The requirement for liturgical music to be chant-based was, however, a fluid one in the late Middle Ages, and the situation is not wholly clear because of the difficulty of identifying the chant notes in polyphony with a decorated tenor part (and indeed the chant can migrate between voices).

[38] See Brian Trowell's article on Frye, in *The New Grove Dictionary of Music and Musicians*, ed. Stanley Sadie (London: Macmillan, 1980), VI, 876–79.

[39] Ibid., p. 877.

[40] On this Master, see P. E. Carapezza, "Regina Angelorum in musica picta: Walter Frye e il 'Maître au feuillage brodé'," *Rivista italiana di musicologia*, 10 (1975), 134–54.

[41] These matters are discussed by Reinhold Strohm in *Man and Music*, I: *Antiquity and the Middle Ages*, ed. James McKinnon (London: Macmillan, 1990), pp. 307–08. Strohm claims that Frye's *Ave regina* "was demonstrably well known to the citizens of Bruges in the 1480s" because "the civic wind band must have played it in public" (p. 307), but the documentary evidence that he cites elsewhere does not show that the *Ave regina* played by those minstrels was ever Frye's setting (*Music in Late Medieval Bruges*, rev. ed. [Oxford: Clarendon Press, 1990], p. 87). It is perhaps just as reasonable to suppose that the band improvised over the chant.

[42] The text is quoted from the Sarum version on fol. 169^r of Richard Pynson's *Processionale ad Usum Sarum* (1502; facs. rpt. Kilkenny: Boethius Press, 1980). I have normalized capitalization and the letters u and v.

[43] Manfred Bukofzer, *Studies in Medieval and Renaissance Music* (London: Dent, 1951), pp. 18–20.

[44] Sylvia W. Kenney, *Walter Frye and the Contenance Angloise* (1964; rpt. New York, Da Capo Press, 1980), p. 75.

[45] The thirteenth-century two-voiced setting in W_1 does so; see the facsimile in J. H. Baxter, *An Old St Andrews Music Book* (London: Oxford Univ: Press, 1931), fol. 194^r.

[46] Sylvia W. Kenney, "Four settings of 'Ave regina coelorum'," in *Liber Amicorum Charles van den Borren*, ed. [Albert Vander Linden] (Antwerp: Lloyd Anversois, 1964), 98–104, esp. 102–04.

[47] Kenney, *Walter Frye and the Contenance Angloise*, pp. 69–72.

[48] John Caldwell, *The Oxford History of English Music*, I (Oxford: Clarendon Press, 1991), 151.

[49] Formerly in the Féral Collection, Paris.

[50] Reproduced also in Max J. Friedländer, *Early Netherlandish Painting*, IV: *Hugo van der Goes* (Leyden: Sijthoff, 1969), Pl. 83.

[51] That is, ligatures *cum opposita proprietate* ("with shared propriety"), transcribed as two semibreves; see Richard Rastall, *The Notation of Western Music* (London: Dent, 1983), pp. 51–52, 75.

[52] I use the bar-numbers of Kenney's edition: Walter Frye, *Collected Works*, Corpus Mensurabilis Musicae, 19 ([Rome:] American Institute of Musicology, 1960). Kenney barred regularly in 3/4 time, each bar representing a perfect breve, or three semibreve beats, of the original. The original has no bar-lines.

[53] It is not the Contratenor or any of the known additional voices of Frye's piece.

[54] See my comments in *Two Fifteenth-Century Song Books* (Aberystwyth: Boethius Press, 1990), p. xxix, where it seems possible but unlikely that *Ave maria I say* would have been performed from the surviving copy in Cambridge University Library Add. MS. 5943. On the other hand, the present situation is an easier one: bar 18 is not on the leaf being turned in either voice-part, so the leaf would simply have to be held upright while that bar was sung.

[55] Rather less than half of the piece is shown in this opening, and it is unlikely that the rest of it could be shown on the next opening without unacceptable compression of the notation. It can be assumed, I think, that two more openings are required.

[56] Frye seems to have written the piece in three parts originally. In all such music, however, the Cantus and Tenor parts make good sense together without the Contratenor, which can be regarded as optional; while, on the other hand, the addition of a fourth voice by another composer is common in the chanson repertory and occurred several times in the transmission of Frye's *Ave regina*. We may take it, therefore, that the piece might be performed in two, three, or four parts.

[57] This may not have been intended to be its original destination, however. A (perhaps apocryphal) story of its arrival in Sicily shows that it may have been intended for Genoa, Naples, or Florence; see Carapezza, "Regina Angelorum in musica picta," p. 135, and Strohm, *Music in Late Medieval Bruges*, p. 140. The painting is the center panel of an altarpiece, the side-pieces of which show St. Catherine and St. Barbara.

[58] Kenney, *Walter Frye and the Contenance Angloise*, Pl. 4; Walter Frye, *Collected Works*, [x] and [xi]. The plate on p. [x] of the edition is a close-up of the music only. The whole picture is reproduced in Max J. Friedländer, *Early Netherlandish Painting*, IV, Pl. 111, Supplement 129.

[59] The music *rotulus*, with the music written on several staves down two or more membranes stitched or glued bottom to top, is of course another matter, and some famous examples survive.

[60] See E. A. Bowles, *Musik-leben im 15. Jahrhundert*, Musikgeschichte in Bildern, Bd. III, Lfg. 8 (Leipzig, VEB Deutscher Verlag für Musik, 1977), Pls. 86, 89–91, and perhaps 81. Bowles does not distinguish the *rotulus* from the horizontal strip, but uses the term 'Notenrolle' for both.

[61] Now MS. HM 1173 in the Huntington Library; see James Thorpe, ed., *Book of Hours* (San Marino: Huntington Library, n.d.), Pl. 9. Marmion's illustrations date from c.1460–65.

[62] One note and one rest are missing, and a few pitches are inaccurate.

[63] See Kenney, *Walter Frye and the Contenance Angloise*, pp. 69–70, for a discussion of this text and its structure. The ABCB structure of Frye's *Ave regina* became normal for the genre now known as the "respond-motet"; see John Caldwell, *The Oxford History of English Music*, I, 151.

[64] The book of hours cited in n. 61, if correctly attributed to Simon Marmion, was presumably produced in Valenciennes. It includes two illustrations of the Virgin and Child enthroned between musician-angels (Pls. 5, 16). In the first, the angels are a lutenist and a harpist; but in the latter, groups of three singers on the left and three instrumentalists on the right (harp, cittern, and ?pipe) show some elements—the book, the decorated cope with a medallion—seen in such pictures elsewhere.

[65] The third painting to include Frye's *Ave regina* is a ceiling painting in the oratory of Yolande de Laval at Montreuil-Bellay. This dates from 1480, and is likely to be marginally earlier than those of the Master of the Embroidered Foliage. As I have not yet seen a reproduction of it I am unable to say how it relates to the other two. For a description of the painting, see M. de Grandmaison, "Montreuil-Bellay, a Great Anjou Border Castle," *The Connoisseur* (October 1966), and G. Thibault, "L'oratoire du château de Montreuil-Bellay: Ses anges musiciens," in *Memorie e contributi alla musica dal Medioevo all'età moderna offerti a F. Ghisi nel settantesimo compleanno (1901–1971)* (Bologna, 1971 [*recte* 1974]), I, 209–23.

[66] See n. 41, above.

[67] There are no doubt other paintings that relate more or less closely to the Virgin and Child paintings of the Bruges school showing Frye's *Ave regina*. The altarpiece of the Virgin by the Master of the Evora Altarpiece, for instance (now in the Museu Regional at Evora and the Museu Nacional de Arte Antiga, Lisbon), is a case in point. The centerpiece (at Evora) shows the Virgin and Child surrounded by angels playing instruments, while a group of three angels by the Virgin's right shoulder sing from a single membrane. See Friedländer, *Early Netherlandish Painting*, IV, Pl. 120. Unfortunately the reproduction in this case is too small for the music (or even the type of music) to be identified.

[68] Emanuel Winternitz, *Musical Instruments and Their Symbolism in Western Art*, 2nd ed. (New Haven: Yale Univ. Press, 1979), Pls. 66–67; Kenney, *Walter Frye and the Contenance Anglois*, Pls. 6–9. Strohm also shows the painting in *Man and Music*, ed. McKinnon, I, 305–06; although the text is not incorrect, the caption of Pl. 87a on p. 305 wrongly says that the *Ave regina* shown is Frye's. A reproduction is shown also in Max J. Friedländer, *Early Netherlandish Painting*, VI: *Hans Memlinc and Gerard David* (1971), Pl. 257, and in Winternitz, "Secular musical practice in sacred art," *Early Music*, 3 (1975), 225.

[69] There are twenty surrounding the Virgin in front of the entrance to Heaven, and twenty around the throne of God. Those around the Virgin are in groups of two, four, or eight, depending on how one sees them. It may be that four, the number of the physical universe, was a deliberate choice for that part of the picture showing Mary's physical assumption. The angels around the throne are in asymmetrical groups and clearly demand a more complex explanation. The three supporting angels no doubt mirror the Trinity; the six instrumentalists signify the female marriage number; but the eleven singers, divided as they are into a group of five (the male number) and a group of six (the female number), may symbolize the sacred marriage between Christ the bridegroom and the Virgin, here standing for the Church; See V. F. Hopper, *Medieval Number Symbolism* (1938; rpt. New York: Cooper Square, 1969), pp. 43, 70.

[70] Four saints are depicted on this angel's cope; the iconography of the cope and morse may point towards a religious guild or fraternity.

[71] The first six bars were transcribed by Kenney, "Four Settings of 'Ave regina coelorum'," p. 101, and by Carapezza, "Regina Angelorum in musica picta," p. 154. The note that Kenney gives at the start of the Cantus part is a misreading of the time-signature **O**. I am not aware that the rest of the piece has previously been published. If it has not, one reason is immediately obvious: the result is musically unacceptable because of errors in the notation. It is largely impossible to be sure which notes are incorrect and what they ought to have been. A speculative reconstruction could certainly be attempted, but it could have no pretentions to presenting the piece as the composer expected to hear it.

[72] Strohm refers to this as being "closely related" to Frye's work but wisely does not suggest the nature of the relationship (*Man and Music*, ed. McKinnon, I, 307. Strohm's Pl. 87a (ibid., p. 305) is rather misleading in showing the coped angel and the top supporting angel as if the latter were a singer. The second singer can just be seen in the top corner of this plate.

[73] The opening is given in Johannes Wolf, *Geschichte der Mensural-Notation von 1250–1460* (1904: rpt. Hildesheim: Georg Olms, 1965), p. 203 (No. 49 in Wolf's inventory). The piece has no known concordances. This part of the manuscript was probably copied at Brescia, by an Italian scribe, in the period 1433–40, so the piece in question must antedate any work of Frye's and probably the Washington setting as well. See Heinrich Besseler, "The Manuscript Bologna Biblioteca Universitaria 2216," *Musica Disciplina*, 6 (1952), 39–65. The piece is No. 44, on fol. 31ᵛ, in Besseler's inventory.

[74] Kenney, *Walter Frye and the Contenance Angloise*, p. 154.

[75] Many are in alb and amice, but some are dressed in a colored gown that has no equivalent in liturgical vestments.

[76] The only major source of mensural sacred monody from the fifteenth

century is Cambridge, Magdalene College, Pepys MS. 1236, which includes thirteen pieces in the style. The monodic repertory seems to have no historical connection to earlier secular mensural monody (such as Machaut's), and its style is difficult to distinguish from that of polyphony. The Pepys music is discussed by S. R. Charles in his edition, *The Music of the Pepys MS 1236*, Corpus Mensurabilis Musicae, 40 ([Rome:] American Institute of Musicology, 1967); the manuscript is described by Roger Bowers in *Cambridge Music Manuscripts, 900–1700*, ed. Iain Fenlon (Cambridge: Cambridge Univ. Press, 1982), pp. 111–14. The Pepys music is in black notation, however, and the manuscript dates from c.1460, rather earlier than the paintings under discussion here.

[77] It will be useful to consider briefly a rather later painting not in this immediate tradition in order to gain a wider view of angelic song as depicted in early Netherlandish painting. *The Adoration of the Christ Child* by Jacob van Amsterdam is now in the Museo e Gallerie Nazionali di Capodimonte, Naples, and was painted c.1512–15. The scene around the Christ Child in the manger is painted in considerable detail, but the part that concerns us here is at center front where a single *putto* holds open a music book from which a group of instrument-playing *putti* read. On the left are the players of two ?shawms and a psaltery, while on the right are players of a *buisine* (a long straight trumpet) and a folded trumpet. The immediate difference between this and the earlier pictures is that here there are no singers; we, the viewers, are invited to sing the four-part *Gloria in excelsis* that is notated there, although the instrumentalists are apparently supporting the performance. In the more direct way in which the music is presented to the viewer, this picture belongs to a tradition that eventually flowered in the 1580's with the engraved picture-motets of Johan Sadelar and others.
The setting is of the *Benedictus*-antiphon version of the text, with alleluias.

[78] See Richard Rastall, "Vocal Range and Tessitura in Music from York Play 45," *Music Analysis*, 3, No. 2 (1984), 181–99, and my edition of *Six Songs from the York Mystery Play "The Assumption of the Virgin"* (Newton Abbot: Antico, 1985).

[79] For the scene-structure of Play XLV, see Carolyn Wall, "The Apocryphal and Historical Backgrounds of 'The Appearance of Our Lady to Thomas'," *Mediaeval Studies*, 32 (1970), 172–92, esp. 172–73. Numerology in the York cycle has been barely touched on so far; I discuss the matter in *The Heaven Singing: Music in Early English Religious Drama* (forthcoming), chap. 6.

[80] For a discussion of the pageant wagon and the costs to the Mercers' company, see Alexandra F. Johnston and Margaret Dorrell, "The York Mercers, and their Pageant of Doomsday, 1433–1526," *Leeds Studies in English*, n.s. 6 (1972), 10–35.

[81] For the increase in numbers, see L. W. Cowie, "Worship in the Minster," in *A History of Yorkshire: The City of York*, ed. P. M. Tillot, Victoria County History (London: Oxford Univ. Press, 1961), p. 345.

[82] Discussed in *The Heaven Singing* (forthcoming).

[83] These texts were first discussed by C. Fenno Hoffman, Jr., "The Source of the Words to the Music in York 46," *Modern Language Notes*, 65 (1950), 236–39. (Hoffman, like Wall, used Lucy Toulmin Smith's numbering of the York plays.) Further on the modifications to the texts, see my commentary to the edition (*Six Songs*, p. 7).

[84] *Breviarium ad Usum Insignis Ecclesie Eboracensis*, ed. [S. W. Lawley], Surtees Soc., 71, 75 (1880–82), I, 481.

[85] See Rastall, "Vocal Range and Tessitura," *passim*, and my note on the music in Richard Beadle and Peter Meredith, *The York Play*, Leeds Texts and Monographs, Medieval Drama Facsimiles, 7 (Leeds, University of Leeds School of English, 1983), pp. xli-xlv (the color plates follow this section of the Introduction).

Index

1. Angel roof. Church of St. Wendreda, March, Cambridgeshire. By permission of the Royal Commission on the Historical Monuments of England (Crown copyright).

2. Christ as Judge with angels and saints (nineteenth-century "restoration"). Church of St. Mary, Fairford, Gloucestershire. By permission of the Royal Commission on the Historical Monuments of England (Crown copyright).

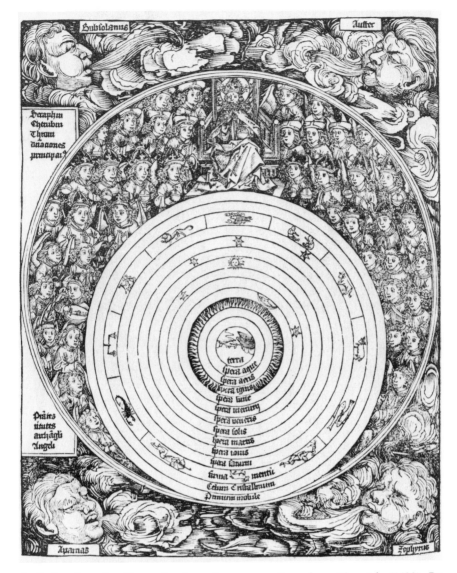

3. God enthroned with angels above the cosmos. *Nuremberg Chronicle* (1493). By permission of the British Library (shelfmark: IC 7452).

4. St. Michael with sword (above), devils, and the damned at the mouth of hell. Wall painting, Östra Vemmerlöv, Skåne, Sweden. Courtesy of the Lund University Institute of Archaeology.

5. St. Peter welcoming the souls to heaven; at the right is the Virgin Mary, crowned. Wall painting, Östra Vemmerlöv, Skåne, Sweden. Courtesy of the Lund University Institute of Archaeology.

6. (above) Communion. Historiated initial. Sarum Missal, Oxford, Trinity College, MS. D.8, fol. 158ᵛ.

7. (at right) Extreme Unction (viaticum). Panel in Seven-Sacrament Window. Church of St. Michael, Doddiscombsleigh, Devon. By permission of the Royal Commission on the Historical Monuments of England (Crown copyright).

8. Extreme Unction (viaticum), showing an attendant kneeling and looking at Host. Panel in Seven-Sacrament Window. All Saints Church, Crudwell, Wiltshire. By permission of the Royal Commission on the Historical Monuments of England (Crown copyright).

9. Eucharist. Elevation of Host. Manuscript illumination. Book of Hours, Brussels, Bibliothèque Royale, MS. 1095, fol. 34ᵛ.

10. Eucharist. Elevation of Host. Panel in Seven-Sacrament Window. Church of St. Michael, Doddiscombsleigh, Devon. By permission of the Royal Commission on the Historical Monuments of England (Crown copyright).

Coute uir feig'ara adam et pota en paradie orudue et faut cite de lon couser er leur deffent le fruit

11. The Garden of Eden. *Bedford Hours*, British Library, Add. MS. 18,850, fol. 14^r. By permission of the British Library.

12. Mary Garden. Woodcut. *Hore Beatissime Virginis Mariae* (1535). By permission of the Durham University Library.

13. Enclosed Garden, with Fountain in center. Henry Hawkins, *Parthenia Sacra* (1633). By permission of Ushaw College, Durham.

14. Jesse Tree Window. Church at Llanrhaeadr-yng-Nghinmeirch, Denbigh.

15. (at left) Angel emptying censer. Apocalypse scene. Great East Window, York Minster. By permission of the Royal Commission on the Historical Monuments of England (Crown copyright).

16. (above) Angel swinging censer. Angel Choir, Lincoln Cathedral. By permission of the Royal Commission on the Historical Monuments of England (Crown copyright).

17. Angel and Three Maries at Tomb. *Benedictional of St. Ethelwold*, British Library, Add. MS. 45,598, fol. 51ᵛ. By permission of the British Library.

18. Resurrection. Roof boss (oak) formerly in the nave, York Minster. Engraving from John Browne's drawing.

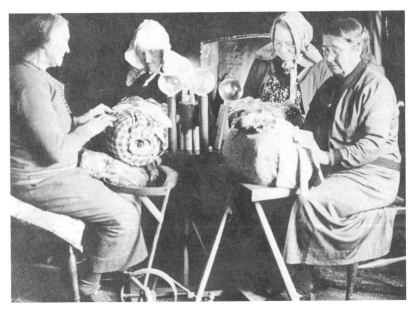

19. The work of four lacemakers lit by a candle and four condensers arranged on a candle stool. Courtesy of Blaise Castle House Museum, Bristol City Museums and Art Gallery (TD 1940).

20. Jerusalem. Mosaic, S. Maria Maggiore, Rome (c.430–39).

21. Apse mosaic, S. Pudenziana, Rome (c.400). By permission of Alinari/Art Resource, New York.

22. Heavenly Jerusalem. Valenciennes Apocalypse. Valenciennes, Bibliothèque Municipale, MS. 99, fol. 38.

23. Heavenly Jerusalem. Bamberg Apocalypse. Bamberg, Staatsbibliothek, Cod. 140, fol. 55.

24. Vault frescoes, entrance bays, San Pietro al Monte sopra Civate, Lombardy (early twelfth-century).

25. Botticelli, *Mystical Crucifixion* (early sixteenth-century). Fogg Art Museum. Courtesy of the Fogg Art Museum, Harvard University Museums, and the Friends of the Fogg Museum Art Fund.

26. "Florentines succoring the Sienese." *Biadaiolo Fiorentino* (c.1340). Florence, Biblioteca Laurenziana, MS. Tempi 3. Photo courtesy of Biblioteca Medicea-Laurenziana.

27. St. Francis and the Simple Man. Fresco, upper church, Assisi (c.1300).

28. Ambroglio Lorenzetti, *The Effects of Good Government in the City*. Fresco, Palazzo Pubblico, Siena (1338–39).

29. Ambroglio Lorenzetti, *The Effects of Good Government in the Countryside*. Fresco, Palazzo Pubblico, Siena (1338–39).

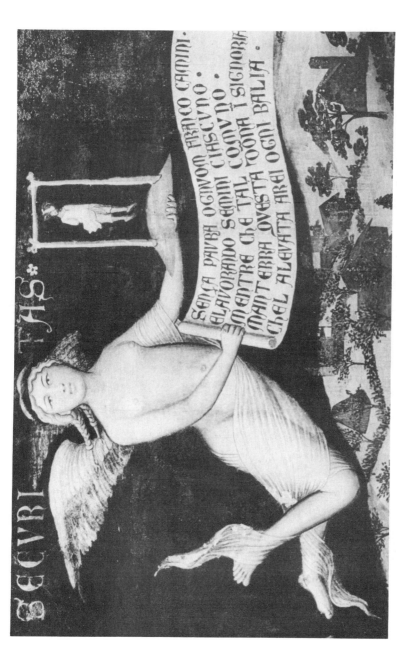

30. Securitas. Detail from Ambroglio Lorenzetti, *The Effects of Good Government in the City*. By permission of Alinari/Art Resource, New York.

31. Broletto, Brescia. Courtyard and tower (early thirteenth-century) looking toward the southwest.